# NOBODY'S HERO

## A Reluctant March Through The Middle East

L D JONES

Order this book online at www.trafford.com/07-1952
or email orders@trafford.com

Most Trafford titles are also available at major online book retailers.



Note for Librarians: A cataloguing record for this book is available from Library and Archives Canada at www.collectionscanada.ca/amicus/index-e.html

ISBN: 978-1-4251-4583-5

*We at Trafford believe that it is the responsibility of us all, as both individuals and corporations, to make choices that are environmentally and socially sound. You, in turn, are supporting this responsible conduct each time you purchase a Trafford book, or make use of our publishing services. To find out how you are helping, please visit www.trafford.com/responsiblepublishing.html*

*Our mission is to efficiently provide the world's finest, most comprehensive book publishing service, enabling every author to experience success. To find out how to publish your book, your way, and have it available worldwide, visit us online at www.trafford.com/10510*

www.trafford.com

**North America & international**
toll-free: 1 888 232 4444 (USA & Canada)
phone: 250 383 6864 • fax: 250 383 6804 • email: info@trafford.com

**The United Kingdom & Europe**
phone: +44 (0)1865 722 113 • local rate: 0845 230 9601
facsimile: +44 (0)1865 722 868 • email: info.uk@trafford.com

10 9 8 7 6 5 4 3 2 1

# PROLOGUE.

SPILLING THE BEANS on the military has become a favourite topic on news headlines in recent years. It seems the nation craves "the shocking truth" behind the public frontage, yet in reality, the secretive world that is the British Armed forces retains much of its mystery for the many, but then, with such aggressive PR and a lawful authority beyond its rightful stature, it's little wonder that the truth never really gets out.

Perhaps you may think you saw the whole conflict on the news and have great faith in the integrity of the reporting news channels. In truth, this is probably justly held in most cases but maybe they didn't see quite as clear a picture as appeared on their coverage. Maybe they only saw what the military wanted them to see. Perhaps even the briefest glimpse beyond the façade was never on offer to them. This doesn't mean that the truth behind that façade isn't there.

My part in all of this? Well, I can't tell you where Shergar went. I've never met Lord Lucan and I can't tell you who pushed Robert Maxwell (if anyone did, of course). There is a bloke who works my local chip shop. He swears he's Elvis. He's probably the right age and height but to me, his delusion just seems like someone else's idea. I don't buy it. I'm no grand conspirator or revolutionary and I don't really buy into most of these underhand theories. That really isn't what this is all about but there is a truth on offer and it's something that most people haven't even considered.

To blow the whistle, spill the beans, dish the dirt or disclose official information is, similarly, not my chosen cup of tea. I simply wish to put across an account, which starts and ends far from the expected norm and contains many bizarre facets on the way. This is simply gritty reality, without embellishment. Consider this, if you will; if you find this account surprising, you should have tried it from my perspective. It cost me five pairs of pants.

My part in all of this; I'm not ex SAS or even any sort of special forces type. I'm not even a soldier really. There's very little awe and mystery as far as I'm concerned and I probably wouldn't impress Shania Twain much, nor do I try. I don't ask for respect. I don't ask for sympathy, nor do I ask you to share my views, indeed I would prefer you to make your own judgement. My views are only important in as much as they qualify my state of mind and perhaps justify my decisions, to an extent. I simply request nothing more than your attention, for a little while, to see exactly what it was like walking in my footsteps.

Further to this, in order to qualify my position further; I'm not super-fit, I've got a reasonable sized bald patch on the back of my head and a bit of back ache. I don't have to confess to a bit of spare tyre around my midriff but here and now, I offer this admission freely. I haven't killed anyone, though I thought about it a few times. I'm just a man, albeit with a capable mind (My one just claim). I'm nobody's hero.

Unfortunately for me, my lack of star-quality didn't really seem to matter when this cast-list was assembled. Availability appeared to be the key factor and regardless of my complete lack of training, experience and desire to do so, I would be taking part. You'll see from here that a tale of heroic masculinity is beyond expectation, so what we really have is something which qualifies loosely as a first-hand account of the invasion of Iraq from a reluctant participant, albeit presented in a satirical, irreverent fashion. It also highlights, rather starkly, the irrelevance of the men on the ground, with so much risk, for so little gain and so little effect. In this latter sentence, we also eradicate the possibility of me being "A Walter Mitty Character". My personal importance, to this once great nation, shall be demonstrated perfectly by its duty of care over me.

At this point, I should but won't make an apology. I was informed, upon my first submission of the manuscript for this project, that it required more narrative detailing the camaraderie and heroism displayed by the characters involved in order to be commercially viable. I took some issue with this, in as much as it suggested a desire, from the knowing public, to believe exactly what they wanted to believe, to bask in the romance and the glory of it all, rather than being exposed to the truth.

Surely this is not the case. At least I would hope not. I would rather be faced with disappointment than live in false hope, clinging to a set of manufactured beliefs. I believe that most people agree. I believe that heroes don't win wars nowadays, regardless of the public's desire for it. I happen to think the truth is more important and I'm not sorry for that. If you want a tale of old fashioned British heroism, read something written by someone who didn't go and doesn't really know. The crux of the matter is this; ladybirds and beetles are generally perceived very differently but genetically, there isn't much to tell between them. This is simply a question of perception. I can't change a history that's already happened. Neither can I un-write what's already written. I simply wish to add my own perspective to a subject that is still very much wide open for debate.

To finalise my stance on the matter, I also wish to state that I do not intend to name names. There are individuals contained with this text, whose conduct could well be the cause of great shame, likewise, some could also take great pride in their actions. In the interest of fairness, I do not wish to identify any such individual by name. I believe that to name, shame and blame others, whilst maintaining my own anonymity, would be particularly unsporting. Incidentally, my name? It's J R Hartley.

# CHAPTER I; FROM WHENCE IT CAME.

POLITICIANS MAKE DECISIONS about the future of our country on a regular basis but mostly we don't really notice a few pence on a packet of cigarettes or an increase of funding for the NHS (particularly as it's largely lost amongst the bureaucrats and bean-counters anyway nowadays). Mostly we wouldn't even notice if they all just upped and left either, despite their insistence to the contrary.

One such decision that was made, however, was given after a brief discussion over cup of tea between Tony Blair and Her majesty the Queen on 7th January 2003. It seemed that he was to go, cap in hand, and offer a detailed account in relation to the imminent threat to national security offered by Iraq's weapons of mass destruction. This was apparently paramount and we could all be wiped out within forty five minutes, so it was "really, really important that we invaded Iraq, your majesty." (Note from author; I was not present for this conversation and can only speculate about what was actually said, but we can all picture the sentimental puppy dog eyes and big, broad smile).

Either way, her majesty, having been "honestly and truthfully" informed by good old Tony of the threat posed by Saddam and Iraq, gave consent for the call up of the general reserve, a most desperate measure, only to be used in desperate times, no less. I would expect that my reaction to this was similar to that of a great many ex-soldiers around the country, being a rapidly twitching arsehole and rather unsavoury view of the conduct of "Good old Tony".

Over the previous few months, we'd been exposed to a large number of issues within Iraq, which all seemed to make the invasion of said country a little more likely. There was of course, the very valid reason that Saddam Hussein's regime was brutal and murderous. This was obviously a human rights issue, much like Robert Mugabe's awful regime in Zimbabwe, though, oddly, we haven't been there, though I can't imagine why. There was also a strong suggestion that Saddam was inherently a terrorist and had links to Al Qaeda, and that he was sheltering Osama Bin Laden (who the Americans really, really want to get hold of, apparently).

Now, the issue I had with this is that everyone seems to have links to Al Qaeda nowadays, whether its Spanish people who would rather not be Spanish, who are blowing up bits of Spain, or un-credited explosions in India, London or Pakistan, it's all seemingly carried out by the same people, in the name of Islam. Maybe they all have links to Al Qaeda. Maybe everyone could be linked to Al Qaeda, given the correct level of hysteria. I, for one, was quite fond of an Indian girl in my class at school. Maybe that's me in the club too. Please don't tell anyone.

Maybe these links to Al Qaeda come from the same intelligence sources as all the intelligence linking people to communism from the previous forty-odd years. In fact, we know they do, don't we? All things being equal, if you replayed a speech of Ronald Reagan's concerning Nicaragua and Communism in the eighties, it would sound very similar to the recent ramblings of George W over Iraq. Very similar indeed, in fact, worryingly so, given the dire consequences. This perhaps suggests something along the lines of manufacturing a pantomime villain but surely the Americans wouldn't do that, would they? Perhaps it's a co-incidence that Al Qaeda now lurks like an invisible spectre in the background of the western world in much the same way as the commies did. Maybe when American children grow up and stop believing in the Bogeyman, they simply need something else to fear.

If considered as a concept, the Al Qaeda part sounds even less likely in any case. The term Al Qaeda, when translated, has any number of meanings, mostly centred on it being something like a foundation, or fundamental underpinning. As an entity, it doesn't, can't really exist. Surely the watching world must realise that all the terrorists in the world, fighting all their separate causes, couldn't simply unite as one organisation, with a common goal. Surely the American insistence to the contrary must be greeted with the ridicule it deserves. I find it strange that everyone believes it.

Another, entirely separate (though still included under the terrorist banner) issue was Saddam's chemical and nuclear weapons programme, which would surely threaten the future of all humanity if left undisturbed. Further to that, he was supposedly some type of sexual deviant and had a taste for bad artwork and cheap Portuguese wine, the Philistine. On reflection, perhaps I'd better not call him that.

Nobody mentioned oil. Nobody mentioned a bitter American resentment of Saddam dating back 12 years. Nobody said unfinished business. Nobody said venting American anger, following the awful events of September 11th 2001. It was all about moral obligation. These were the official reasons given at the time. Officially and actually are most certainly two different things. Furthermore, I personally didn't feel morally obliged to go and invade a country. I would have much preferred to stay at home, with the missus and flushing toilet.

Good for me then, that my involvement was beginning to seem less and less likely over the next few weeks. The invasion, whilst officially still in the negotiation stages, was imminently looming over the political horizon, whilst I had heard nothing. I had assumed that, due to my so-called specialist skills, (which, in truth, existed only on paper) I would either be called up as a matter of priority, or not needed at all. The longer time went on, the less likely it seemed I would be involved.

The Army had told me, as they told the vast majority, upon leaving, that I would be sorely missed. I was, officially, an electronics technician (which was seemingly one of the more desirable trades, of the many on offer from the armed forces), of impressive repute and had achieved qualification and experience above the average. I was one of a few people that had become qualified to repair Phoenix, the Army's all singing, all dancing unmanned reconnaissance aircraft.

The sad truth of this, however, was that the aircraft itself never sang and it certainly didn't dance. In fact it only ever flew sporadically. It was really an out of date six hundred and fifty million pound white elephant (Price correct at time of going to press). Furthermore, it required no particular expertise to repair either. The truth about me was that I had been a decent tradesman but a poor soldier and in my two years of civilian life, my soldiering skills had deteriorated alarmingly quickly.

Since leaving the armed forces, my lot in life had flourished into something which offered infinitely more promise than my military career ever had (even before I saw through the lies at the beginning). Like many were at the time, I had become heavily involved in property developing and was beginning to make some solid money. I was soon to be married to a delightful young woman, who I will not embarrass by describing further and who should hereby be known simply as the missus. I was living in a rather smart detached house, in a very pleasant area and also working at my father's company as a motor fitter in the other hours my life had to offer. It's fair to say that things were going well and I had left the army well and truly behind. My life had been taken over by hard work, a glass of wine and a Sunday morning lie in. Soldiering wasn't on the agenda anymore.

Four weeks after the decision to declare a national emergency and call out the reserve, my future brother-in-law, having left the Army a few weeks before myself, received his call-up papers. The mood was one of disbelief and disappointment. He certainly wasn't happy and I could strongly sympathise with him. The British Army is undermanned and over-committed but that was in no way his fault, yet it was he who would be made to suffer for the shortcomings of others, it seemed, well, at the time anyway. Personally, although I was upset for him, it appeared that my chances of being called up were greatly reduced, as I had been both senior in rank to him and part of a trade group which was seemingly in far greater demand. It defied logic to call me up after him but then logic was never the Army's chosen tool.

It came as a monumentally unpleasant shock when, less than a week later, the day after valentine's day, my compulsory call-up papers landed on the doormat, with a life-changing slap. After a nice evening with the missus the night before, we had decided to extend matters to a champagne breakfast and a possible resumption of the things adults do. The postman delivered a large brown envelope and expecting it to be something completely different, I went downstairs to open it. I had recently applied to join the police and was anticipating notification of the next stage of my application. As I opened the envelope, my thoughts changed from a career move I was genuinely looking forward to, to one I could only look back on with deepest regret.

Unfortunately, the champagne didn't get out of the fridge, as its taste would have been horribly soured. The compulsory call-out of the TA and general reserve had suddenly wiped the smile from my face with a firm hand I had long since forgotten the feel of. It seemed I suddenly had a legal obligation to support the war effort. I had no moral obligation, of that, I was certain. As far as I was concerned, "Good old Tony" and George W could go and poke themselves up the arse.

I remember when I signed up for the Army. I could do a minimum of three years and three months and get out if I didn't like it. I would be transferred onto the reserve list but that didn't matter because the general reserve hadn't been called up for almost fifty years. Furthermore, I would probably do the full twenty two years because I would be forever playing sport, or away on adventure training and I would be promoted very quickly and be paid an awful lot of money for what seemed to be an enormous, fulfilling, beer drinking challenge. On the downside, I might occasionally have to spend six months in a war zone but then I would hardly notice because I would be permanently drunk. Like a twat, I fell for it. Make of that what you will. I can only offer that I was young and naïve.

In retrospect, I find it odd that I had to sign a few documents and no one from the Army signed anything. It really was simply a huge scam and I fell for it, hook line and sinker. It seemed that of all the qualities required of a soldier, integrity wasn't one of them, particularly when working in the recruiting office. The nature of a handshake has been long since forgotten by many a dishonest man and he shook my hand without ever knowing that in times gone by, it was meant to signify that you were unarmed and bore no ill-intent. I took it at this meaning but that was probably the first time I discovered that a verbal agreement, made between two men, is completely worthless. The price of learning this turned out to be much higher than initially expected, I later found.

The small print on a deal which had already turned sour for me jumped out and grabbed me firmly by the bollocks. There didn't seem to be much I could do when an organisation (This is overstating their case, to some extent), which had used and abused me for the best part of six years decided it wanted yet another pound of flesh from my already stricken hide. I accept that for some people, the Army can be a loving wife but for an increasing number, it has developed into a treacherous mistress, intent on ruin. I felt trapped. For nearly two years, I had been master of my own destiny, but from that moment on, I was drawn into the inevitability of the Army system.

The letter informed me that this was a compulsory mobilisation of the TA and general reserve. It also said that I was to report to a place called the Reserves Training and Mobilisation Centre at Chilwell, near Nottingham, on the 28th February. It said that if I were pronounced medically fit, I would be issued new kit and equipment and taken back onto the regular strength of the Army. It seemed that somehow, I had incurred a debt to society, although I didn't know how.

The letter said quite a lot, in terms of legalities and threats of prosecution. It didn't say much in terms of anything I actually wanted to know, though. There was no mention of where I would go, what I would do, when I would come back or even what may happen beyond day one of my engagement. Seemingly, the need to know bit started precisely at this point. I felt I needed to know. Unfortunately, they didn't. The army's capacity for looking after the interests of those in its employ had picked up exactly where it left off, as far as I was concerned. In fact, as far as "Good Old Tony" and George W were concerned, it seemed that I could go and poke myself up the arse.

The letter also said that I should make adequate financial provision for my family and that I should try to arrange adequate life assurance cover. There was more than a hint of a one way trip in the wording of it. In addition to the general heartache, the timing of it really didn't suit me financially either. I had always had money in the bank and I had always had life assurance, however, I had recently thrown all the cash into bricks and mortar – I owned three houses – and ceased my life assurance policies, to reduce costs. These papers wouldn't have been welcomed at any time but for me, they arrived precisely at the wrong time.

By this point, I was starting to despair at my latest misfortune at the hands of the Army. I decided to go and see my parents, who lived close by, to discuss the matter. It was there that I usually sought my wisest council in most matters as, at twenty seven years old, I had finally become mature enough to know that they knew best all along. The missus had pre-empted our visit with a cautionary telephone call. Their preparation for my visit was obvious, as my mother already appeared worried, yet my father looked more like a stern parent, who was about to put his errant child in his place.

My mother said little, as the discussion between my father and I became slightly heated, which was very rare. His point of view was a very logical one. He was and still is a very successful businessman. His perspective was that I had signed the contract and I was legally bound to honour it. He believed, logically and sensibly, that the Army wouldn't just pluck someone from the street and send them to invade a country, whilst trained soldiers occupy lesser duties at home. He believed that I would be filling in for staffing shortages in a camp somewhere in Europe.

He didn't think, for one minute, that anyone was stupid enough to send untrained soldiers into war, not in the new millennium. My perspective was that the Army was and always has been run by incompetents, who have no care or conscience over the lives they waste. There is, of course, a good deal of history to support this view, from the few who lived to tell the tale. Like the errant child, I also thought it simply wasn't fair.

I had a further argument centred on human rights legislation and the complete lack of parity with all other aspects of British society. Asylum seekers, upon their entry to Great Britain, have various rights, which the country must immediately support them with, regardless of cost. Prisoners, detained at her Majesty's pleasure for their crimes and misdemeanours also have these human rights. These are all in accordance with the human rights act of 2000 and must be rigorously conformed with, at all costs.

Several aspects of this legislation, which were relevant to me and my call up were; Firstly, and most importantly, the right to life, then there's my right to freedom of thought, conscience and religion, my right to respect for my private and family life, my right to liberty and security and what about the prohibition of forced labour? There are others, all of which were in force at the time. The law in England and Wales allows that these could be breached, only in times of national emergency. It is worth pointing out there is no other group of people who can have their human rights breached in this way. (Note from author; I duly acknowledge that this may seem simply that I am airing my point of view and indeed, it certainly is a thing which must be cleared from my chest but this point of view is a necessity in itself and is divisive in the telling of this account).

It would have been fine if that was it but my point was this; if I had been in prison, I wouldn't have been called. Similarly, if I had been dishonourably discharged from the armed forces, for drugs related offences or similar, I wouldn't have been called. The only people they could call up were the ones who had behaved properly whilst in the Army and abided by the law having left it. Step forward one reluctant law abiding citizen, with an exemplary record of past military service. It didn't matter how much tax

I'd paid, it seemed I still had a hefty debt to society and payment was due. Many times previously, I'd observed that a soldier could receive the same thing as a punishment or reward. This will be proven in detail later.

Later that day, with my wisest council having failed me for once, the missus suggested that a spot of retail therapy may be just the thing to cool my boiling anger. Unfortunately, upon our arrival in the town centre, we were greeted by a demonstration against the proposed invasion of Iraq. The scruffy oik, with megaphone in one hand and petition in the other, might as well have just accepted the inevitable. His message wasn't reaching me at all. I didn't bother signing the petition, as I had already signed it twice in previous weeks. Unfortunately, these signatures, like thousands, possibly millions of others, counted for nothing. In the name of democracy, the western world had already dictated the future of the middle-east.

Nothing seemed to be taking my mind away from my predicament and matters soured further upon our return home, to the house I owned, paid heavy taxes on and wouldn't be allowed to live in, in a fortnight (At this point, if you press your nose close to the page, you may smell the bitterness). I switched on the television set and was greeted by the sight of apparently around two million people protesting against the war. They gathered in Hyde Park, to listen to Ken Livingstone attempting to provide a viable case for peace. It seemed an admirable attempt, whatever his motives were. To give him due credit, he seemed to understand the point of such a gathering. Peace is only possible if it is presented as a realistic alternative to war, rather than a distant ideal.

From there, things degenerated into the usual drivel. A pop star, shouting and singing the word "peace" repeatedly, does not a successful campaign make but Ms Dynamite(e)'s ramblings appeared eloquent, when compared to the offering by the guest of honour, the incredibly reverend Jesse Jackson. This, Jesse, was your big moment.

The unease on Ken Livingstone's face was easy to see as the man who seemingly finished second (or third) in every major political campaign he's entered, began to shout, rant and rave on no particular subject, offering no particular wisdom, wasting the opportunity, before a massive world audience, to put across a structured argument for peace, or maybe just a speech of stirring sentiment and humanity. He bathed in a moment of pure self indulgence, whilst I sat waist deep in self pity.

By the end of Jesse's raucous demonstration of ineptitude, the whole world was left certain of something they had suspected all along. Peace is just an unattainable dream. It's something to wish for, when you blow out the candles on your birthday cake. It's a myth, made all the more romantic by the dreamers and idealists of this world. I don't think anyone told Jesse though. Let me hear you all say "Peace". No, it didn't work, did it?

## CHAPTER 2;
## THE DIFFICULTY OF ACCEPTANCE.

THE REMAINING TWELVE days of freedom I had left threw up some very odd and unfortunate answers to my questions. After several calls to the help-line, concerning topics such as where I may go, or for how long, or what I was doing, or what I would be paid, I found out that they weren't actually the people I was supposed to be speaking to. The help-line number on my and presumably everyone else's call-up papers was, bizarrely enough, the wrong number.

It was in fact, the number for the regular Army's pay department, which probably explained why no one knew anything. (To some, this may demonstrate an incredible lack of competence within the Armed forces system. Indeed, I had been out of the Army for so long that it surprised me but the reality of it is that this is very much the norm.) A quick call to directory enquiries gave me the number for the Reserves Training and Mobilisation Centre (RTMC) Chilwell and suddenly the picture became clearer, albeit in a restricted fashion.

I would be at RTMC for a day and a half, where I would undergo medical and dental examinations and, if healthy enough, I would be issued new kit and sent to a camp in Grantham where, over a period of four days, they would take me from the civilian I had become, to the lean, mean, fighting machine I never was. It seemed a tall order. The time after Grantham wasn't their concern and, as such, they knew nothing of what to expect. I hadn't learned much but at least I knew roughly what the first week would consist of. As far as the Army was concerned, I knew exactly what I "Needed to know".

I went to work as normal but found myself to be discussing my situation with everyone, rather than getting on with my job. Being the managing director's son, I was not always everyone's first choice for conversation but people did seem genuinely surprised and sympathetic towards my predicament. Reassuringly, they all seemed to share my father's belief that I would not end up anywhere near the Middle East. They all shared my view that I was, regardless of my military history, a civilian like any other on the shop floor. They, like me, knew I wasn't a soldier. None of them had any military experience but they had all formed the collective view that "The Army's not that fuckin' stupid" as to send me to invade another country.

Some even mocked me, singing the Dad's Army theme and suggesting possible roles I may be fit for. As I was previously known as Corporal Jones in my former life, my ears received this easily and I offered no disagreement. (Neither did I acknowledge the scintillating wit required for such humour) I guessed that to get me back up to a decent soldiering standard would really take a good few weeks training. The four days on offer might just get me back to a standard to be put on standby for the fireman's strike, or some other benign duty, nothing more. The only doubts in my mind were caused by my knowledge of the lack of common sense and compassion employed within the Army system. I knew that the four days might just be sufficient to put a tick in my box, where it said "Trained soldier", thereby forcibly separating the official and actual at the outset.

I decided that the best thing I could do was to accept my situation and try to make the best preparation possible, for the missus' sake. I called an insurance company and attempted to get some prices for life insurance. I told them my situation and awaited the answer. After a few seconds, the manager came on and politely refused to insure me in any capacity. I couldn't disagree with them either. It didn't seem that there could be much of a profit in it for them, given the risks. I suddenly found myself as uninsurable as a seventeen-year-old with a fast car and a speeding conviction. Even the dog who always says "Oh Yes" muttered expletives under his breath.

I also knew that the mortgage on the house we lived in was solely in my name and hence, I had to check if that mortgage policy had sufficient life cover in it to pay out in the event of my death. It would have been bad enough me meeting an unfortunate end as a result of Tony and George's pact of shite (Which the insurance companies felt was fairly likely, it seemed) but it didn't seem fair that the missus should become homeless as a result of this.

I called the company dealing with the life cover part of my mortgage and explained my situation. She went away to check the details of my policy and came back with a reassuring tone of voice. "Yes Mr. Jones, the policy will pay out in the event of your death, be that from old age, illness, accidental or pretty much anything." Then, obviously turning the page, she continued. "Yes, it'll pay out for almost anything…With the exception of an act of war." I gathered my thoughts for a second then asked her to confirm that that was the only eventuality in which they wouldn't pay out. She did, I thanked her and put the phone down. For illustration's sake, I would guess I muttered something like "Bastard" at this point.

It's fair to say that this wasn't a good day. Upon her return from work, I broke the news, as implausible as it seemed, to the missus, who took it with false good cheer and optimism for my sake. Then, with false good cheer and optimism for her sake, I set about making the tea. At this point, I feared that eating could prove difficult due to the solid grimace which had set itself in my jaw-line. I also noted, at this time, that I was barely able to taste my food. This, I put down purely to my agitated state, which was also preventing me from sleeping or concentrating an anything other than my impending doom.

I watched the news, which kept throwing up little snippets of motivation to invade Iraq. There were a few leaked reports, or photocopies at least and a few articles concerning the not-particularly-infamous Al-Samoud missiles but nothing much to actually prove that Saddam Hussein had committed any serious wrongdoing in the last decade or so. The whole world was aware that Saddam Hussein was an evil man but for global public opinion to concur with the desire to invade another country, it takes a lot of mud slinging, to equate to one scrap of tangible evidence. This war was happening with or without that but the gap certainly needed to be closed significantly. Eventually, after creating so much smoke, public opinion would concur that there must be fire, somewhere, even if six months of NATO weapons inspections suggested otherwise.

I gave a little consideration to these so-called leaked reports, the nature of which I still find confusing. Should someone not face trial, following their deliberate disclosure of articles covered within the official secrets act? Surely they would, if the government hadn't intended it to become public knowledge. I feel sure though, that the country buys into this method of revealing information as being genuine. Strange then, that such leaked information always suits the cause of the government of the day. They tell us it's true, so it must be. Maybe not.

Six days before I was due to leap into the unknown, my future brother-in-law was due to donate his pound of flesh for the cause. Having taken the previous week off to sort out his life, as best he could, he duly arrived at RTMC for mobilisation. We waited with baited breath for any snippet of information. I remember selfishly thinking more of the information he could give me, than the predicament he was in. A few hours later, we found out that he had been given numerous forms to fill in upon his arrival and then basically given a sleeping bag, shown to a dorm and told to be up at six o'clock the following morning. Bit of a damp squib, that.

As a newly arrived component of the military machine, he had done exactly as he was told and turned up the next morning to attend his medical and dental inspections and probably to sign a few dozen forms, most of which contained the same information. Then, after finding out the vague suggestion that he might have been in the Army's employment for as long as eight months, came the dampest of squibs, in the form of a failed medical.

Happily enough, although he'd been passed as fit to leave after five-and-a-half physically strenuous years in the Army, it seemed that in two years of Civilian life, his knees had been damaged beyond repair. Casting him aside like an old odd sock, the Army decided that they couldn't take him back and sent him home the same day. He didn't get a tick in the box and unsurprisingly, there were no apologies for the inconvenience or the stress induced, just the promise that they would pay him the £395 call-out gratuity sooner or later, probably later. So, as much as I was relieved to see him return, I was still frustrated at being left entirely in the dark as to my own predicament.

My last few days at work weren't spent as productively as they should have been. I had tried repeatedly to be positive and to put a brave face on it, even to try and look forward to it, to some degree but no matter how hard I tried, I couldn't convince myself. The plain truth was that the last thing I wanted to do was be re-united with my former employers, whatever task they had in mind for me. There were a few more seemingly hilarious remarks from my colleagues at work but in truth, I wasn't entirely appreciative. The resentment of the situation I had managed to get myself into was at the forefront of my thinking and nothing else mattered.

Similarly, my last night with the missus was something of a non-event. I wanted to smile. I wanted to enjoy myself but it just wasn't happening. I couldn't think of much else other than how unfair the situation was. "A right miserable bastard." Was how she put it and she was right. I wish that last night had been different but I have to concede it would have taken a better man than me. All I could produce was bitter resentment of the government policies, which had given rise to this situation. No need to press your nose to the page this time. Trust me it's there.

It seemed to stem back as far as the early nineties when the problems started. The government, without care or wisdom, decided to offer redundancies across the Armed forces in order to cut manning levels and subsequently cut costs. The fancy title was "Options for Change." Economics aside, this was seen by many in the armed forces as the day it all started to go wrong. With fewer men, there was less scope for the niceties, which an Army career can bring. Instead of adventure training, career courses and relaxing during slow periods they were greeted with more duties, more operational tours and a general tightening of the belt. The vicious circle, which the Army now finds itself in, had begun. The solution? Spend more money on recruitment adverts, of course.

With the situation ever worsening, more and more people left. As more people left, the staffing levels became tighter and tighter and so the effect continued until the present day, where the Army is undermanned in almost every trade group during peace-time and completely unable to scale a war-fighting force. National emergency it isn't but the Army is in a mess due to mismanagement and the only people available to bail them out are the people who left the Army for those reasons, the unfortunate bastards on the reserve list.

Certainly, in my case, that was the exact truth. In the soldier's contract, which the Army really only adheres to as and when it sees fit, it states that there should be an interval of two years between one six-month tour and another. After the completion of one, which ran up to seven and a half months, I had asked for a year (Not the two, to which I was entitled) back in the UK, to sort my life out and get my career back on track as I was overdue promotion but unable to complete the necessary courses due to my absence. I was assured that this wouldn't be a problem. Unfortunately, that promise, like many others, was quickly broken and I was packed off to Kosovo for another six-month tour, within four months of my return. There were other reasons for my resignation but the main point was that I couldn't see my way out of the endless cycle of overseas tours I was in.

If I had stayed in, I would certainly have managed to squeeze in another tour between then and this latest kick in the teeth. My case is further illustrated by the fact that at one point during my final months, I was on standby (24 hours notice to move, no less) for the fireman's strike, for the foot and mouth crisis as well as another jaunt back to Kosovo. Unfortunately though, I wasn't actually standing by. I was working extra hours to make up for the work I'd missed whilst in Kosovo and I incurred extra guard duties as well, due to the lack of available manpower. If I had stayed in, I would almost certainly have gone to Afghanistan in the meantime but oddly, I genuinely believe I would have avoided any involvement in the Iraq Debacle. It was the bitterest of bitter pills and I was struggling to swallow.

On the gut-wrenching day of departure, the missus went with me to the train station, where I was to catch a train to Derby station and be picked up from there. It was an odd situation given the events of six days earlier, which were all we had to go on. I didn't know when I would be back. I might well have been back the very next day. I might be gone for the six days and then sent home to wait. I might have been gone for a month or possibly six, or even the awful prospect of eight.

We didn't know anything and when you don't know where you're going, or for how long, it's difficult to say your goodbyes properly. So it was then, that without telling the missus how much I loved her, or how much I would miss her, or how I couldn't stand being away from her, that I left her and my comfortable civilian life behind for a rather uncertain future. I don't suppose she found the situation any better than I did because she never signed on the dotted line and neither had she chosen to spend her life with a soldier. We got together shortly after I left the Army, so she never knew of the Army way of life. It was a point of note that the Army cared even less for her well being than mine and yet she is a civilian and a taxpayer, one of the people the Army is supposed to protect.

# CHAPTER 3; INTO THE SAUSAGE MACHINE.

I LEFT THE train at Derby station and along with the other passengers, shuffled along the platform, banging my luggage on my knees as I jostled my way up the steps. That short walk was where my cosy civilian reality ended. All of those people, the civilians, went to the left. In front of me there was a small white sign, which read "Mob Personnel". The loneliest man on earth trudged down towards a lift and then stairs, which bore the same message. It almost seemed to represent a portal into another reality.

With ironic memories of Mr Ben, I followed the signs downstairs. I was greeted outside by a small foreign man in civilian clothes who spoke only the worst of English. I knew instantly that this man was a Ghurkha and I knew instantly that I was going the right way, despite the fact that I couldn't understand a word he said. I followed his physical directions to a bus waiting around the corner. As I arrived at the bus, I was joined, by some similarly downtrodden and uncertain-looking people.

As has always been the case with the Army, it was time to stand around and wait. We had to wait for fifty-odd other "Mobilised Personnel" to arrive and then we would be off, to be processed in the "Sausage Machine" that was RTMC Chilwell. As we stood there, six or seven of us, I said nothing, preferring to listen to the others for a while and attempt to gather information. As usual, one man proclaimed himself to be the absolute expert over all matters and proceeded to tell us that we were all going away for eight months to fill in for the lack of manning in Germany. Apparently, everyone was doing the same thing. I judged that he seemed too certain and sure of his information to actually know what the hell he was talking about and guessed that he had elected himself for the role of group bull-shitter. It was a point of note though, that he was quite happy to go away for eight months, well, unless this was more bull-shit.

The difference in motivation between these people and me was vast. There was one clear reason for this. I asked around the other half-dozen people standing there. All of them were current TA personnel. None of them had served with the regular Army before and they all seemed to have a healthy curiosity of the situation. One said he hoped to get out to Iraq. None disagreed. I said nothing further. They hadn't experienced the unpleasantness of the British Army before and I had, at length. To them, it was a hobby, which they enjoyed and which they were about to experience full-time. Furthermore, as they all excitedly declared, this would satisfy their TA commitments for the year. This didn't initially register with me.

I asked for an explanation and it basically meant that this call-up would allow them not to see the TA again for the rest of the year and still collect their bounty. The bounty, a point of irritation with regular soldiers, is something the TA receive, for fulfilling their commitments of whatever days and weekends they are supposed to attend during a year. It comes in at around £1300 tax-free and the regular soldier doesn't get a sniff. As a reservist, I also got nothing, not even a fiver, so to start with, all the TA soldiers were better off than myself. Couple this with the fact that they volunteered to sign on for the TA a lot more recently than I signed (Within the previous twelve months) and the difference in enthusiasm is obvious. I sat on the bus alone and chose not to listen to any more "information" provided by "the expert".

As the bus filled up, I was greeted by the sight of a lot of middle-aged men, who all looked at least slightly more enthusiastic than I did. No one knew much more than I did about what would happen but I knew better about how it would be carried out. I knew how we would be treated and how it would make me feel. For them, that was still to be discovered. I attempted to make conversation with no one. All I knew is that for all I disbelieved "the expert", I couldn't face eight months away from my life. This would be my third tour in just over four years, which was a lot, considering I'd been out of the Army for almost two. For the majority of the rest, it would be their first and if the engagement went to form, most probably, their last.

We arrived at the ill-maintained, depressingly designed shit-hole, which is RTMC Chilwell and were driven into a huge hangar building and told, not asked, to leave the bus. At this point, I was reminded just how ill mannered the Army set-up is. I have always considered myself to be a polite person from a decent upbringing and I find that the use of please and thank you and the like have always gone a long way. It was a point that during my Army career, I was criticised by some for being too polite. I bore this criticism out and pointed out that I wanted people to co-operate willingly with me, rather than reluctantly do as they were told. I address people politely because I would rather be addressed politely myself but that's not the way with the Army. It never has been.

A Loud and uninspiring voice, belonging to a burly, inarticulate infantry sergeant, boomed out the order. "Right, switch your mobile phones off because they'll crash the computer system." Unsurprisingly, this was the standard instruction, which this particular component part of the Army had been programmed to give. Doubtless, he had been told this by a senior man and hadn't thought to question the implausibility of it. This was the first of many such portions of ridiculous bullshit we were to be spoon-fed. Sensibly, he could have asked us to turn them off, just to be polite during the briefings we were about to receive but the Army always relies on the "Aggressive Bullshit" method of instruction. I turned off my phone because, unlike many other men I was about to encounter, I am not an ignorant arse-hole, or at least, I try not to be.

We were herded like sheep into a large briefing area, told to sit down and then told, very briefly that we would have to form a queue to perform the first of many sittings of paperwork, (most of which was pointless, the rest of which would be lost in the system). Like the inmates we had become, with the doors locked behind us, we slowly shuffled forward and identified ourselves as the men on the list and took several different sheets of paper, a urine sample tube and countless other uninteresting nick-knacks to sit down at our next briefing. A Geordie voice muttered; "This is a fuckin' load of shit, isn't it?" A number of heads nodded their agreement.

The next briefing, presented by a monotone Irish Artillery Officer (who sounded very much like an IRA terrorist, explaining that he knew your address) was about the general purpose of our time at Chilwell. "Don't ask any questions about where you might be going from here. We're only here to process you to the next stage. All we've been told is that you've been called up for eight months. We don't know where you're going or what you're doing but you might find out when you get to Grantham tomorrow night." With that, a thousand questions were put on hold until the following night.

This stage of the Sausage Machine was simply to "process" us into the Army and then on to Grantham. He then told us, in officer speak, that we would be pissed about something rotten for a couple of days and warned us, in his stern, flat, monotone voice, "Keep your sense of humour". This man was amongst the most uninspiring people I have ever encountered. The same Geordie voice muttered "Ignorant cunt". The same heads nodded. "The expert" looked smug at the verification of his claims. The machine rolled on.

The next stage was to fill in half-a-dozen forms or so and then sit and wait for the chubby female sergeant to loudly shout "next" which, after fifteen minutes or so, she duly did. I stepped forward and verified that I was, or at least I had been the name, rank and number she offered me. She opened a file and pulled out an envelope and tipped the contents out onto the table. Like a ghost from the past there was my ID card, with a picture of my former self, staring back at me. I confirmed that he had been the idiot who got me into this mess and also took my dog tags back from her, the same ones that he had worn before he wised up to the scam. I swore under my breath and reluctantly agreed that they had me by the balls and I couldn't do a thing about it.

We were then shuffled around several other briefings before the last and oddest of them all, the Anthrax briefing. Here we were greeted by the chief medical officer, a chubby, middle-aged Major, who spoke with several plums in his mouth and came across as incredibly assured and well informed. In fact, he came across almost as the world authority on both the Anthrax virus and vaccine, informing us at length that the vaccine was perfectly safe and that without it, we might well die a horrible death. The lengthy instructional video too demonstrated just how necessary the jab was.

Indeed, the delightful Shobna Pakrahvan (She's a jobbing actress/TV presenter, paid to articulate the Army's point of view on the subject) demonstrated that the virus is invisible, can be easily inhaled and has no smell. Surely any British soldier worth his salt would want protection from such a disease with a nice, safe vaccine. Any sane individual could tell she was reading an autocue and hadn't got a clue about what she was preaching. Then again, we were all in a darkened room, with no voice of reason to tell us otherwise. Surely this scam couldn't work.

A point of alarming curiosity to me was that to have the vaccine, the British soldier had to sign a disclaimer first. They didn't explain this part in any detail but then it was only a signature on a piece of paper, it wouldn't affect your rights at all, they said. The disclaimer seemed genuinely irrelevant in the Army's presentation, just as it had quickly become in the minds of all around me. It wasn't so irrelevant that we could have the jab without signing it though. My mind wandered towards the plausibility of ex-soldier's claims for Gulf war Syndrome from the previous conflict. Maybe they had a disclaimer too.

Later, we were shown to our accommodation, namely small grubby rooms with lots of beds. We were issued a sleeping bag each and told to be up at six the following morning for what would be a tiring day. It seemed all I could do was attempt to strike up conversation with my fellow inmates and see if anyone had anything useful to say. That was where I first encountered a man who should only be known as my mate Dave.

I told him my situation and he told me that he was Ex-Army and had been a member of The TA until quite recently. He had one child, a little boy and his wife was expecting their second in about three months time. It seemed to me that anyone with any sense would have allowed him to simply go home to where he was surely needed most, rather than just be included in the vast number of people to be mobilised. Unfortunately, we had left the common sense world behind. We were back in the Army, where common sense counts for nothing and the system rules over everything.

All Dave represented to the Army was a man who belonged to a particular trade group, which was officially in big demand. It was capable of taking into account nothing else, other than the question of whether he was medically fit to serve. If he was, he was going wherever they sent him, box ticked, without any individual consideration. If he wasn't, he would be allowed home. In these times of morality, political correctness and human rights for all, it seemed unfair that a two-hundred-year-old system, which had been failing for years, had the final say on his immediate future, rather than his being judged as an individual case. Morally and sensibly, that man should have been allowed home, to be with his family but then, the system is inflexible in the extreme and cannot take morality into account.

We discussed a few notions of attempting to fail the following morning's medical. It was also suggested to me to tell the dentist I had chronic toothache. (This would be very problematic because, at twenty seven, I didn't even have any fillings). All of the ideas appealed but I don't think I ever genuinely believed that I was going to manage it. The truth was that I was fit and healthy and wasn't about to get away with anything on medical grounds. I think I knew it then but until they passed me medically fit, I still had hope.

After our discussions on the practicalities of the medical, most of the other men returned to the dreary squalor of the room, to sleep. I remember feeling a genuine point of annoyance that I couldn't go to sleep when I wanted. I had to wait for everyone else as well. I hadn't slept in communal accommodation for five or six years at that point and had taken my own personal space for granted. Amongst other things I used to take for granted were a nice, comfortable king size double bed and carpet on the floor.

I was also pretty despondent to be joined by a middle-aged Jock who, whilst picking the filth from between his pungent, cheesy feet, informed me that the Army, without the influence of common sense, had sent some TA and reservists to the gulf already. I argued the toss about the sensibilities of such an action with him but he seemed absolutely certain of his information. I didn't take this to heart. The Army is probably the largest and most complex rumour machine in existence and everyone's sure of everything, until it turns out to be total rubbish.

This said, even though I knew full well that sending this motley bunch of middle-aged ex-soldiers and non-soldiers into a war would be a ridiculously stupid thing to do, I also knew that many ridiculous things happen in the Army. The Army's rules are firmly set in stone and few of the so-called hierarchy have the decency or courage to challenge them on common sense grounds. In fact, most of them lack the common sense in any case.

So it was that I laid uncomfortably in my uncomfortable bed, (green plastic mattress anyone?) in a room full of strangers, contemplating the morality of such matters, whilst gently contemplating sleep. I knew this was unlikely as I had far too much on my mind and I have always been a light sleeper. On top of this, I knew that, of the twenty or so men in the room, one fucking arsehole would snore like a pig and keep me awake all-night. I hate snoring. I don't snore and it always seems that the people who do haven't made much effort to prevent it. It all just seems so inconsiderate and it really makes my blood boil.

Sure enough, within a few minutes, the Jock of absolute certainty, with the cheesy feet, almost ruptured my eardrum with his first, thunderous burst of inhalation. So loud was it that it drew a number of complaints from around the room. I woke him up and informed him that he had been snoring and politely asked him if he could attempt not to do so. It worked for a few minutes. An hour or so later, I woke him up again and told him that he was getting firmly and squarely on my tits and told him, without manners, that I would prefer it if he stopped. He didn't, so after another hour or so, I gathered my mattress and sleeping bag and headed for the corridor. I spent the rest of that depressing, sleepless night out there, with two other males who mentioned "Fucking snoring like a bastard pig". Already, I was missing the good things that life had to offer but then, when you make deal with the Devil…

## CHAPTER 4; WHATEVER HAPPENS IS INEVITABLE.

I AWOKE FROM my few minutes of peaceful sleep, to be greeted by the sight of a few naked men making the first moves towards manning the sinks and ablutions. With some vague memory of my former life, I decided that I needed to get myself washed and dressed before it became a queuing matter and before it appeared that the sinks had been used as toilets. Sure enough, around ten minutes after I'd readied myself, the corridor was filled with around a hundred men waiting to wash, shave and liberally scratch their bollocks. It wasn't a pretty sight and was certainly a lot less pleasant than waking up next to the missus. I couldn't remember the last time I saw ten dicks before breakfast and I wasn't looking forward to the next time either.

After a heavily greased but reasonably edible breakfast (There had to be a high point somewhere), it was back into the hangar for another briefing, to fill in a few more forms before we were sent to be medically approved for service. Personally, I had mixed emotions on this subject as I wanted to be pronounced fit, so as not to jeopardise my application for the Police Force. Unfortunately, this also meant that I had to endure whatever mindless scheme the Army had planned for me. If I was passed fit, that was it, box ticked. I was on the boat and I would have to endure whatever stormy weather it sailed into. I had no way of influencing my immediate future.

I went to the medical centre and along with everyone else, sat and waited for my turn, whilst filling in a few forms. After that, I had to fill my urine sample tube, which looked a tall order, as I had already been that morning. I managed to go into the cubicle and squeeze out nearly half of the amount I needed. Fortunately, it was quite yellow, so it would still look okay when I topped it up with tap water. I scribbled my name on it and handed it in. It was a piece of piss.

Whilst I waited, I came across a strange situation. There was a man before me, whom I would guess to have been in his late forties, complaining bitterly about having failed his medical due to a back problem. He seemed genuinely angry at not being allowed to go to war. I asked him why he was so upset to miss out on something that surely no one in his right mind would want to do.

"You don't actually want to go do you?" I asked.

"Well, next time there's a war on I'll be too old." He replied.

"I think the doctor's just told you you're too old this time."

"Yeah but its something I want to experience."

"Fucking hell, do you want me to donate a few healthy body parts?"

"You might not fuckin' pass it yet."

"I'm not that lucky mate." I replied, genuinely amazed that anyone would want to experience such a thing. For me, ignorance would have been more than blissful. I had all the military experience I wanted. I'd seen a few unpleasant things in Kosovo but not much in the way of action. Still, this was enough to tell me I didn't want to see anymore. Unfortunately, I fully expected to pass the medical and gain more unneeded military experience.

The medical consisted of the usual heart rate, blood pressure, sight and hearing and height and weight checks, followed by a thorough examination with a doctor. It was at this point that I could be deemed medically unfit; however it looked unlikely, as I had woken feeling exceptionally fresh and healthy, despite my lack of sleep. In fact, I felt curiously healthy. I wasn't tired at all and I didn't have an aching joint anywhere on my body. I would say that, at the time when I most needed to be unwell or injured, my body was functioning better than it ever had.

My blood pressure was perfect. I had no backache and he couldn't find a creak or groan on any joint. I was, as he proclaimed, in perfect working order. He had a brief, if very uncomfortable grope of my testicles, although not in a personal manner. I don't think he was that impressed by my physical well being. Nonetheless, it was plain to see that I was medically fit. Suddenly feeling resigned to my fate I made a subtle and very gentle enquiry into whether he would consider making me officially unfit for service on some minor technicality that we may be able to agree upon. Unfortunately, there were two honest men in that room, the doctor, who was having none of it and myself, who probably wouldn't have taken the option, even if it were available. I was desperate to leave but I managed to keep my integrity, even if it was a close-run thing.

That was and always had been my problem. I had always been too honest and decent with the Army and had only ever been punished for it. Working for my father, it would have been quite simple to concoct some vague story to cover my absence for business reasons. There is even a standard procedure for it and I have no doubts that, if either myself, or my father had been a more dishonest man, then I would not have been there. Another option would have been to simply throw the papers in the dustbin and pretend I'd never seen them. They didn't arrive by recorded delivery, so there wouldn't have been any problems on that front either. Quite what would have happened afterwards was unclear at that point but I certainly wouldn't have been going through that particular experience at that moment had I not responded as requested.

Once I'd made this schoolboy error, which I decided, was my last, as far as the Army is concerned, I was theirs to punish in any way they saw fit, regardless of my lack of crime. As I passed through the dental inspection, I was, for once, counting myself to be very unlucky for having very healthy teeth. The inevitable pronunciation of my medical fitness had happened and all that was left was to be issued with my kit. At this time, I guessed that the issue of kit would, as ever, be haphazard and would burden me with numerous unnecessary items, whilst failing to satisfy my requirements properly.

A curiosity for my kit issue was that when I left the Army, I had retained several items of equipment and clothing, which collectively had been called my reservist's call-out kit. I was quite surprised that they told me not to take that with me (given its name and nature) and that they would issue me with all the clothing and equipment I needed. Here is where I found there to be two definitions of the word need. I also made a mental note to burn my reservist's call-out kit, if or when I returned.

All the clothing and equipment they thought I needed would be issued to me there and then, thrown at me in great heaps. It came as a surprise that, if I was supposed to be going to the Gulf, as was rumoured, they would issue me with an entire compliment of brand-new green kit. Surely the desert combats would have been better. As ever though, I wasn't making the decision and whether it was right or wrong, whether I really needed it or not, I was issued with greens. Another box ticked.

It was a waste of time, effort and taxpayer's money but that's the system. Everything is done on a large scale and in a uniformed manner. No one actually stops to think about the requirements of the individual. As long as the clothing store has provided the soldier with some kit then the job is done. For an instance, my NBC (Nuclear, Biological, Chemical) protection suit would only have fit a malnourished midget and yet I was made to accept it as they didn't have any in my size and yet they had to issue me with one (box ticked). The standard, if slopey-shouldered answer to this and many other problems is that "It will all be sorted out when you arrive at your unit." Knowing how things really were, I took this to mean, "You will have to spend ages running around like an idiot, trying to sort it out but this will only take place when you get to your unit." Again, strictly speaking, it wasn't a lie.

After I had been issued with my mountain of useless clothing and equipment, I had to go back to the booking in desk and sign just one more form to be "allowed" back into the Army. This form was to accept that I was subject to Army law, which meant that there really was no way back. Suddenly, it sounded like I had a choice.

"What if I don't sign?" I asked.

"We'll charge you with AWOL or desertion and throw you in prison for a few months." Replied the monotone Irish Artillery officer, whose nose, by this time, was looking very tempting for a stray fist or two.

"I suppose its inevitable then." I replied as I accepted defeat.

"Yeah, just sign there and then quickly go and get yourself into your uniform." He offered, in his flat, charm-less manner.

That was my fate sealed. I had just officially volunteered to serve with the British Army. I may have done it under threat of prosecution and I hadn't wanted to but they had forced me to volunteer to sign. It takes a clever man to beat the Army system and I was too stunned to contemplate trying. It seemed unfair and I did feel as though I was being bullied by a particularly unfair regime but I didn't have many options. Furthermore, I really didn't appreciate his arrogant tone. I had one last question then I would be reluctantly putting on the uniform.

"I haven't got my rifle yet. Could you tell me when I get it issued please?"

"I said, put your uniform on then come and sit back here and you'll be told when you get your rifle." He mouthed, rather too aggressively for what had, until then, been a relatively civil conversation.

"No you didn't. You just said to get changed. You're making that last bit up, aren't you?" I replied, much to his disbelief.

"Don't answer me back." He rasped.

"Alright sir, keep your sense of humour, not that you've ever had one… you fucking useless ring-piece." I replied. I didn't care much about incurring his wrath at that point. It looked to me like I'd already been given the consequences, so pissing him off really didn't matter. In fact, upsetting any senior officer really didn't matter. It wouldn't change my fate. What the hell were they going to do to me, send me to the Gulf war? In any case, he didn't reply. I'd guess it wasn't the first time he'd been called that. My little bout of insubordination, within a minute of signing on for service, might have been a new record but I wouldn't have much time to bathe in the freedom of being a condemned man.

I reluctantly, yet hurriedly pulled on my uniform, which felt more uncomfortable and aggravating than it ever had before. Within minutes, I was issued my rifle and told, along with everyone else, that I needed to get my quarter-of-a-tonne of useless kit onto the back of a lorry and to get myself lined up on parade and wait for our coaches to arrive. Of the hundred and fifty or so people arriving on the same day as myself, seventy-seven had survived the medical, of which, seventy-four were TA and three were reservists. All were male. Some of the TA people even looked happy to be there. I wasn't and I was determined not to go quietly.

Our bus journey was an uneventful one and as we arrived in Grantham, where we would spend the next four days training, I began to feel trapped. No one else seemed alarmed that we weren't allowed to leave camp. I certainly was. It was a lonely feeling, almost as though everyone else had accepted his or her fate and I alone was questioning our predicament. There were rumours abound that we were all going to Iraq but they were only rumours. No one knew anything for sure and there were still a few rumours abounding that we would be sat on our backsides in Germany for a few weeks, and then sent home.

The briefing, as we arrived in Grantham, was presented by a rather jovial and seemingly pleasant Sergeant Major from the Green Jackets. He did tell us the unfortunate fact that we wouldn't find out what would happen to us until three days later and that it wasn't his business anyway but other than that, it all seemed to be quite pleasant and relaxed. It was a far more pleasant atmosphere than we were expecting but everyone wanted to know exactly what would happen next. We all had to get used to being kept in the dark because that's simply the way it is.

After another struggle to unload our masses of baggage, we were shown to our accommodation. It was luxurious compared to Chilwell as there were only eight men in our room. It was reasonably clean too and the showers didn't seem to be too disgusting so a few days there might be a pleasant respite after the tense unpleasantness we'd just experienced. Furthermore, I'd managed to shake off the Jock snoring machine with the cheesy feet. As the bar was only a hundred and fifty yards away, it seemed things were indeed looking promising.

Unsurprisingly, given the ratio of numbers, I was again in a room full of Stabs (TA) and it seemed to me that they were all far too interested in matters military, even in their spare time. They all just seemed so keen and interested but then, this was their hobby, I supposed. Looking around the room, I noticed a copy of Bravo Two Zero and a couple of other works of fiction by Andy McNab. Personally, given our predicament, I would rather read anything else but it seemed that some of these men just couldn't get enough of it. I called them a bunch of Stab twats and then went to sleep. No one snored.

# CHAPTER 5; PREPARING FOR AN UNCERTAIN FUTURE.

AS WAS RAPIDLY becoming the norm, we were up at six for what had been described as a rigorous training course. The enthusiasm for anything above "vaguely testing" was sadly missing and, in real terms, if there were any particularly arduous tests to pass, I was more than happy to fail. The thought of not passing the course did spring to mind but then I had heard that like a great many military courses, it was attendance only. It stands to reason really because if it was difficult in any way, then people would fail it in droves.

It was here that the Army had a huge problem. They had to bring what was in principle, a group of civilians, up to a standard to be possibly deployed into a combat zone. In my view, to get me back up to a decent standard of soldiering should have taken a few weeks of hard training, which I would have failed through lack of enthusiasm alone. The people at Grantham didn't have the time and the people they were training didn't have the inclination. They were in an impossible situation of having to send people out without proper training because there was no other option. If they had tried to bring everyone up to the required standard, then a large percentage of men would have fallen by the wayside. We were all aware of this before the training started. No one was fooling anyone.

There was also another problem, in addition to the fact that the training was woefully inadequate, it was also misdirected, as the bit we were getting was outdated, by approximately fifty years. This sounds like an odd statement but consider, if you will, the nature and location of war over recent years. It makes you wonder why the British Army wears Green anymore. The standard Army training bears a close resemblance to that required for foot-mounted infantry combat in central Europe, in trees and woodland. This obviously draws from its' experiences in World War two, which is when the current training doctrine was formed. This is what the standard Army basic training package is directed towards. We were getting a brief snippet of this. This, to me seemed a little bit odd. If you were returning to competitive football after a two year absence, you wouldn't prepare for it with a few games of cricket, now would you? Perhaps a brief snippet of Desert warfare techniques would have been more relevant.

The training itself was to be taken by the Green Jackets, which was a good thing because they ran it in a very relaxed atmosphere. I knew that my state of mind wouldn't take some arsehole shouting the odds at me, so their reasonable approach was very much appreciated. So, on that first morning of training, a Sunday, of all days, we were politely asked to enter the classroom, one of the many rickety Porta-Cabins in use by the Army, for our first lesson, which, comfortably enough, was first-aid in the battlefield.

The Army, ever reliant on standard practice and uniformity of instruction, has a video aid for every single subject to be instructed. There are probably hundreds of different Army instructional videos in existence and the vast majority of them are total and utter shite. Some, like the classic "Too Fat to Fight" are useless but totally hilarious. Most of them are just useless. Fortunately, our instructor for the morning had the same view and had decided to throw it out in favour of something far more interesting.

"Right then gents, I've got a video for you all to watch. I don't know if any of you will get out to the Gulf but if you do, here's a clip, which shows some of the injuries you might encounter." He offered cheerfully.

After a few seconds, we were greeted with, not the standard Army rubbish but the opening sequence of; Saving Private Ryan. Never has a film offered, more realistically, a demonstration of the horrors of war. The total chaos and the mindless waste of human life are most starkly demonstrated. A group of men sent carelessly into battle, with no thought spared for their well being, just the job they had to do. It also shows the random factors, which can contribute to a man's death in a war, where you don't necessarily have to do anything wrong to die, you just have to be in the wrong place at the wrong time. It also demonstrates just how unimportant the life of each individual soldier was. The true nature of expendability is shown in depth in ten minutes of film. Watching it, I suddenly realised that, although my chances of survival were infinitely greater than theirs, my life was no more important to my own government.

I had to laugh along with everyone else at the immense sickness of the joke he'd played but I couldn't escape the feeling that we were just the modern day equivalent of the scene being played out before us. We were just a number of men, called in forcibly by the government, to add weight of numbers to the "war effort". This is the only comparison I may draw with myself and the men who fought in the Second World War, though. They at least achieved something worthwhile and acted entirely in the national interest, well if we believe British history, which, admittedly, may have been slightly influenced by propaganda. They endured an ordeal, which I cannot begin to comprehend, however, in the total insignificance of one individual and the care afforded to each, we shared common ground. The difference is that the rest of the civilised world had taken huge steps in human rights terms since, whereas the British Army still lives within a two-hundred-year-old regime.

It wasn't that the British Army would deliberately send us to our deaths. It was that the British Army didn't care what happened to us at all. They didn't care about my mate Dave's family. They didn't care if my missus ran off with the milkman. They certainly didn't care if I was unhappy or whether I agreed with the war. All they cared about was making sure I fulfilled my side of the bargain. My side of the bargain, such as it was, was to basically do everything the Army told me to. They could and still can, renegotiate my contract terms, without my consent and if I don't come running when they want me, I will be thrown in prison.

They don't have to keep to their terms, if it doesn't suit either. The upshot of this absolute authority is that they don't need to care because I can't do anything except fulfil my duties, which are whatever they specify. I left the Army with an excellent reference and on good terms, having served them to the best of my abilities and been thoroughly let down by them in return but none of that mattered. They had absolute authority over me and I could do nothing about it. If they wanted to send me, completely untrained, into a war and mock my fears as they went, they could. My position in all of this was one of such little importance that all I could do was laugh along with them.

When broken down into component parts, the film did actually serve an instructional purpose. In it is contained one example of just about every war-wound available. The catalogue of injuries is vast and there was more than enough to give a very realistic and graphic example of every injury we were being "trained" to treat. That we attended the course was never in doubt. That the instruction was of an acceptable standard was also true. The question mark was whether everyone in the room was capable of recognising and dealing with all the injuries we had been shown. I had doubts over several people in the room, not least myself but, nonetheless, we were all given a tick in the box to say we were competent and sent on our way, after lunch (I never call it lunch but the Army does) to our next lesson, which, boringly enough, was vehicle recognition.

Vehicle recognition is and probably always has been a monumentally boring subject. There are some people who try their hardest to sparkle at it and demonstrate their immense knowledge of the fighting machines of all the world's armies. I paid attention to the British vehicles, most of which I knew and also the American ones. It was pointed out that the American ones would be easy to recognise because they would be shooting at us. Given their track record, this seemed a fair point.

We were then shown the vast selection of all-very-similar Iraqi tanks. They ranged from the T55 to the T72 and basically all of them looked just as shit as each other. These were the tanks which you wouldn't want in "Top Trumps" They would be no match for our Challenger 2's, which were almost officially the best tanks in the world, we were told. That was probably one of the few true statements we heard. We were then shown the rest of Saddam's fleet, most of which was old and battered Russian kit. It was plain to see that they didn't have much in the way of a war fighting force. If we did get out to Iraq, it would be a walk-over; we were assured by the "hardened war veteran" who was instructing. I felt a little patronised by this, as did a lot of the Stabs who knew a lot more than they were given credit for. I felt that this individual was guilty of talking a good game but it was plainly obvious he hadn't been in long enough to have experienced one, so it seemed to me that we had encountered another bull-shitter. He wouldn't be the last.

Before we could retire to the bar for the evening, we had to undergo a weapons handling test, in order to be allowed to shoot on the ranges the following day. This was the only part of the training it was possible to fail, so I enquired about the consequences. My answer was that I wouldn't be able to zero my weapon, as I wouldn't be allowed to fire it on the ranges. I would still proceed onto the next stage, whether I was deemed capable of handling a rifle or not. It wasn't the answer I was looking for. It was odd though, that they were willing to send someone into war, who was deemed unfit to handle a rifle. Odd, but not the oddest I was to encounter.

Later on, I was cheered to find that Liverpool had won the League cup, although slightly disappointed to find that I'd missed it completely as it seemed that the outside world had barely registered our absence and decided to carry on without us already. It is a strange feeling to be removed from your own life and then watch it carry on without you and this was just the first symptom of it. We did manage to catch the news on T.V. later on and all the talk was of whether the war would be avoided due to Saddam Hussein being exiled in one of a number of possible countries. I was hoping for this outcome but I would have been surprised if Saddam Hussein had co-operated quietly and left. That just didn't seem to be his way.

The night passed into an alcoholic blur as a group of desperate men turned wholeheartedly towards drinking for the solution to their problems. It worked too, as although my situation hadn't changed in the slightest, it did seem to be far more amusing with a few pints inside me. We drank until the bar closed, which, given that I would be firing a rifle for the first time in over three years the following morning, possibly wasn't the wisest course of action.

Nonetheless, as the morning came, we went out to the ranges, taking our hangovers with us. The whole bus stank of alcoholic breath as we were driven to the ranges. I would have doubted my ability to drive a car legally at that point but picking up a weapon and pointing it down the range seemed a simple enough task. As long as I kept it pointing down the range I wouldn't kill anyone. Having said this, if I had killed someone, I may have escaped punishment on the grounds that I was anything but a trained soldier. Due consideration was also given to shooting one of my toes off but I don't think I had the bottle for it.

So, with a steady hand and a slightly blurred eye, I addressed the target for the first five round grouping. We were only shooting from a hundred metres and it wasn't windy so there was no chance of me missing, or rather, no excuse for me missing. I knew I wasn't going to miss the target completely but the thing with a grouping is to get all your shots as close together as possible and I anticipated a liberal distribution of holes spread around the target, making it impossible to zero the rifle. I fired the five shots and waited for the verdict.

After a pause of five minutes or so and many mutterings and radio conversations, each man of the group of twenty who were firing was given the verdict on which direction the sights on his rifle needed to be adjusted. I was addressed by a young, fresh-faced boy, who held the same rank as I did.

"Don't touch anything mate, you're spot-on." He declared.

"Fuck off; I've never been spot-on in my life. Have you got the right target?"

He confirmed that he had and that we were to fire a confirmatory group of twenty rounds into the target, just to check that the weapon was zeroed correctly. I proceeded to do this and was later told that I had achieved a grouping of under one-hundred-millimetres for all twenty rounds. It wasn't marksmanship stuff but it was a decent standard for someone who hadn't fired in such a long time. In retrospect, it was probably better than I had been before I left the Army. Maybe it was the alcohol swimming around my veins. Maybe he'd got the wrong target.

Before we began the irritating and very mundane task of weapon cleaning, we were given a pat on the back and encouraged for our efforts. Jolly nice chaps those Green Jackets were. If only things would have stayed like that. I don't believe that I have had a more pleasant day on the ranges before in all my time in the Army. It was conducted in a most civilised and relaxed manner, almost enjoyable.

Before we set off back to the camp on the bus, the stores system took the odd step of issuing some REME tradesmen with a toolbox. Why this wasn't done back at the camp was unclear, as they had been brought from there and would only have to be lugged back there when we'd finished. Much to my confusion and amusement, I didn't get one. My mate Dave and several others did. How their faces lit up when they realised the reality of having to carry their rifle and all their range gear onto the bus with the heaviest and most awkward toolbox in the world in their other hand. These items weren't received gratefully.

We arrived back in camp and in contrast to the surprising lack of time wasting, which had occurred at Grantham, we were told to wait outside the Armoury, until someone turned up with the keys. This was where I heard something I hadn't heard in a long time, namely a standard squaddie conversation. It was so stereotyped it was difficult to believe but I had certainly heard this same conversation a thousand times before. The Army seems to have a strange effect on the individual, almost forcing him to get into character for a role he is playing. Suddenly, they laugh at things they would have been appalled at a week earlier. Suddenly, they are all single men talking about dirty sex with ugly women and drinking pints of piss and puke.

A middle-aged married man came across as more than a little odd when describing his technique for progress with the opposite sex. It came as no surprise to me to hear that he sets low standards and fails to achieve them and that "going ugly early" made sense because you were at least guaranteed "something to shag at the end of the night". These things have been discovered and endlessly discussed by thousands of young men in the Army for years and the falseness of it irritated me considerably.

Why a man of forty-odd or so feels the need to behave like a teenager is beyond me but that's the Army. It's all a big role-playing game, where men pretend to be something that they aren't in order to fit in with the majority. No one really enjoys drinking piss and if mentioned in the wrong company, these actions can be a source of embarrassment. Looking back, I'm glad I had enough character not to have to fit in with everyone all the time.

As it was, that was when that other false persona reared its ugly head, namely the senior rank. When the Armoury doors opened, we found that the queuing system didn't make sense any longer and certain members of the TA, who had been regular soldiers in their time, suddenly believed that they should go to the front of the queue. These men, who had long since left the Army and taken employment as taxi-drivers or security guards, suddenly found themselves in a position of power again. Suddenly, the man immediately to my rear was no longer an unintelligent, institutionalised man who couldn't get on with life. He was suddenly transformed into that holiest of entities, a Sergeant and had to behave like one.

The Army is full of these weak men who behave perfectly in accordance with their rank. I think it's because they don't have the strength of character to allow their personality to shine through. It quickly becomes tiresome when a man of no particular intelligence suddenly believes his opinion carries more weight in conversation than it reasonably should due to the rank and status afforded to him by a system that operates entirely without intelligent input.

It is a point of annoyance that everyone within the armed forces has to behave in a certain manner, which has to be entirely in accordance with his or her rank. They have to shape their lives around a label, which is given to them by a system, which has to have a name and number to identify everything. They become whatever rank they are labelled as and are treated with the respect due to the rank they wear. I find it difficult to respect the people who behave entirely according to rank and I found it hard to behave like a lance-Corporal again, particularly when my own previous military standing, vague as it had become, had, at times exceeded this.

I have always been myself, first and foremost. I have always formed my own opinions and had my own ideas. I always had a problem following orders if they didn't make sense. The point of fact is that I don't necessarily respect a man because he wears a particular rank. I tend to find that I respect people who are intelligent, or of strong character, or just plain decent, rather than address them by rank. The rank system is only there to compensate for a lack of judgement. That lack of judgement was to be seen all around us.

The senior rank pushed his way passed us, without so much as an excuse me, or a thank you. If this were a civilian organisation, I would have put him straight but the Army system tells us that such behaviour is perfectly acceptable, as he was the senior man. I brushed off this minor irritation and allowed myself to pity him for living his life in such a way. The reality was, happily for me and sadly for him, that the situation was only temporary.

As we retired for the day and before the night passed into an alcoholic blur once more, we were greeted with a newsflash, which told us that US intelligence personnel (they must be rare) had apprehended a man whom they believed knew the whereabouts of Osama Bin Laden. I wondered if, a day or two later, they may announce that he was shacked up in Baghdad, having coffee with Saddam. It seemed to be just another handful of mud to throw at Iraq. I think the official term is propaganda, which to me, just sounds like more lies.

Another curiosity came to my attention when we bumped into the range officer in the bar. Seemingly a decent man, he recognised us from the day's efforts and came over to speak to us. After a while, a very odd detail came out about the ranges we had been using that day. They were manually-operated, staffed by twenty men or so and these staff had to be sourced from somewhere. The people who were manning the ranges for that period had been sourced from the Army display team in Warminster. That, in itself makes perfect sense as they were under-employed at that time and the Army must always make best use of its' available manpower.

The thing that didn't make sense was that most of them were electronic-control-equipment technicians, which was the exact same trade discipline as I was. There I was thinking that there were none spare. Surely there couldn't have been any spare anywhere, or the Army wouldn't have felt the need to call me up, under the threat of prosecution. It irritated me to think that there were regular Army soldiers, who didn't need to be re-trained, who were already employed to do exactly the same job as I had been commanded to, who were obviously available and who should surely have been used, before calling me up. Unfortunately, I couldn't do anything about it but just accept that the Army needs no logical or sensible justification to do anything. The Army merely acts on the wishes of the government of the day, in accordance with its own, ancient system of operation of course.

# CHAPTER 6; HAVEN'T I SMELLED THIS BEFORE?

WE'D ALL SEEN the timetable for the four days training at Grantham. We all knew exactly what was coming next and some were decidedly unhappy about it. I knew I hadn't got a problem with it but some looked decidedly nervous at the prospect of entering the gas chamber, or whatever politically correct name they have to give it nowadays. This was one of my few strong suits but there were a few who had only encountered the discomfort of CS gas only once and they were wary.

Not that we were thrown into it straight away. There was a lot of rubbish to be talked about for a few hours first. The most useless and yet the most intuitive lesson of the morning was the first, namely, "Actions upon encountering a nuclear blast". The pointless nature of this was easily outweighed by the comedic values of its content. It is pretty certain that when witnessing a nuclear blast, one of the steps you may just take, is to die a sudden horrible death but there are others too, apparently.

The first thing you must do; is to lay down with your hands under your body and your head pointed towards the blast. I think this is to either protect your head from minor impacts with the helmet or, should a particularly large piece of debris come along, to make sure the part where the nerves send the pain to is switched off, well before it gets there.

Without panicking, or pissing yourself, or saying your final goodbyes to the wife and kids, you must be aware that, at all times, you have a duty. That duty is to take note of the direction of the blast, relative to your own position and to count the time between flash and bang, in order to calculate the distance. This is then to be reported up the chain of command, which, if it hasn't been vaporised in the blast, will know exactly what to do, apparently. I think the point of the training is to make you realise that there's not much you can do, besides attempting to follow the drills. It paints a none-too-cheerful picture but then, none of us believed that Saddam Hussein had a nuclear capability. So, further talk of eardrums exploding, eyeballs popping out and your bladder bursting due to the external pressures were simply a mildly comedic irrelevance.

The rest of the morning was taken up with standard chemical warfare drills. Most of this amounts to little more than getting your mask on properly, in good time. After that, everything else pails into insignificance. There are some useful drills, like changing the filter canister in a chemical environment. That's the nervous one where people have to hold their breath, close their eyes and attempt to unscrew the old one and then replace it. Some find it difficult to re-thread the new one with their eyes closed and it can be a general source of panic. There are drills for eating and drinking and for urination and defocation but none of these are particularly important, or effective. The mask will save your life in the first place and its one of the few pieces of British equipment I have ever had any genuine faith in. There are methods of working in a chemical environment for days on end but I'd be surprised if this was ever really necessary.

The afternoon was to be occupied with that most pleasant of tasks, the gas chamber itself. We were all lined up in groups of nine and, in turn, taken into the chamber. Until then, the Green Jackets had been very decent and polite towards us at all times but they couldn't let us go without a little bit of cruelty. We nine entered the chamber and the door was closed behind us.

The Army always test using CS gas. It is a particularly effective method as you get quite heartily punished if you get the drills wrong. CS gas is an irritant. It (almost certainly) causes no lasting damage and yet temporarily, it renders the recipient blind and unable to breathe. I have no idea what a prolonged dose would do because a few seconds has always been enough for me. It makes the skin sting and burns right to the back of the throat and nostrils. Conversely, I did once see someone who was immune and was totally unaffected and it presented a most bizarre sight, when absolutely nothing happened to him but this is very rare indeed.

Normally, certainly after the first ever time you enter a CS chamber during your basic training, there is no need to take a lungful of the stuff but it has to be done in the first instance to enable the soldier to get a realistic grasp of the unpleasantness of it. After that, every time the soldier enters a gas chamber, it is only to test the fit of the respirator and to perform drills. If these are correct, the soldier need never get more than a vague whiff of CS again. Having left the Army, I wasn't expecting to smell it again but this was where the little bit of deliberate cruelty came in. I would ask you to make you own opinions over this but would also point out that there is a relevant chapter relating to acts of torture in the current human rights legislation.

In the chamber, which was quite a claustrophobic little room, with windows above eye-level, we were to run around and perform aerobic exercises. These are quite difficult in a thick over-suit with a mask on because the suit restricts movement and the mask restricts breathing – heavily. After a few seconds of this, most in the chamber were beginning to perspire and were well out of breath. All this movement, we were told, was to test the fit of the respirator. I knew that testing the fit of the respirator could be achieved, simply by movement of the head and upper body, however, we needed to run and jump around, we were told.

The filter canister on my respirator was also faulty and letting in a little bit of CS. It was unpleasant but nothing to panic about. Once we had decided that everyone's mask fitted properly, it was time to remove them and walk out of the chamber. Apparently, we had to take our masks off in the chamber, in order to prove to us that there actually was CS being used because a member of an earlier group had questioned this. This was nothing more than the usual flimsy Army reasoning and I don't even think the instructor believed it, bearing in mind that you could see clouds of the stuff all around the room. Nonetheless, it was time to get a nose, throat and eye full of it.

I took off my mask, held my breath and closed my eyes as tightly as I could manage, whilst still looking for the way out. The concentration of gas used in the chamber felt particularly strong and my face was burning as well as my eyes. As if to prove the nature of his lie, the arsehole held me inside the chamber until I had to breathe and get and proper lung-full of it. I saw no logical reasoning for this. It was just one man, who was qualified as an NBC instructor, attempting to use his position to bully people for his own amusement. Oddly, he let go of me as soon as I tried to pull his mask off, even showing mild symptoms of panic. This said, I still got a proper dose.

Personally, I could always see a need for cruelty on the part of the army physical training instructors, as the soldier sometimes needs motivation to find his physical limits. The part of an NBC instructor, in my eyes, was simply to instruct and advise and this man had missed the point and was simply abusing his position. As I emerged into the fresh air, the CS stung all the more, due to the clammy sweat on my face and my freshly opened pores. It stung badly, particularly around my eyes and looking around, as best I could, it was plain to see that everyone else was in a similar state. I certainly hadn't needed to experience that again. Still, it was another tick in the box on the route to becoming a "fully trained soldier" again.

Once the chamber of horrors was put to one side and the general tang of CS was washed from the skin with cold water, it was time to relax for a little while before the main briefing that evening. The briefing that evening was the one we had all been waiting for. There had been countless rumours all week and everyone was gasping to find out just what the hell was going to happen to us. I was nervous but I tried to tell myself that the worst thing that could happen, although it shouldn't be possible, was to be sent to Iraq and that couldn't possibly last six months and besides which, it didn't look particularly scary anyway. Unfortunately, I was having some difficulty convincing myself.

We pushed our way into the briefing room and sat listening to the second in command (I think) of RTMC rabbit on about all the procedures and generally indulge himself in the audience forcibly provided for him. No one was interested. All anyone wanted to know was "What the bloody hell was going on". Eventually his double chins and pink cheeks wobbled their way to a point where he forgot about himself for a minute and got back to the purpose of his job. "Anyway, I'm sure you just all want to know which units you're going to and where." He offered, to muffled applause.

He read off the lists of a few other units before he came to Third Royal Horse Artillery. I had been attached to the Artillery in Kosovo and spent three years with them in Britain and the prospect of another stint really didn't flick my switch. The Artillery have a very well deserved reputation for treating their attached personnel very poorly and having been a victim of this before, I wasn't greatly pleased to hear my name on that list, although it seemed inevitable, given my luck with the Army. On the plus side though, most of the people I'd taken a liking to were going there, so it could have been worse.

The plan was that we would be driven to their home barracks in Germany and meet up with their rear party, before we were either flown straight out to Iraq, or kept on rear party duties. That was it, nothing more. After all the rubbish he'd spewed out for the previous half an hour, he still couldn't tell us where we were going to end up, or for how long. Such things may have been nice to know for a man who had been made to put his life on hold for this period, however long it was. It may have been nice for the missus to know too but no one knew anything. I knew then though, in the back of my mind, that I wasn't going to end up in Germany.

For me, the Army had been a constant source of bad luck, from the day I joined, to the day I left. I knew exactly what the worst-case scenario was and I knew that I would end up with precisely that. As I'd said to the missus before my departure; "If there's one ticket to Iraq, out of five thousand people, it'll will have my name on it".

I remember some of the bad luck I had in the Army. I remember once being given a posting preference form and being told to write where in the world I would prefer to be posted. All I remember was that I could see the benefits of going to Germany or abroad but if I was in the UK, I would, at least, be able to go home more often. I filled in the form, requesting to be posted "Anywhere in the world except the South of England" as that just represented a long drive home, with no plus points. Shortly afterwards, my posting came through for Larkhill, a completely desolate shit-hole, just thirty-five miles from the south coast. It's a story I've told before, much to everyone's amusement but it must be said that three years is a long time to spend in the only place on earth you requested not to be. It was nothing personal, just bad luck, I reasoned, as the person who made the decision to post me there had never met me and was never likely to. In hindsight, it was a bloody good job too.

I was struggling to contain my anger at the predicament I'd been forced into and was approaching a point where I felt the need to let off steam. The man who waffled on about nothing before me was the only person I could see to try to blame for the situation and he wasn't going to leave the room with a smile on his face. He could stand up there, speaking as eloquently as one might, easily earning his fifty-grand a year and then it would be off home to the wife and kids. He could stand and dictate my future to me without having to face the consequences of it. He had a very comfortable, cosy existence, much like the one I had established for myself away from the Army and was forcibly being deprived of.

People were asking questions of him, most of which he didn't have answers to. He didn't seem at all apologetic for his lack of knowledge. In my eyes, he demonstrated all the care of a man who would leave the room and forget all about everyone in it instantly. He didn't seem particularly concerned about anyone's circumstances but he was about to become well aware of mine because I had a question. I waited for my chance, for a quiet moment, then set off speaking, quite loudly; "I don't want to go to Iraq because I don't think I have any duty to go, so what would you do if I just jumped over the fence tonight and did a runner?"

He looked shocked as the applause resonated around the room. These weren't the muffled cheers of earlier either. This was clapping and stamping of feet, accompanied by a few whistles and shouts. There was only one man in the room who wasn't pleased to hear that and I think he really did have a sudden urge to leave the room. He stood, flustered for a few seconds before attempting to present a reasoned response. The system provided one for him but it took him a few seconds to think what it might be.

"Well, we'd send the military police to your house to pick you up and you would be tried for AWOL or desertion and locked up." He stuttered.

"Would it be for less than six months?" I snapped, before he had time to gather his thoughts. Cue more applause.

"I don't know. You must remember the Army system. You won't win." He said with a depressing air of finality. No further applause.

I knew I wouldn't win. I also knew before he spoke that, when he eventually thought of it, that would have been his exact response. I knew that because I knew the position I was in. I didn't even have the right to pop home and say a proper goodbye to the missus. I had no rights whatsoever. All I could do was go to war without the proper equipment or training, if the Army decided to send me. Whether it was hell or not, I would probably live to tell the tale and hence it wasn't worth ruining my entire future for. Furthermore, I had to think about someone else other than myself and how my criminal record might have affected the future I would share with her.

At that point though, the choice between six months in Iraq and possibly ruining my career prospects forever was a very slim one. If I had no one else to think about, I think I would have jumped the fence and taken my chances, after possibly giving chubby chops a right hander on the way. Strange that the missus was keeping me on the straight and narrow from such a distance, without even knowing it. I knew I'd pushed as far as I could, for the time being. At least Chubby chops wouldn't forget me in a hurry. The briefing petered out to nothing and after a few pats on the back and a bit of dead eye from Chubby, I found myself alone outside.

As it was, I decided to ring the missus and tell her the monumentally bad news, which she just didn't deserve. I told her that it looked like I was probably going to Iraq. I remember feeling more upset at the length of time I would be away than the place, or nature of my employment. To her credit, she managed to find some strength from somewhere, which was fortunate, because one of us needed to.

I don't always consider myself to be a strong man and that was one of my moments of particular weakness. I wish I could have taken it on the chin, like a man seemingly should but I just wasn't good enough. I wasn't man enough. It's fair to say that I was in a bit of a mess and looking back, I think I should have been the one to reassure her. As it was though, she showed enough strength for the both of us.

After twenty minutes or so, I ended the call to the missus and immediately decided to drop the bombshell on my parents. I think I had a more resentful and angry tone for this call, most probably in opposition to my father's stance over the whole issue. I don't remember my exact words but I do remember asking him if he still thought it was fair. He didn't answer my question. He just tried to reassure me that it would all be alright, and that I'd be safely home in one piece before I knew it. These were the answers to questions I hadn't even asked, so it must have been some measure of his concern that, for the first time in my life, I would be doing something markedly more hazardous than crossing the road.

I was wrong to be angry towards him. He deals in real-life business where people are forced, by law, to behave with at least a scrap of decency. He expected the Army to behave reasonably and sensibly. He didn't realise that, as there is little to challenge military law, the Army were going to do what the fuck they liked with his son and there was nothing he could do. I think that realisation hurt him enough without me pointing it out to him.

That was the second time that night I had wished to be a stronger, better man but it just wasn't to be. If I could have turned back the clock, there were a few things I would change. Maybe I would just have liked to have been better all round but I simply wasn't. I'll just have to live with that because I'll never forget it and I'll never be able to put it right. My mother asked if I would be allowed home for a day or so, to say my goodbyes properly. I'm sure, to her, it seemed a perfectly sensible question.

# CHAPTER 7; ALL THE THINGS YOU WANTED TO KNOW (BUT COULDN'T BE ARSED TO ASK).

THE FINAL DAY of our "training" began with the usual hangover from the heavy drowning of heavy sorrows. It was information day, when we would be told all the "intelligence" gathered about Iraq, "just in case" we were being sent there. I decided to try and take some of it in because I had a feeling that I would be seeing it for real soon enough. Despite the lack of certainty and strong suggestions to the contrary, I thought I'd had enough subtle hints.

A young officer, probably about twenty-two years old, began instructing us on the position in Iraq. He must have felt a little awkward, as I was one of only three other men in the room who were still in their twenties. The other thirty and forty-something's listened, as he imparted his seemingly vast knowledge upon us. We were told about the number of men in all the Armies in the Middle East. Iraq's million or so troops vastly outnumbered our own hundred thousand or so, which made a promising start.

I noted then that our once famed armed forces drew favourable comparison with few, if any of the other countries prominent in world politics. Tony Blair had decided to send forty thousand or so troops to Iraq, in support of the US. Most people would be surprised to find that this number contained people who weren't even in the Army. I was certainly surprised to find that he'd included me. It seemed that I had been in the Army all along; I just hadn't been made aware. If he can count me amongst his forty thousand troops, I just wonder exactly how the unemployment figures are calculated. There were seventy-seven men in the room, all of which were officially trained soldiers, ready for war. The official figure was seventy-seven, whereas the truthful figure was a lot closer to zero, or possibly exactly zero. Looking around the room, I realised that our armed forces are in a pretty bad state. Lies, damn lies, statistics and then Blair's official line, seemed the correct order of things.

It was also mentioned that Iraq's troops were poorly armed and many had very low morale, as they had been forced into war by a brutal and evil regime, which they strongly opposed. A lot of them were close to deserting or surrendering, even before the war had begun. They had almost no serviceable equipment and their supply chain was faltering. Apparently, incredibly, some of their troops were barely trained, simply just men plucked from the street and thrown into war. I found it difficult to believe that any regime could be so callous, be it Iraq or Britain. A few people in the room muttered comedically about the similarities between our positions and theirs. The only difference I saw was that I had been plucked from a much nicer street, which I pay more money to live on, than my Iraqi counterparts. Oh, and the flushing toilet.

My mind began to wander from the monotonous bullshit filtering through the air to a picture of what my immediate future may represent. I found it difficult to accept that there could be a man fighting to defend a regime, against his own will and better interests, from another man who was attacking him, also against his own will and better interests. Furthermore, it went completely against my conscience. If this war genuinely was about human rights, then Bob Geldof would have had a whip-round for them, rather than bombing the living shit out of the place and killing thousands. If it were down to me, I would have politely asked that reluctant Iraqi soldier to leave the battlefield, rather than have his death on my conscience. I see no honour in any man dying for a cause he doesn't believe in. Similarly, I see no honour in killing for such a cause.

We were told some fairly uninteresting things about Iraq and about its leader and his cronies. A pretty evil picture was painted before us and whether there was a grain of truth in it or not, if it's the only source of information given (which it was), then it's difficult to argue. Certainly I found it difficult to argue with my colleagues, who were slowly being convinced by the endless one-sided propaganda we received. My sceptical voice pointed out one fact to them all; governments have lied to their people and their armies for centuries. Perhaps the British aren't quite as bad as the Americans but thanks, in no small part to Tony Blair; Britain becomes more like an American State every day.

Britain has stood shoulder to shoulder with the US since September 11$^{th}$ and has come to a point where it stands alone in its unfailing support. I doubt that the favour would be reciprocated, if the need should ever arise. Certainly, they failed to include the IRA in their hypocritical "Global war on terrorism" but then, some US voters have been known to show appreciation to their cause. Their war on terrorism did include Iraq though, even though no Iraqi had carried out an act of terrorism against the US at that point. Odd that, I thought.

With that rubbish out of the way, it was time for the scare-mongering tactics. We had the brief about landmines, accompanied by the video, which we all found extremely informative. Towards the end of the brief, the standard practice is to show some motivational pictures of the horrific deaths and injuries to be incurred from landmines. In truth, they weren't pleasant. There were legs removed, vast holes in torsos, a picture of a torso with no limbs and strangely, a seemingly erect penis still attached and a body ripped to pieces. They showed us what happens to a man's body inside a tank struck by an anti-tank mine. It had been almost completely incinerated and there were worse images too. The thing was, as unpleasant as it was to watch, it didn't change anything for me because I had already decided I didn't want to be blown to pieces by a landmine. The closing image, as it has been for some years, was of a surgeon removing shrapnel from a man's shredded genitals. I don't know who he is (or was) but he appeared to have suffered a most unpleasant fate and most men suddenly felt very vulnerable just watching the film.

After that cheery subject, we were treated to a briefing about if the fate worse than death itself happened, namely, being taken prisoner of war. I'd heard this briefing before too but it doesn't prevent the statement; "You will almost certainly be raped." from having the desired effect. They go on to tell you about being beaten up and threatened with a variety of painful punishments and the twisted mind-games they will most-likely employ on you. It doesn't sound too cheery but we are endlessly reminded that we must only give "the big six" of, name, rank, number, religion, blood group and some other detail that they repeated over and over again whilst I was thinking about something else entirely. They say this because this is in accordance with the Geneva Convention. Curiously, I would guess that if my back passage was bleeding from enforced anal penetration I really wouldn't be too interested in the big six or the Geneva Convention because both had already failed this soldier (loosely termed). Seemingly, as far as the Iraqi's were concerned, I didn't need to poke myself up the arse, because they had the tools, the know-how and the desire.

In an attempt to maintain the light-hearted tone, we were then given the health brief. They showed us the beautiful images of rotting feet and genitals and the general disgust of being unclean in the field. We were shown the lovely creatures we may encounter on our travels, namely scorpions and the incredibly unpleasant camel spider (apparently, it will inject you with anaesthetic and eat as much as it likes). By the time the snakes and other nasties had arrived I had already lost interest. This place, quite obviously, was unfit for human habitation.

I didn't really listen to the lecture about fluid intake because they started off with the strange statement that to survive in a desert environment, a man would need to drink ten to twelve litres of water a day. I switched off at that point because there was no way I could consume that much water and we probably wouldn't be able to get our hands on that amount every day anyway. I consoled myself with the knowledge that if I was still sweating, my mouth wasn't too dry and my urine wasn't too yellow, I would probably be alright. Rocket science it most certainly isn't. I certainly didn't need the flowchart with "Increased thirst?" at the top.

Having wasted sufficient time forcing useless information into my increasingly reluctant mind, the briefings ended and all we had to do then was to pack our bags for our departure the following morning, which took about ten minutes and then go to the bar. I wanted to get particularly drunk that night, as I wasn't only saying goodbye to my life in England for a while but my beloved John Smith's bitter too.

As we sat in the bar, merrily drinking away, we were stunned to encounter our most recent past on the television screen. There it was on the six-o'clock news, RTMC Chilwell, in all its glory. They were interviewing an attractive(ish), young(ish), blonde(ish) TA woman, who was being mobilised. It was quite a surprise to see how the Army had managed to show such an acceptable public face for what was, in its entirety a completely immoral bullying exercise but there she was. Unsurprisingly, she was an officer, a Major, going to a field hospital, if I remember right, which probably meant that she would be doubling her civilian income for the time she was out there.

Oddly, she seemed to know exactly where she was going and for how long. Even more oddly, given her favourable circumstances, she was "a little apprehensive" about being paid fifty grand a year to work miles back from where anything was being fired. She was also relishing the challenge, of course and was quite happy to "do her duty". She wasn't lying and no one was feeding her lines, she was simply hand picked to give a good impression. Things would have been dramatically different if they had chosen my mate Dave, or myself, or any one of our group but that just isn't the way. That part of the truth just wouldn't have been acceptable to the British public, hence their drastic economy with it.

## CHAPTER 8; AN UNNECESSARILY LONG JOURNEY.

WE HAD TO weigh in our mountains of baggage individually. The weight and bulk of it was strangely increased by the addition of three twenty-four hour ration packs. The explanation for this was that we were to hand them over to the chefs upon our arrival because, if we were sent to the Gulf, there may be no food. This didn't make sense, as the ration packs were intended for individual use by the soldier and didn't need a chef to be cooked, neither did it make sense to hand over your rations if their was no food. The general consensus was that, if there was no food then we'd be alright for a few days. After that, it was uncertain. We, of course commended the British Armed forces on its planning at this point.

Eight o'clock in the morning seemed like a reasonable enough time to start the day's proceedings. We had to weigh in our baggage and then be further processed through the medical tent, where we would have the Anthrax immunisation. The curiosity about this is that a lot of people had been very wary about the nature of it and the safety aspects concerned. We had received two briefings in the last few days from the chief medical officer about just how safe and how effective it was. He'd mentioned again that the disclaimer (Yes, that's a disclaimer) didn't affect our rights in any way and that the only downside of having it was the immediate symptoms, which only lasted for a few days.

Most of our group had voiced their concerns but seemed to have been convinced by this man's claims. I personally didn't know enough about it to decide whether it was safe or not. I had heard his ramblings but unsurprisingly, we hadn't heard any argument against it. I am still unsure whether I was right or wrong but I observed one thing, which was consistent with everything about the armed forces and it was upon this that I based my scepticism.

The Army, as it had upon my enlistment, had made various verbal promises. There was nothing in writing, which meant that there was no commitment to the individual. None of these promises were honoured.

If I had signed the disclaimer, all that would have existed officially was a piece of paper, which stated that I volunteered to have the injection and accepted the consequences. The verbal promises and recommendations of the staff involved would count for nothing. They weren't recorded anywhere. I already knew that a verbal promise from the Army was worthless in its entirety. I'd wised up to their scheme, albeit a little too late.

Nonetheless, even though a large number of our group had voiced their concerns, they signed the disclaimer and had the injection. As ever before, the Army made a string of promises but the soldier made the written and physical commitment. It didn't surprise me either, because we were told that less than one percent of regular soldiers had refused the injection and there had been no problems with anyone. Such statements go a long way towards convincing the indecisive. Apparently, they had had only two refusals from all of the three thousand mobilised troops passing through the system at that point, so to refuse was a genuine oddity.

As far as I was concerned, unless I had a written guarantee that there were no long-term lasting side effects, I was going to be number three. I asked the plummy Major to provide for me a written guarantee of the safety of the injection. I said that I was prepared to accept an allergic reaction and the short-term side effects but I wanted him to guarantee that nothing else would happen. He cheerfully agreed to perform this task and scrawled, in his best handwriting, a statement, which finished "I anticipate no long term damaging side effects."

"This says anticipate. It doesn't say that there won't be. It wouldn't stand up in court, would it?" I asked.

"Well, are you going to be taking me to court?" He asked, sounding offended.

"I will if I get any problems, yes."

"Well, you're asking to sign on the behalf of the company, which provides the vaccine and I can't guarantee something on their behalf. You can never say never with medicine."

"What, do you mean that you can't guarantee that something won't go wrong?" I asked, attempting to sound surprised by something I already knew.

"Of course I can't." He replied, finally and, of course, correctly.

"But you stood up on that stage the other day and said that it was perfectly safe. They were you're exact words. This vaccine is perfectly safe, you said. I remember it and so does everyone else who has now had the vaccine on your recommendation. I just want you to put that promise in writing because I've had a lot of promises from the Army before and they all turned out to be lies."

"Well, I'm sorry but if you won't accept my word then I don't see how I can deal with you. It's beyond me, so you'll just have to manage without. Don't have the injection, if you don't want it." He snorted, obviously quite annoyed.

I knew I wasn't having the jab anyway. I knew he wouldn't be able to give me a written guarantee and it was unfair of me to ask. I also knew that when he told everyone that it was perfectly safe, it wasn't legally binding. I still don't know whether the injection is safe and neither did he, that much was obvious. The fact that a lot of people have had it doesn't sway me in any direction. A lot of women had thalidomide. Of the seventy-seven people in the group, seventy-five had the injection and yet days earlier, most were sceptical. In this period, we had seen no tangible evidence of the safety of the injection whatsoever. It had just been recommended to us, by a man whose job it was to make sure as many people had the jab as possible.

Having had the injection, or not, we were then told to sit and wait for our transport. It was around ten o'clock in the morning and the bus didn't come until half past three in the afternoon. It made little sense but then, who were we to complain? We sat and read newspapers and watched television and ate and slept and generally did anything possible to waste the time until the buses arrived.

The buses, when they did arrive, were going to take all seventy-seven of us to our respective camps in Germany, where we would find out just what was going to happen to us. This seemed the only way forward, so, having manhandled tons of baggage into the back of our accompanying lorry, we got on the bus for what was going to be a very long ride. It wasn't too grisly a prospect in the short-term, though because there would be plenty of alcohol flowing on the ferry crossing.

If my second term of employment with the Army had ended there and then, I would have had to say that it hadn't been too bad. The training, if worthless, had been given in good spirit and I had met some very decent people and consumed quite a lot of beer. That first week wasn't too bad at all really, it was just unfortunate that the second week promised to be quite tragic and wouldn't offer improvement for a long time after. This point saw a very distinct change of heart for me. All the way, people had been asking me if I was going to do a bunk and I hadn't given a straight answer but that situation had to change.

As much as I hated the position I was in, I decided that all I could do was accept it. I'd tried to change things but it didn't seem possible so I decided to knuckle down and try to make the best of the time I had. I think this was the correct approach because it wouldn't be fair on whoever I ended up with to have to put up with such a miserable, counter-productive bastard.

Morale is hard to come by in difficult times and I realised that I needed to try my hardest to be positive, whatever the weather. I decided that, rightly or wrongly, I had a duty and I was going to fulfil that to the best of my abilities because I had to. I was determined to be an asset to the cause, even though I didn't believe in it.

As was expected, the beer was flowing well on the ferry. My three good friends and I had managed to bag a cabin together and although it was very compact, it was the most luxurious place we'd encountered in a week. We drank as much beer as we could possibly get down our throats that night, as we all expected not to see a pint again for a while. At around two o'clock in the morning, we decided that enough was enough and retired for the night.

After a brief blink of sleep, six o'clock came and it was time to stagger out of bed. I had difficulty getting down from my bunk as I was still feeling the effects of alcohol. My situation was made worse by the fact that I had developed a heavy cold during my sleep. All four of us were displaying the symptoms of the side effects of the vaccine and yet I seemed to be suffering the worst. It looked like, despite all my protests, I'd been vaccinated by proxy. I hadn't had a cold for years before that, so I was particularly annoyed. Nonetheless, I made by best effort to look extremely ill and pretend to be dying, like most men when they have a sniffle.

After a none-too-traditional greasy breakfast, (Who has fish?) we were quickly herded back onto the bus and got rolling towards our destination. Oddly, there seemed a sudden enthusiasm for watching war films on the bus's video set-up. This wasn't for me. I'm not a particular fan of most of them and I really cannot stand "Full Metal Jacket". I decided, rather than wallowing in my recently established usual self-pity, I would wallow in the symptoms of my recently established illness. I managed a few hours of open-mouthed, drooling sleep then woke and wiped the saliva from my chin to find that we had arrived in Rhiendahlen. This made no sense to me, as we had all been told that we were headed for different camps to link up with the rear-parties of our respected regiments but there had been a last-minute change of plan apparently. From experience, I guessed that this "last minute" change was probably really suggested in the first or second minute. We entered the camp and a Sergeant-Major got on the bus to explain the situation.

"Right ladies and gentlemen, you'll all be staying here for the next forty-eight hours and then you'll all be on a flight out to Kuwait." He said flatly. He continued his instructions, telling us where our accommodation was and other places of interest but I got the distinct impression that all this paled into nothing after his opening line. Looking around the bus, there were quite a few shocked expressions. Even those who claimed to know they were going to the Gulf looked surprised at how suddenly and abruptly it was happening. I found it hard to believe that I could be taken from my cosy civilian existence and flown into the middle of a war-zone just nine days later. It was a frightening prospect. My realisation that I had "rumbled" the Army in their latest burst of bullshit did little to stop my bottom lip quivering. I pretended to go back to sleep for a while. At least, if my eyes were closed, nothing could leak out.

We went through the mundane struggle of getting our baggage and filling in another twenty-or-so forms before we were sent to another briefing. At this point, with a hangover, a cold, a fuzzy head from lack of sleep and a generally confused mind, I was finding things a little difficult. There was supposed to be a representative from each regiment to meet us there and tell us exactly what was going on. Unfortunately, although there was a representative from all the other regiments, there wasn't one from Third Royal Horse Artillery, so we were very much in the dark. This wasn't a surprise because I hadn't had a clue what was happening since I left the missus at the train station a week earlier. There was only one thing I was certain of and that was the unsavoury fact that we were all going to the Gulf. There was no-one to ask about the rest.

On a more pleasant note, after the briefing, our time was our own until we had to check in for our flight, so we retired to the accommodation. The Twenty-five man rooms we'd been given were clean enough but I wasn't about to get used to a bunk bed, even though that would be a luxury compared to the facilities after the plane landed in Kuwait. I decided that I was in need of a shower. To my surprise, they were all large, individual cubicles, rather than the communal facilities we had been used to. They were very private and as privacy was at a premium, I decided to make best use of it. We all need ways of relieving tension.

# CHAPTER 9;
# THE BRAVEST OF MEN.

I AWOKE, WITH a heavier version of the cold and hangover combination I'd taken to bed with me the night before. We would have the whole day off, to do as we pleased, possibly just the calm before the storm but a welcome bonus, nonetheless. We had to be up stupidly early the following morning to weigh in our baggage a ridiculous sixteen hours before our flight was due to take off, so the plan was to prepare early then go to the bar early and get smashed early and hopefully, go to bed early too, but that was optional. This was where living one-day-at-a-time began.

We had the option to go to the stores in the morning, to attempt to sort out our shortages of kit and equipment. I took my NBC suit with me to try and swap it for an adult-size. Unsurprisingly, they had no suits to fit. To tell the truth, they had absolutely sod-all and no one actually managed to get anything from them whatsoever. Apparently, everything was in a container, floating somewhere between there and the Gulf. It seemed plausible for the Army to just send all its clothing and equipment, wholesale, to the Gulf, as it had done exactly the same with its mobilised personnel. Again, we commended them on their planning and preparation.

We decided to hit the bar early that afternoon, just to make sure we would be nice and drunk for the flight. With a bit of luck, they wouldn't let us on board. The bar was full of young, regular Army boys, most in their late teens and early twenties. To them, a group of thirty and forty-somethings and one man in his late twenties must have looked like a real bunch of old-stagers. We were all dressed in just the clothes we'd had lying around and generally looked a bunch of bedraggled scruffs. We didn't really care though because we knew where we were going and fashion wasn't a pre-requisite. This bunch of arrogant louts didn't seem to appreciate this and they were only too willing to mock.

The ignorance of it struck me starkly. These men, all of them past their physical peak, most of them completely out of touch with the art of soldiering and some without any military experience to speak of, surely deserved utmost respect. They all knew their physical limitations. They were all well aware that they were past it and most didn't believe that they had a duty to serve a very questionable cause but they had all turned up and done the decent thing. They had all come to serve their country, in whatever capacity and however unreasonable the demands placed upon them. They were prepared to give their all for Britain and in my eyes, these men deserve far greater credit than any afforded to their regular Army equivalents, whether you get the "same bang for you buck" or not. These husbands, fathers and in some cases, grandfathers had answered the call and were prepared to offer the little bit they had left. These men did not deserve to be treated like this.

I do not necessarily include myself in their number. I was (and still am, unsurprisingly) younger and fitter then they were and I had a good deal more military experience and knowledge than most. I may not have had the support and training of the regular Army and I may have been far short of soldiering match fitness (that analogy again) but despite my vague, yet dramatically exaggerated, illness, I knew I was physically fit and strong. I knew I wouldn't be lagging behind the rest. Some of these men knew full well that they weren't fit enough to be there and yet they still went, come what may. Their courage and decency stood in stark contrast to the young men before us.

One of these brash, indoctrinated young squaddies, obviously up for a rumble, attempted to wind up the Geordie, who was significantly older and wiser and had simply had gone to the bar for a quiet pint. Soon enough, the mouthy little boy soldier was attempting to prove his masculinity by squaring up to the North East of England's finest and I felt the need to interrupt matters and try to calm things down. Unfortunately, before I could move, the Geordie had him by the throat and his huge, vice-like hands were exerting a pressure that this young boy hadn't encountered before. With his legs dangling beneath him like two pieces of string, he suddenly looked quite scared and became rather apologetic. The Geordie's words went something like "Listen you little prick, If I rip you're fucking head off, they might just take me off the flight to Kuwait tomorrow, so it makes no difference to me". It seemed the point had been made. Perhaps I too had underestimated this group of ageing men.

The young boy decided to back down and attempted to strike up a more reasonable and polite conversation. The Geordie wasn't having any of it but I think he got the message that a group of men facing such an uncertain future really didn't care too much about little boys looking for Saturday night action. He was attempting to politely ask his third or fourth question when the Geordie tired of the façade and told him to fuck off. That was pretty much the end of that. I later found that the Geordie had been "A top rumbler" in his day.

With that unsavoury incident swept away by an almighty hand, we soon set about the serious business of drinking and the beer began to flow at a commendable rate. The evening started to move on, into a far more relaxed, alcoholic haze, which dimmed the senses and judgement of all involved. Later that night another of my TA colleagues was having a little difficulty phoning his wife. It seemed that maybe jealousy had got the better of him and that he was worried all wasn't how it was supposed to be at home. He had tried to call but she was out. This didn't strike me as particularly odd as it was Saturday night but it was a problem to him.

I asked him if he thought his wife loved him. He replied that she did. I asked him if he was sure. He replied that he was perfectly sure that his wife loved him. I asked him, if he was sure, what the problem was with her not being in the house when he expected her to be. He said that there probably wasn't one. I told him to keep thinking like that because we would be away for along time and there was no sense in ruining you home life just because you can't be part of it. I told him that she would probably be very upset and worried but that she shouldn't have to stay in the house. I think the things I told him were the same things we all wanted to hear too.

He agreed and when he called later, he found that she had nipped out to get a DVD to watch to take her mind off things. I had found his problem very easy to solve because it was an obvious natural reaction in most men. I had already had that same natural reaction some days earlier and had just about managed to think my way around it and come to the same conclusion. Some men don't manage this and I can certainly sympathise with their problems. I don't think that there was a man out there who hadn't considering chinning the milkman upon his return, just on the off-chance. The probable exception was my mate Dave but then his concerns were of an entirely different kind.

The night's sleep, such as it was, lasted for about five hours. We had to be in the gymnasium to weigh in our baggage at a quarter to four in the morning. Our plane didn't fly until eight o'clock that evening, (no misprint) so it would be a case of hurry up and wait, yet again. There were supposed to be two lorries to help us transport our bags up to the gymnasium but, as we expected, they didn't turn up. We waited for a while and then decided to make the monumental effort of carrying our own sixty kilograms of bulky baggage for a quarter of a mile, a bit of a stiff task, with a hangover.

As we arrived breathlessly, we saw the lorries setting off, back towards our accommodation. The job was already done, so this was, as ever, an empty gesture.

"We've sorted the lorries out for you." Declared a man in civilian clothes, who obviously had a position (Which he considered to be) of some importance.

"You've sorted fuck all out. You lot haven't been able to sort fuck all out since we arrived. You're all fucking wank." Came a reply from behind me via Newcastle. "It's difficult to be impressed." I offered, slightly more mildly, as I struggled past him with my baggage.

After we weighed in and said our happy goodbyes to our stupidly heavy bags, we went for a bit of breakfast. It was noted by many that there were a lot of regular Army personnel sat in there, involved in assisting with our deployment, who didn't seem to be doing very much. It seemed wrong that all of these trained soldiers, some of whom actually wanted to go to the Gulf, would be under-employed in Germany, whilst the TA and reserves invaded another country on their behalf. It would have made better sense for us to fill their roles and for them to go to the Gulf but we all knew that this wasn't possible.

The problem is, when the Army has a manpower requirement, it has to pick from the biggest pools. The system isn't capable of finding a few men from one unit and a few from another as the various Commanding Officers of the units adopt a "Train set ownership" method of retaining their staff, making up reasons to retain them, in the face of such requests. The Army therefore have to source vast quantities of men in one big step. The TA and general reserve list is one such large source of available manpower. Everyone on it simply represents a name, rank, number and trade discipline. They are chosen for what they represent on paper. It is a wholly impersonal system, which operates only in an official capacity. Actuality is disregarded entirely. This also allows pockets of fully trained soldiers to be spread about the country, doing nothing, whilst the Army frantically mobilises anyone it can get its' hands on, into a war-zone.

A few irritable hours passed and we were driven to Hanover Airport, to sit and wait for another few irritable hours, until our flight took off. We could easily have managed a full night's sleep and still had over eight hours to waste, waiting for buses and planes that day, instead of twelve. I would have liked to complain to whoever planned the whole operation but I get the distinct impression that no one actually had. I tried to make best use of my time by calling the missus on my mobile phone. I had to do this, regardless of cost because the phones were being forcibly confiscated upon our arrival in Kuwait and we wouldn't be speaking to our loved-ones for the foreseeable future.

I made my last call to the missus and eventually, after what seemed like an age, we were called to board the plane. As we walked onto the runway, I got the distinct impression that I had seen the Aircraft, a Boeing seven-four-seven, somewhere before and in retrospect, I think it was on one of those late seventies disaster films. It was an absolute heap of shit. It had none of the facilities of modern airliners and resembled something more akin to a flying cattle-truck. I squeezed myself into my seat, which felt uncomfortable, worn and very tired, a bit like me. The plane shuddered into life and after a few creaks and groans, ambled from the runway, leaving the safety of Europe behind, to start the long journey to the Middle East. I've never been a fan spending hours on end on a plane and in the ten hours we spent on that plane, my knees set like concrete several times. Why that couldn't have happened on the morning of my medical at Chilwell, I'll never know.

The flight seemed incredibly long. The food was awful, the plane was noisy and almost everything rattled and vibrated on it. The air was thick with bad breath and body odour and the toilets soon began to stink. It was the most unpleasant flight I had ever known but as bad as it was, I didn't want it to end. The end of that flight signalled the start of something entirely different and only the group bull-shitter seemed to be looking forward to it.

# CHAPTER 10; OUT OF THE SAUSAGE MACHINE, INTO THE FIRE.

WE ARRIVED AT the makeshift airport at around three o'clock in the morning, Kuwaiti time. The first thing I saw, as I left the reassuring security of the aircraft was an armed American soldier, on duty on the runway. Looking around, there were many such people, all dressed in American spec desert combats. The airfield, as ramshackle as it appeared to be, was heavily guarded. My only previous experience of living in a war zone was Kosovo and with that one footstep, that experience had already begun to feel like a very tame and lame memory. There was no doubt in my mind that we were well and truly in the shit.

Shuffling along down the row of huge, immaculate, American marquees, it was almost possible to comprehend the scale of the American operation there. By comparison, we arrived at a slightly smaller, scruffy-looking marquee, which looked like an old, unwanted version of the rest. This, unsurprisingly, was the British area. We were told to squeeze inside for, unsurprisingly, another briefing and to fill in a few more forms. This was where we had to "Swipe into theatre", which meant that we had to show our ID card and officially be booked into the Middle East. As we expected, we were told that use of mobile phones was prohibited and that there would be serious repercussions for anyone caught doing so.

After that thoroughly un-enjoyable experience, we were allowed a hot dog each, which, after such a long journey, wasn't nearly enough and then told that it was time to get on our bus. Walking towards the buses, it was plain to see that the vast number of American soldiers all had identical, serviceable desert-coloured combats. There wasn't one person in a scruffy-looking uniform, or in a different colour uniform. It drew an unfavourable comparison with the British, who must have appeared more like a disorganised rabble in green, by comparison. We certainly felt every bit the poor relations.

Our transport to wherever it was we were going (again, we didn't have a clue), was of an equally unimpressive nature. The driver also looked more than a little dubious. A Geordie voice suggested it was "Bin Laden's brother". He was wearing the standard issue grubby dress-type smock, the standard Middle-Eastern beard and the mark one desert-welly (flip-flops) and what can only be described as a tea-towel on his head. The new, politically correct Army (another public façade) tells us we shouldn't form racial stereotypes but this man was plainly a tea-towel-head and was liberally referred to as such. I see no problem with that description. It makes no mention of skin colour, religion or ethnic origin. It simply refers to the fact that he appeared to be wearing what looked like a tea towel on his head, which, if he was happy with it, was good enough for me.

The Army's policy on racism is particularly poorly administered. As ever, it was drawn up with a heavy hand and a small mind, with little sensible consideration. It doesn't go much further than a statement that there will be absolutely no racism within the ranks and the Army definitely isn't a racist organisation. It also states that there will be no positive discrimination on grounds of race or gender and officially, this never happens.

As with most public organisations, the official version of events isn't always a close representation of the truth. The Army claims to be free of racism and yet by its very nature it has to be racist. I don't imply any wrongdoing here. It's simply that as an organisation, it surely ought not to be subject to the same rules on racism because it is, first and foremost, a nationalistic organisation. It acts for the British interest, on behalf on Britain. It is British and should be allowed to be proud of it. It has to discriminate because when fighting a war against another nationality, it is necessary to take aggressive action against that country. If that isn't racism, I don't know what is and yet, the Army isn't a racist organisation, officially.

The Army is apparently subject to and abides by all the employment laws in the UK, which, in turn, abides by EC employment law, to a point. I doubt that any other organisation would be allowed to forcibly re-employ one of its ex-employees under threat of prosecution though. I also doubt that it would be allowed to subject its ex-employees to such sub-human living conditions either. Any other organisation would be forced to provide all the necessary equipment for its ex-employee to do his job as well but then, in any other organisation, the ex-employee would have the right of complaint and legal recompense.

The Army has a problem on these grounds. On the one hand, it is an equal opportunities employer, attempting to adhere to EC employment law. On the other hand, it operates above civilian law and has a vastly different role to any civilian organisation and as such, isn't subject to any laws. Certainly my compulsory call-up and subsequent treatment contravened EC employment laws and the previously mentioned human rights laws. The Army must be aware of this and yet it maintains its public façade of operating within the employment laws in the UK, officially. Believe me, the further you get in, the dafter it gets.

So it was with our transport. I'm sure I have been on that bus before, possibly as an away supporter with Chesterfield, when it was trashed by the Mansfield supporters, on one of our many happy visits (it was always worth it for the three points though). Quite how this wreck had ended up in service in Kuwait was beyond me but this thirty-year-old heap was going to take us to our destination, they said. Everyone got on board, without questioning the roadworthiness of the vehicle or the ability of the driver. It's just a fact with the Army that you get what you're given and this beaten up old bus was the transport provided for us. There was no right of complaint or reasonable alternative.

We squeezed on and, with no air-conditioning, it was far too-warm, even at four o'clock in the morning. It was very uncomfortable and stuffy and sleep was impossible. Nonetheless, we were all determined to try. It was so warm, I was beginning to see the merits of wearing a tea-towel on your head and a few cast a jealous eye over the flip-flops. Bin Laden's brother dropped the handbrake and with a little pressure on the aforementioned footwear, we set off for a destination, which I assume he alone knew the whereabouts of.

Try as I did, sleep wouldn't descend upon me but I certainly wasn't finding grogginess difficult to come by. After a while, I think I was starting to become de-hydrated, due to the conditions. To my dismay, I couldn't lay my hands on the flowchart, or any water. The darkness passed by the windows in steady, bumpy rhythm and after an indeterminate and very disorientating time on the bus, the sun came up, revealing the desolate nature of our new home. Soon, we arrived at a camp, which I didn't get the name of, seemingly located precisely in the middle of nowhere.

We were invited to again reclaim our baggage, which was a monumental tussle (Given that everyone was issued with the same type and any distinguishing features were quickly becoming dusty) and then we were told that before we got to the serious matter of getting us to our respective regiments, it was time for breakfast. This notion made me happy as I could have easily eaten at least the back-end of a horse and was feeling sick and light-headed, due to hunger. A few minutes later, upon seeing my breakfast, I think I decided I would have preferred the back-end of a horse, rather than the abysmal fare on offer.

We entered the huge marquee and stood in line, with our white plastic trays, waiting for our food to be roughly thrown in our direction. The "Chefs" duly obliged and within seconds, I was the recipient of a heavily thrown ladle-full of sticky dried egg, stodgy beans and a strange long grey sausage, which had the appearance of a very long, boiled, dog's dick. The grey hard-boiled duck egg was optional. At least the bread was edible.

The scene, in which we were reluctantly involved, may well have played out like a scene from prison, with the ladles of "slop" being thrown so roughly onto our plates. We certainly weren't free men but any comparisons with prison must end there, because prisoners were infinitely better off than we were. It was a point that, at that time, my morale was such that I wished I had elected to take the prison option because at least the missus could visit me there but then, I hadn't expected the law abiding option to be so much worse. They even get Sky telly, for Christ's sake.

Having thrown half of the beans, almost all of the stodgy egg and the entirety of the dog's dick in the dustbin, which was overflowing with similar platefuls, it was time to find out some information, or so we thought. We went back outside and sat down on our baggage, in the middle of the desert, with the sun beating down and the sand blowing hard into our eyes. Some of the TA, who were due to be posted with the Scots Dragoon's, found that they didn't have far to go, as they were only on the other side of the berm. (A berm, or burn, or whatever its proper name turned out to be, was a mound of earth, which had been formed into a straight line, for the purpose of creating cover on an incredibly flat landscape. From a distance, you would easily hide a tank behind one and it would merely appear to be a flat part of the flat horizon). A curious point of note was that there was a huge supply of long, thick orange pipes all over the place. I couldn't quite picture what they were for.

After a few minutes, most of them came back to get their baggage. Some seemed in good spirits and some, seemingly the REME tradesmen, looked quite agitated and annoyed.

"They're saying they don't want any REME TA." Said one, who was due to be posted there as a mechanic. "Apparently, they haven't asked for them and they don't need them, so I don't know what's happening."

I offered my commiserations and we said our goodbyes as he disappeared around the berm, to find out just exactly what the British Army had planned for him, although it sounded as though they didn't have much of a plan at all. We sat down again and waited. As before, there was no one from Third-Royal-Horse-Artillery to meet us. We watched as our buses drove away and we waited for someone to tell us just what the bloody hell was going on. No one approached us. It's fair to say that things had gone a little quiet.

We sat for three hours, in the desert, with the sand blowing into our eyes and the sun beating down. Sensibly, I tried to cover the bald patch but in reality, I really did need the sun-hat, which I was supposed to have been issued. I hadn't taken much in the way of kit and equipment to Chilwell. Forgetting exactly how Army life used to be, I'd foolishly believed the Army's promise that they would issue me with all the kit and equipment I needed. I had an Army issue sun hat in the loft at home, which I could have quite easily brought with me, if only I'd known.

That was the first of many genuine low-points in my morale. Dumped out there in the desert, with no supplies and no transport, I suddenly realised jut how dependent upon the Army I was. We needed them to provide everything for us. Without them, we couldn't survive. Sat down there, I realised just how unimportant I was to the British government. It really was quite a depressing feeling. Periodically, we had attempted to grab hold of someone to find out some information but apparently, we were no one's problem. It was up to the unit, who were conspicuous by their absence.

After the aforementioned three hours, a lorry stopped in front of us. Out of the back jumped a man with a beret on, wearing an Artillery cap-badge. He was about to walk straight past us, when the Geordie piped up.

"Are you from 3RHA mate?" He asked.

"Yeah, why?" Was the reply.

The Geordie then proceeded to have a Geordie conversation with him, which consisted of more howay's and alreet's than I'd ever heard in one go and it seemed that we were going to get a lift to wherever they were on the back of this lorry, a Bedford four-tonner (As seen in the slow lane of many a Britsh Motorway, with cheerful-looking troops in the back). The Geordie confirmed this with possibly his most eloquent request of the morning.

"Fuckin' howay, let's fuckin' gan lads, get yer fuckin' stuff, howay."

We were on the back of the lorry within seconds. The regiment didn't know anything about our arrival and ours had been a chance meeting but to actually get to relative sanctuary of the unit, rather than sit out in the desert, was a source of great relief to all of us. We didn't know how we would be received at the unit but at least it looked like we might get food and water and somewhere to sleep.

After a short drive, we arrived at an indistinguishable shit-hole, which looked remarkably similar to our previous location. We were told that we were twenty-odd kilometres south of the Iraqi border and yes, we were in range of Iraq's heavy Artillery and a few sleepless nights were assured. Again, we were dumped on the ground with our baggage and told that we weren't his problem but that he would alert someone to our presence and we would be sorted out quite quickly, with a bit of luck.

After a surprisingly short delay of around half an hour, we were greeted by a relatively young one-pip lieutenant. Apparently, such an individual had been bestowed the task of being the second-in-command of the workshops, which was where we were meant to be (though it was unclear exactly who meant us to be there). Apparently they had no idea that we were coming but we had at least, become their problem. We were going to get food and water, it seemed. Morale soared to a point just above chronic depression.

After giving a few details, we were allowed into the unit and greeted by the Officer Commanding workshops, a man who, despite the trails and tribulations of life, was always immaculately groomed. Not to put to fine a point on it, he was a right posing bastard. I had known him from my time in the Army and found him to be a decent enough man, so things were really looking up. It even looked like we might get somewhere to sleep.

The OC went on to confirm that he had absolutely no idea we were coming. He told us that the regiment hadn't requested for any extra manpower to be sent from the UK and that he didn't know why we were there. The regiment's manpower problems had been sorted almost entirely by bringing in almost the entirety of another Artillery regiment and they were surprised that we had been sent there at all. Nonetheless, he did say that they were down a couple of men and that they certainly could use two or three vehicle mechanics.

I wasn't one of those but he said that, although he had no particular need for a man of my trade group, he would probably be able to find a use for me. So too, with the Armourers, he already had a full compliment of men and four more had been sent from the TA but in fairness, he wasn't wrong to accept the extra men. I think he probably wanted less than a third of us but accepted the rest because we had come a long way and our only other option was sitting out in the desert. I was certainly relieved to find a home. This relief tempered my anger at having been forcibly plucked from my cosy civilian existence and sent out to the Gulf for no reason whatsoever. I had at least expected, when called-up under threat of prosecution, to be needed in some capacity, by someone.

He brought us something like up to speed with the grand scheme of things and told us what was likely to happen in the immediate future. In short, he told us the "plan" for us to invade Iraq. It was proper old boy scout's stuff, drawing maps in the sand, with a stick and telling us a few possible eventualities. I was genuinely impressed with his apparent know-how and although the "plan" seemed absolutely ridiculous, it was put across in admirable fashion.

The plan, in its simplest terms, was to stage a brief, heavy aerial bombing campaign, followed up immediately by vast quantities of Artillery shells and then a surge into Iraq. If they hadn't surrendered after this initial "Shock and Awe" stage then, we were apparently going to have bit of a rethink. That was as far as the plan went. That and the small detail that, for the first time in British military history, the Artillery would roll in first and the other small detail that the workshops, myself now included, would be rolling in with them. As a reservist, who wasn't actually in the Army who had recently discovered he had no reason for being in the Gulf, I found myself amazed at the microscopically short straw I'd managed to draw.

He allocated us all to the most reasonably relevant position he could find. Mine was to be part of the section whose job it was repair all the thermal imaging and sights equipment, which seemed a fairly sensible place for me. I had some experience of thermal imaging whilst working on Phoenix, so even if I hadn't encountered the equipment I would be working on, I would at least be able to understand it in principle. Having said this, we expected little in the way of technical work and more in the way of war-fighting, which rendered my skills even less relevant. At least I would be going to war with other similarly-un-soldier-like tradesmen though.

I was shown to the back of a truck, another old Bedford Four-tonner. The back of this thirty-five year-old-heap was going to be my home for the foreseeable future and possibly beyond. The problem was, the two men already living in it didn't know, until that point. It came as a little bit of a shock to them, to be suddenly told that they had to find room for another body in an already crowded space. Nonetheless, to their credit, they accommodated me as best they could and my new home was to be on the floor, with my head hanging out of the back door. It wasn't much but a place to sleep was something I desperately needed. I was sorted, to some extent. We quickly addressed priorities and a cup of tea was soon in my grateful hand. Not a bad reception from these two, I thought. It was as good as I could have hoped for. At least I had a roof over my head, albeit canvass.

Later, we had a briefing from the Artificer Sergeant Major (ASM) of the workshops. He seemed a decent enough bloke despite his "Saddam" moustache but I was a little annoyed when he advised us to have faith in the system because "The system works". I had no faith in the system at all because I knew it had already failed us on numerous occasions. It was his way of attempting to tell us that all the supply shortages we were suffering were only temporary and all would be sorted before we went over the border. He was right to pacify us but I'm not sure if he believed the advice he was giving.

At that point, when we were officially on twelve hours notice to move into Iraq, most men at the unit had no "Bullet-proof" Kevlar plates in their body armour. Hardly anyone had any desert combats, or desert boots. We couldn't get hold of any sunglasses or goggles, which made it very uncomfortable on the eyes, with all the sand constantly blowing around. None of this concerned me too much though because I would have flatly refused to enter Iraq at that point because we had no bullets. We weren't just short of them. We had none at all. Other people complained about the lack of various things like flares and smoke grenades but I wasn't interested in those, I was just concerned that I may need to shoot someone fairly soon and I didn't have the means. Mine was a reasonable stance, I thought.

I tried to get my hands on a few of the niceties, which should have been available from the workshops stores. I asked for goggles, sunscreen and insect repellent. I was told that, although a few of these things were available, I couldn't have them, as I wasn't part of the unit. It was frustrating, standing there with the rest of the TA men, watching him hand out all of the things we needed, to people who were behind us in the queue. We got nothing. As far as he was concerned, we weren't his problem. He only wanted to look after the people who belonged to the unit. The poor relations, those urchins who turned up at the last minute, could suffer without. My frustration, as he handed out the last of his supplies, was beginning to boil again. We left empty handed and feeling very much that the system hadn't worked for us.

As if to further my depression, it was then suggested, in a rather clumsily delivered briefing, that we must sanitise ourselves. Surprisingly, this had nothing to do with the welcome notion of cleansing our dirty and sweaty bodies. It was a de-humanisation process. I didn't think it was an unnecessary task but it was still quite distressing to perform. On the pre-tense of potentially being taken prisoner of war, it is necessary to remove anything, which may personalise or identify something about yourself. Anything, which might have your address on it, or photographs or anything particular to your family has to go. This is to deny your potential captors access to anything other than the information they are supposed to have. It is another reason why the mobile phones were confiscated. I would imagine that no-one's wife would wish to speak to the people holding their husband prisoner, or to be threatened by them. On the other hand, if they got through to my mother, I would probably be home in days, with a written apology.

The whole exercise is to help the would-be-prisoner maintain an indistinctive and uninteresting appearance, so as to avoid being singled out for special treatment. Understanding the reasoning behind it doesn't make it any easier to hand over all the things, which remind you of home though. I remember feeling that that was the point when I became closer to Iraq than I was to my own life, which suddenly seemed like a distant memory. Wearily, I trudged back to the truck, sat down in the back and wrote my first "Bluey" (forces mail envelope) to the missus. I don't remember making a great effort to be cheerful.

## CHAPTER II; YES MEN AND SUPER EGOS.

I AWOKE THE following morning after a poor and often interrupted night's sleep. That was the first time I would wake up and spend ten seconds trying to deal with the reality I found myself in. I wasn't so detached from my life as to completely forget everything about it and so I found myself literally dreaming of home. These happy thoughts contrasted completely with the harsh reality of waking up somewhere near the Iraqi border. "Oh bollocks, I'm here" was the first realisation upon waking and the morning became the hardest part of the day. The only thing, if there was anything, to look forward to, was breakfast, so one of the first tasks of the morning was to amble along towards the American tent at the allotted time, in order to scrounge some, which they were happy to provide, we were told.

Unfortunately, as we arrived at the American food tent, it turned out that we were too late. They had stopped serving and we should have turned up half an hour earlier, as we had been told. We'd turned up at precisely the time we were told to at the previous night's briefing. This, it turned out, had been the first of many poor or problematic briefings given to us by a man who was quickly becoming a figure of ridicule. He seemed to be slowly acquiring the unlikely tag of the "over-promoted buffoon", although some already referred to him as "That twat".

It is a problem in the Army, that there are many people who have been promoted above and beyond their mental capabilities and here was a prime example. The problem was, we depended on him for our information and he struggled to pass on even the simplest of messages. When fifty people miss breakfast due to the failings of one weak individual, who has more responsibility than he can rightly handle, it is a cause for a rapid fall in collective morale and ours duly plummeted.

I decided, as annoyed as I was, that I might as well attempt to clean myself up and to polish my boots. It had been a long time since I had had to keep myself clean without the use of running water, so the culture shock was there to be felt and smelt. I knew that, as hard as I may try, it would be a long time before I would feel properly clean again. It was just a case of trying to keep the sweaty parts clean enough to prevent infection. No one, with the exception of the OC workshops, with his hair gel, managed to keep their self genuinely clean.

Later in the day and somewhat incredibly, dinner turned out to be an even bigger disappointment than breakfast. We queued up for half an hour, in order to get hold of some of the American rations, which were being handed out. The British Army had to beg food from the Americans in those first few days because the system wasn't working. The unfortunate thing was that, when begging for food, it can be difficult to beg for enough to satisfy everyone in theatre. The disappointment was obvious when, as we neared the front of the queue, they suddenly declared that there was nothing left. Looking behind me, it seemed that there were a hundred or so similarly disappointed faces. "The fuckin' Brits are like Oliver Bastard Twist." Exclaimed a frustrated Geordie voice, before we all trudged back to our lorries, bellies 'a' rumbling.

The newspapers made a big song and dance over the lack of food for the troops but in my view, it shouldn't have merited so much attention. The situation wasn't life threatening in any way. True, it was unpleasant but nothing to get excited about. This isn't to say that I wasn't hungry, indeed I was painfully so, it was just that as far as I was concerned, we had a number of far more significant problems.

Another problem, of varying significance, was the situation with the "Welfare telephone". The Army maintains that it has a more than adequate welfare system to cater for everyone's emotional needs, with each soldier being given a phone-card, which gives an entitlement of twenty minutes per week. The problem with this, in practice, was that the workshops only had one telephone between nearly sixty men. As ever with the Artillery, they made sure that they had plenty of phones before considering their attached personnel and the workshops got the left-overs, namely a slightly wonky, unreliable phone with a permanently flat battery, which was just enough to fulfil the minimum requirement, without ever being genuinely adequate. Further to this, there seemed to be no provision for phone-cards for any of the TA. Certainly, the Army welfare system wasn't working for me at all but then I should have expected it, having served with the Artillery before.

My despair at the situation seemed limitless. I wanted to ring the missus, just to explain why I'd suddenly seemed to disappear off the face of the earth and that everything was mostly alright really and that there was no need to worry that much. I think, in her position, alone at home, without any explanation of the situation, someone needed to put her mind at rest but yet again the Army system failed the both of us. There was only one reason why I counted myself fortunate and that was down to the people around me. Where the system failed, human decency succeeded and it looked like I would get my wish. The Section Artificer, a man who's first principle of management was to look after the people under his command, came to my assistance.

The nine minutes or so, which were left on the phone-card he gave me, were probably the most prized of my possessions at that time. The relief at being able to contact the missus was immense and I owed it to the monumental decency of one man, rather than the Army itself. His was an act of exceptional generosity, which I can never forget. Unfortunately, my frustrations with the system were soon to be further aroused, when I got the phone and found that I couldn't get a signal and the battery was flat. I'm sure that this situation did little for the missus, who didn't even know if the plane had landed safely. I would have to wait a little while and so would she. At least I knew it would happen, though.

A curiosity arose later in the day. Another "soldier" I was in company with (This man will remain unnamed and without description, for his own sake) had checked the serial number on my rifle for no apparent reason but had said nothing about it. I didn't twig just why he'd done so until a young woman from another regiment turned up, demanding to speak to him about her rifle. It seemed that there had been a mass search for her rifle all morning because someone had mistakenly taken it, leaving their own instead, after washing that morning. She had noticed instantly and reported it, whereas the unnamed man hadn't noticed for a couple of hours, until he'd heard the rumours.

There was little fuss made of it officially, save for a couple of haughty bollockings for the culprit, which sent him into a proper sulk. It wasn't a pleasant sight as he protested that it really didn't matter what weapon he had, as long as he had one. This was my oddest conundrum to date. I was a resolute non-believer in all matters military and yet I found myself lecturing him about combat effectiveness and the need to maintain your own weapon, which is zeroed to your own eye. I found it strange that I, of all people, should have to tell him this, as he was a fully trained serving soldier.

It probably stood as testament to my basic training from years earlier. As much as I'd forgotten most things about being a soldier, there were certain things, which were harshly and repeatedly drilled into my head and which I can probably never forget. If I had neglected my rifle in any way, I was made to run a couple of miles with it above my head, arms throbbing and later on, they would punish the rest of the platoon again, for one man's error.

These were harsh lessons but they were well learned. It seemed that in later years, the basic training syllabus wasn't allowed to incorporate such harshness and the lessons maybe weren't quite drilled home. I felt that, perhaps in weakening this syllabus, the Army had lost one of its best and most effective tools and perhaps taken the substance out of what is an incredibly well-learned lesson for the majority. Certainly this individual, though younger and far more recently trained than I was, hadn't quite had the military education I received and had gained a reputation for losing or not caring for equipment.

I didn't think that shouting and screaming at him at this late stage would achieve anything though, so I tried to explain myself calmly. I have never given over to the shouting mentality of the Army. It just isn't my way but I had to admit that all the shouting and screaming and bullying of my basic training platoon staff had had some positive effect on me. I just found it odd that I was living by principles, which I hadn't encountered in over seven years. I only hoped that it would be enough because to all intents and purposes, I was chasing the game as well, though no-one had yet found me out, due to my apparent outward calmness.

This said, I really did find myself ill at ease with life in the Middle East. It was too hot, too dusty and there were too many flies. The helicopters, which constantly flew overhead, were too noisy and my eyes were constantly streaming, due to the sand blowing around. This was where another decent man bailed me out, with the offer of a pair of goggles. Fortunately, he'd brought a spare pair with him and suddenly, I was particularly grateful to be able to walk around with my eyes open and actually see where I was going. This said, I really couldn't understand just why anyone would choose to live in such a place. I'd had enough after that first twenty-four hours.

The second twenty-four hours in theatre got off to a much better start. We actually made breakfast and although it wasn't by any means pleasant, it was a huge improvement over the previous meal. There was no dog's dick and some of the egg was almost edible. I wasn't surprised by this as a lot of the food needed to be sourced locally, so the first few days would inevitably be the worst and improvement would occur naturally. Only to a point where the food was actually marginally better than eating dog-shit, though, warned my mate Dave.

We were due to be on the receiving end of a speech from the Commanding Officer, which is when six-hundred men have to stand around in baking-hot temperatures and wait for the most self-important arsehole at the unit to turn up and generally blather on about any old self-promoting shite. It wasn't fun in the forty-five degree heat, without a sun-hat or sunscreen but after forty minutes or so, he decided to turn up and stand on the top of the Artillery Piece, which had been placed there for just such a purpose, to address us, his loyal subjects.

I expected, or should I say I had hoped to be inspired by a speech, which marked preparation for war but as with most of the things my ears had been forced to receive, I was disappointed. We were told to expect war within a week, which sounded a little vague and that we would see some horrible sights and that some of us wouldn't be coming back. I would say that the first minute of that speech contained some of the most uninspiring words I had ever encountered. Everyone knows war isn't safe or pleasant but to point this out at the outset would seem to be the exact opposite of motivation.

He then told everyone at the regiment that we were all doing the right thing and that we had to "Square it away with our conscience" because this course of action was right and any other school of thought was wrong. This didn't sit easily with me because I had genuine doubts about the morality of such a war and didn't appreciate being told what to think. I had just about accepted that we had a job to do and that we were going to do it to the best of our abilities but I don't think for a minute that it was necessary for me to agree with it in principle. It seemed foolish to make such a statement because it could only ever draw dissenting voices, (there were quite a few) such was its heavy-handed nature. This speech may only have worked for those people who believed wholeheartedly in the Army system and that number was shrinking fast.

We were told that Britain had no friends in the international community and that we had to go in, in support of America, or face international isolation. I found this statement to be the closest to the truth of the ones we'd heard, yet it seemed a little contradictory to the statement about it being the right thing to do. I was becoming less and less convinced with every word.

A new level of de-motivation was reached when he felt that he had to quote an American general, in order to "further inspire" his men. He made mention of the protest against the war in America and that the Americans were going to war to give the Iraqi people the same right of protest. It was a fight for freedom and that we should shake any peace protesters we meet firmly by the hand because we fought to protect such rights. Furthermore, when doing so, we should wink at that peace protestor's girlfriend because having seen just how manly the war-fighting soldier is, she may decide that her peace-protesting boyfriend is a pussy.

I think this was about the biggest insult my intelligence had ever received. I can't believe that the Americans fall for that kind of rubbish and it makes me cringe to think that such words were used in British Military circles. I didn't heckle the Commanding Officer but I was certainly aware that he was capable of monumental stupidity. It was said firstly with "American Sincerity", which puts it well beneath plausibility and furthermore, it came from an almost Neanderthal point of view. I certainly didn't believe that the Iraqi's would be granted such freedom as a direct result of this conflict and I have never found women to be quite so easily impressed. I went from a point of acceptance of the job in hand, to wondering just why on earth we were there. Several heads nodded to the muttered suggestion that "He's a fucking idiot".

To motivate people at the outset of the war is surely not to point out the negatives of the horrors of war, or the likelihood of death. Surely, it would be better to concentrate on the positives, like the courage, skill and determination of the men before him. It would be better to emphasise his belief that his was the finest regiment in the land and that they, with an aggressive stance and reliance on teamwork, would surely flatten all before them. Everyone is aware that they may well not come back alive, or they may lose a friend but these facts motivate no one. The message, in its simplest form must surely be that there is a job to be done and everyone must collectively grab the bull by the horns. To quote another man, from another country as motivation is surely a poor attempt to justify a questionable cause. He didn't need to justify the cause because each and every man was stuck with it, whether he agreed or not. Few people seemed impressed with what had been one of the weakest speeches I had ever heard.

We were then addressed by the Padre (Regimental vicar), who, after telling one of the poorest jokes in history, went about the process of giving us total absolution. Apparently, in the eyes of the lord, each and every man before him was to be absolved of blame or guilt for any wrongdoing for the entirety of his life, until that point. It seemed a strange thing to do and it was a strange thing to receive but, having been guilty of bullying the overweight effeminate kid at school (Still sorry about that), I was grateful for at least something to show in return for my efforts. Such a practice probably goes a long way to confirm the grave nature of what we were about to undertake and despite my lack of religious inclination, I felt a little strange listening to the Padre speak.

Later that day a man, who could only ever be known as the Scandinavian (or similar) and I, found that we had a job to do. This came as a complete surprise to me as it had looked unlikely that I would be involved in any of the repair work as most of it was done before I arrived and the rest was awaiting spares, which were unlikely to arrive in 2003. Furthermore, not having worked on the equipment before and being a little out of touch with matters military, I would be a little off the pace. My value to the unit, even if there had been a job for me, was questionable. Nonetheless, the thought of partaking in a bit of engineering practice with the Nordic God held at least some appeal.

We drove away up the dirt track, towards the dusty gun-park, (grand title, for an area of desert, which looked the same as any other) in our dusty Land rover. On our way, we encountered something of an oddity. We saw the three Challenger 2 tanks lined up for a press shoot and in the immediate background, we were surprised to see most of the regiment playing football on what appeared to be a hastily marked out pitch. These men, who had been preparing equipment and digging holes all morning, had suddenly started a game of football, which coincided with the arrival of the watching eyes of the world.

The surprise faded quickly when we saw the cameras. It was all just part of the public façade of the Army. They had been made to work hard all morning and would spend most of the night working equally hard, yet the public perception was that most of the work was done and "Our Boys" were getting a bit of leisure time. Certainly, we were unsurprised, upon our return, to see that the cameras had gone and everyone was back to work, digging trenches. This is standard practice within the Armed forces. Indeed, such falseness of impression has given rise to a situation where every member of the Royal family believes that the Army smells of wet paint but out in that desert, there was a lot more than a lick of paint between the public image and the truth.

It is interesting to hear the occasional unsubstantiated rumour in the newspapers about just how bad things are in the Army and just how starkly these contrast with the public statement. This game of football took place when a leading General had just stated to the press that the British troops had life a little too comfortable in the Gulf. I do not wish to call him a liar. I only wish to state that when he arrived and had a look around, the mess was tidied away and the regiments he visited portrayed a false image to him too. The people who may have thrown up a problematic question or statement to him were warned against it and the hierarchy of these regiments closed ranks and gave a resounding thumbs up, when asked if everything was ok. This is standard practice in the Army. It is the system. Yes, it happened with us too.

In reality this false public image occurs in almost every situation, in every way of life, wherever you are in the world, from the rowing couple portraying a picture of marital bliss in public, to a man wearing a wig and a woman not leaving the house without make-up. It is all false and human society, as a whole, is full of falseness. No one has any difficulties accepting these falsehoods, it is the act of washing dirty linen in public, which is frowned upon by those involved and ridiculed by those who aren't. No one likes to have their own embarrassing truths revealed and yet the whole world loves a scandal.

The problem with the Army is that all the hierarchy within are also involved in this denial, rather than at least attempting to face up to the problems at hand. All the dirt is quickly brushed under the carpet, time and time again and everyone pretends that it just doesn't exist. The Army is a closed shop, where everyone pretends everything is fine, whilst being perfectly well aware that it isn't. No one rocks the boat. Some may occasionally raise an issue but none dare make too much noise for the fear of jeopardising their own career.

The reason why the system survives in an almost unchanged state, despite its obvious failures is a simple one to explain. It survives because without ever existing as a living entity, it rules over everything within it. The need for personal opinion and judgement is almost totally removed by the system, such is its' rigidity. The system selects people for promotion by attempting to fit them to a rigid template, not by assessing their intelligence or abilities outright. The system continually allows talented individuals to slip by, because they didn't quite tick the right box.

This gives rise to the Army system of people assuming the correct personality for their rank status. If everyone knows their own station in life and behaves according to their rank then the rigid systematic template will survive indefinitely because there is no one to challenge it. The Army system, if administered correctly, should consist of "Yes Men" and "Super egos", which, in simple terms, makes it an autocracy. In the eyes of the Army, the person with the highest rank in the room has absolute authority. If that is a Corporal, then so be it and all should assume the role of "Yes Men" to his "Super Ego". His authority on any subject should be unchallengeable. If a person of higher rank enters the room, then he must assume the "Super Ego" mantle and the Corporal, being of lesser rank, must fall in with the "Yes Men". This system should continue all the way up until whatever Field Marshall enters the room and becomes the "Ultimate Super Ego" who has superiority over everyone in the room and has an authority, which is unchallengeable. All beneath are subsequently rendered "Yes Men".

People who fit easily into this template and act within the authority afforded them; quite obviously find it easy to succeed within the Army. Indeed, people showing a greater belief in the Army system often find that that belief is repaid as they are deemed a round peg for a round hole. This system of promotion ensures that the man at the top of the tree, being the absolute autocrat himself, is the roundest peg in the roundest hole and the system survives indefinitely, due to this. As with any trends, there are exceptions but anyone with revolutionary thoughts would need to hide their intent alarmingly well for many years before having the authority to put anything into practice.

It is a regime, which is mirrored almost exactly by the one it was tasked to remove, namely the Dictatorship government of Iraq. In it, all are subservient to one man and in his absence, subservient to the man immediately beneath him in rank. Everyone must try to protect the status quo and anyone found to be rocking the boat must be quickly punished. No one dare speak publicly of the problems within, for fear of the repercussions and the people who are best suited to serve the system are handsomely rewarded. For Saddam Hussein, read "Ultimate Super Ego". For "Ultimate Super Ego" read dictator. The public image bore distinct similarities in its falseness. It is little surprise then, that the Iraqi governmental template has changed little since it was first set out when the British Empire dictated rule over the area.

To challenge the Army system in this way may seem idealistic. It may seem an impossible task to change something, which has been set in stone for such a long time and as such, my criticism of it may appear a little fanciful but then to claim that a war on dictatorship would result in peace and democracy is also more than a little hopeful. In attempting to put the world to rights we must all be aware that the world is a big place and we, in our infinite wisdom, are not perfect either.

My place within our regime was officially to be a Lance-Corporal, or one up from the bottom. I found though, that during my later years in the Army and upon my return, that I belonged somewhere out to the left of the Army, rather than being one of its' component parts. I found, both during my later years in the Army and again after my recall, that my position in the Army is naturally incorrect. I did not blindly follow the orders of the man most senior, as I found I usually had a disagreement in principle with those orders. I found myself constantly carrying out tasks, which I knew to be pointless and having to take the long way around solving any problem due to the lack of vision of those in command. In short, rightly or wrongly, I considered myself too intelligent and creative to work comfortably within such a rigid system. I found it curtailed my freedom of thought and strangled any ideas I may have. I was as poorly suited to the Army as the Army was to me and as such, my decision to leave ought to have been allowed to be final.

Further frustration was readily available in the shape of the one-pip lieutenant, to whom I was officially sub-ordinate. He had little military experience, save for his initial training and the preparation for the deployment to Iraq and yet he bore a full compliment of the arrogance, which is deeply instilled into each and every Sandhurst Graduate. The fundamental underpinning of the Sandhurst training method is to remove any thoughts of manners or decency from the command process and this chap had obviously passed comfortably.

The young officer cadet is taught that the use of manners, or any tone of voice, which is vaguely equivalent, is strictly prohibited. This school of thought dates back to a time when an officer was a gentleman (and behaved as such; how times have changed) and had a very distinct class superiority over the men he under his command. The teaching is from a time when any man wearing a suit and tie was called sir and the working-man had no aspirations above abject poverty. In this time, most of the Army's officers were sourced from higher society and most of its' other ranks were plucked from the prison gates, having been threatened with a spell due to some misdemeanour. The class divide between the origins of the officer and the soldier in today's Army is rarely so great and yet the Army's class system stands as rigid as stone. As a relative outsider, I felt duty bound to bridge the gap.

After sitting in the back of the command vehicle, listening to several of his unnecessarily abrupt commands, I decided that I ought to offer him the benefit of my knowledge and experience. This represents no vast reservoir but would easily burst the banks of his tiny trickle of judgement. I attempted to tell him that the modern soldier, having served in several operational theatres, is deserving of respect and should properly be addressed more politely and equally. I also told him that manners go a long way when attempting to convince someone to co-operate with you.

"People don't have to co-operate with me. They have to do as I tell them." He replied.

"Do you think I'll do everything you tell me to do?" I asked.

"Probably not but then you'd have to face the consequences."

"Having been plucked from my comfortable house and sent right into the middle of a war-zone, I have to wonder exactly what the consequences are."

"I don't suppose there's much to threaten you with."

"No but here I am co-operating willingly because in general, people have spoken to me in a reasonable manner and because I'm a reasonable man. Things might be different if people shouted and screamed at me. I'd probably just ignore them because I respond to human decency, like the vast majority of people". I continued.

"Well that's the Army and you're stuck with it." He said finally.

I had to admit that, as many times as I'd heard that answer, I still found it completely annoying but in his case, I took it as being the closest thing to an acceptance of my point, as he'd nothing more to offer than the company motto. In my eyes, there is no justification for bad manners and as such, I will always have a valid point in any such argument. Having made my point and hopefully provided a little food for thought, I made my excuses and opened the door, only to be greeted by huge, swirling clouds of dust.

Leaving that cheery little subject behind, I stumbled outside to address far more pressing matters. Unfortunately, I had also stumbled outside into a wild and very thick sandstorm. Even with my goggles on, I still couldn't see more than five feet in front of me. It was dark and my goggles were instantly enveloped with dust. I got my bearings from the vehicle and set off, hopefully in the direction of the toilets. The toilets were of an upright plastic cubicle variety a similar type to those used at a lot of outdoor events in Britain. The unfortunate thing is that, as this was the Army, they were to be used over a far longer period and kept in a far more disgusting state.

I staggered the fifty yards or so to the first cubicle and yanked open the door, which almost blew off in my hand, due to the wind. After a brief struggle, I decided I needed to empty my bowels more than I needed to feel clean and threw myself into the pitch darkness of the cubicle, closing the door behind me. It was relatively sheltered from the direct forces of the sandstorm, save for the large vent at the top, which allowed in plenty of dust. In the darkness and without the torch that the Army hadn't provided me with, it was difficult to estimate the depth of the slurry already deposited but from the smell, I deduced there to be quite a pile. These cubicles were used exclusively for defecation. To urinate in them would simply have caused them to overflow, hence all the huge orange pipes, which, in this location, had been sunk into the ground, to use as urinals, known as desert roses, I'd recently discovered. There was no privacy when using them, as they were simply out in the open, for all to see. I had grown accustomed to privacy in civilian life but after running water, flushing toilets and my bed, I decided I wouldn't miss it so much.

I dropped my trousers and plonked myself down onto the pot. For once, I was glad not to have been blessed with anything more than moderately proportioned genitalia, as anything swinging far below would surely have trawled the slurry at length. I made as quick a job of it as possible and stood up to wipe. I didn't want to get my hands in, because there wasn't running water to clean them, should I finger the carnage below. The curiosity was that when the General had said we had it too comfortable, he was right to a point because this was going to be the last time we would see the toilet cubicles for weeks and things would only get worse. We wouldn't be taking such luxurious facilities with us into Iraq.

To my further dismay, upon my stumbling, hazardous return to my wagon, I found that several pairs of pants and socks, which I had hung out to dry prior to the sandstorm, wouldn't be making the journey either. I didn't really need any more problems but a shortage of underpants looked liked being something else I to deal with. It wasn't high on the list.

# CHAPTER 12;
# THE ENTRANCE TO SHIT CREEK.

WE WERE DUE to move a little nearer the Iraqi border, although we weren't told exactly where or why. We were just told that we would move up with the regiment and they would be going somewhere near the border. There was never any clear reasoning for the workshops to follow the guns so closely, as we weren't even scaled to repair the equipment in theatre at the time. In my eyes, it seemed reasonably sensible for soft-skinned vehicles, such as the lorries and Land-Rovers we were using, to go in a good distance behind the armour of the guns.

Throwing caution and any reasonable consideration aside yet again, the plan was to closely follow the guns all the way into Iraq. It seemed that the hierarchy had missed the workshop's role in all of this, as each separate battery of guns had its' own compliment of workshops personnel with them, to support their equipment's immediate needs. As there were no spares and no equipment immediately en route, it seemed that the workshops were almost entirely redundant in the grand scheme of things, so the plan was simply to follow everyone else into Iraq, as quickly as we could, without actually performing our role. We had a duty to invade Iraq because we had all been "taking the money for long enough", according to the OC Workshops. The statement that "It's time to give something back" may well have motivated everyone else but it just didn't fit the bill for me.

The daily routine was that the workshops was supporting itself, as an infantry unit would, rather than genuinely providing a service to the unit it was supposed to be supporting. The workshops were irrelevant to the war, just as I was irrelevant to the workshops. There was almost no output, as far as supporting the regiment was concerned. I realised that my place in all of this was no more than that of an unexpected visitor to a unit of uninvolved bystanders (Here we eradicate the Walter Mitty factor completely).

Before the off, I just had time to attempt to sort out the wages crisis, which I was sure was about to happen. Having given my bank details at

Chilwell, in order that they may sort out my wages, I was surprised to be told that I was on a lower rate of pay than when I was in the Army before, so I needed to sort this matter, as well as addressing my concerns that my wages situation would go horribly wrong due to the Army's notoriously inadequate administration system. I just wanted to make sure that the missus would be able to pay the bills at home, as she already had enough to worry about. Unfortunately, having attempted to speak to the clerks about it for the fourth time, I found that they knew nothing about my situation and had no way of contacting Britain at all, let alone Chilwell.

Unsurprisingly, my wages weren't their problem and they didn't know how to deal with it. This situation certainly wasn't the unit's fault, as they knew nothing of the impending arrival of any TA or reservists. It did highlight the problem that, having dragged me out to the Gulf, the Army system had no measures in place to cater for my financial or welfare needs. Indeed, my situation with the missus at home wasn't catered for in any way. Whether she knew anything about my health or whereabouts, or whether she received any money to pay the mortgage really didn't matter to them. All that mattered was that I was sent out to the Gulf. The commitment stopped there. Disappointed and genuinely concerned, I trudged back to the wagon and continued the process of loading up various piles of our equipment. All I could really do was worry.

The appearance of our vehicles told a story about the more immediate problems we faced though. Out in an obviously sand-coloured desert, they stood out, as sore as the sorest of thumbs in Army green and black. There had been no time to paint them prior to their departure from Germany and despite several promises of desert paint, they were still green and were going to roll over the border into Iraq as green as the trees they were supposed to blend in with. This pretty much summed up the plight of an Army in the desert, in green vehicles, with green combats, boots designed for cold weather and no bullets. I forgot about my wages for a while because I wasn't sure that I would ever be able to spend them anyway. At that moment, it felt like we were being pushed hard right up shit creek and the Army had provided us with no paddles.

The workshops attempted to form up into a convoy that afternoon. I say attempted because watching all the lorries sink into the soft sand and the general disorganisation of it all was a most comical sight. Surely enough, when it all went wrong, tempers began to fray and several senior figures within the workshops began to shout the odds. The people shouting the odds weren't those at the top of the command chain but those lesser individuals who were caught in the middle, in a position of management without genuine authority. These people needed to be seen to shout, otherwise their immediate superiors would question why they weren't

"Managing" their staff correctly. Nobody was actually angry about it at all. It was just the military system's automated response.

The voices got louder as the scene got sillier until it was time to call a halt to proceedings. For most of us, it was a source of amusement as we got the vicious bollocking, which was associated with our rank status. I personally hadn't been involved with any of the fiasco so far, with the exception of attempting to assist a couple of struggling individuals and neither had most of the Corporals and Lance-Corporals I was taking to, yet we got most of the backlash. This shouting, aggressive blame culture is widespread throughout the Army and the results of it were plain to see. Enthusiasm plummeted to a point where most were reluctant to get involved at all. Blame had been apportioned and that was the end of the matter. I would much rather have sought a solution to the problem, which was still there to be found.

A sensible man who had previously voiced his concerns about overloading his lorry was suddenly the culprit as it became firmly bogged in, due to the weight on the back axle. There was much shouting and pointing of the proverbial finger, before he was allowed to suggest a solution to a problem he hadn't caused. A few, who had managed to stay calm when so many people were losing their heads, pitched in and the problem was quickly solved and soon enough, this bizarre Circus was on the road, or rather the dirt track. We were mobile.

The convoy eventually rolled away into the dusky evening, throwing up plumes of dust as it went. It was difficult to follow the vehicle in front, with no headlights on, with the dust blowing in through the window and the strain on the unnamed man's face as he drove was plain to see. We drove for about three-quarters of an hour, into the darkness, before we pulled up in a position, which looked as bland and featureless as the previous one. Someone, with a red-filtered torch (All white light was banned, as we were on blackout) stood around thinking what to do for a while before directing us into something like a position. Our position was approximately twelve kilometres from the Iraqi border, which meant that we were on radio silence. I didn't care too much about this but it did mean that we wouldn't be able to make use of our twenty minutes of phone-calls from there, a fact, which pleased no one, least of all me.

We quickly dismounted and began to unroll the cam-nets. These huge drapes were at least desert-coloured and as they were almost brand-new they provided thick cover over our vehicles, which disguised our location as well as a dark green vehicle can be, in a beige landscape. Camouflaging the vehicles, with the rest of the section, made me feel a little uncomfortable as I realised just how out of touch I was. I hadn't done this for three or four years and as I was of little use, I felt more and more like I was totally unfit for service. The rest of the section completed the task, with little input from me. It was just something else I couldn't remember how to do.

I had also noticed that, for the first time, I was a little nervous of the position I was in. I have always been able to maintain a calm outlook and watch other people panic but at that moment, just the prospect of being so close to Iraq and well in range of their Artillery and missiles frightened me. The nature of artillery and to some extent, missiles, is that they are entirely indiscriminate, in that they kill whoever they land on, or near. It doesn't matter whether the individual has done everything right or everything wrong. You can be the best soldier on the planet but if you're in the wrong place at the wrong time, that's your lot, no questions asked. At that time, a few kilometres south of the Iraqi border, as war was about to break out, felt very much like the wrong place and the wrong time. A sleepless night was guaranteed for all.

The following morning threw up another wrong time, namely the first time to dig a shell-scrape. A shell-scrape is a very shallow trench, which is long enough to lye down in and provides a reasonably safe position from which to engage any enemy. As none of the Army's equipment will actually stop a bullet, despite their claims to the contrary, being in a hole in the ground presents an infinitely safer option, meaning that the need to dig it as well as possible was paramount.

The one snag with the plan was the fact that I personally hate digging. I do tinker in my garden at home but generally try my hardest to avoid actually digging it. Unfortunately, as with everything I'd experienced to that point, I didn't have much of an option, so, in the blistering heat of the morning, we dug out our first shell-scrape. We also dug out a hole for the desert rose, which from here in, would be constructed from used water bottles. We finally dug out a burn pit, as we would have to burn all our own shit from now on.

As we satisfactorily completed our digs, the second in command of the workshops, or One Pip Louis, as we preferred to call him, came to give us a briefing. Apparently, the commander of the Royal Artillery was visiting us that morning and we weren't to mention anything about the chronic lack of ammunition, or the dire kit and equipment situation, or he would become really angry because he'd heard it all before.

As he left, having imparted his complete lack of wisdom upon us, we dismissed his wishes at a stroke. We all knew that he wouldn't have heard it all before and that One Pip was the only person who actually believed the story. The truth was, as with all (Alleged) VIP visits, we must give the impression that everything is great. Certainly, if he came to our section, he would have left with a flea in his ear but we doubted he would be interested enough to walk so far.

Unbeknown to us, the hierarchy had arranged for some "training" to take place to coincide with his visit. It was all based around subjects everyone knew already and would be of little worth at that stage but at least it would be a chance for the unit to look good when the VIP came. At that time, in that situation, I would have undertaken anything rather than to waste the time of tired men but it seemed that the hierarchy weren't strong enough to make such a courageous decision. It seemed that giving a false impression of capability to someone who wouldn't be coming into Iraq with us was far more important than allowing the unit to recuperate during a slow period. Even in the run up to the war, we were still painting the grass the deepest shade of green.

After sitting through a pointless lecture on first-aid, which was clearly aimed at the wrong people (it was geared towards explaining the structure of the medical unit), we were then "taught" prisoner of war handling, which was also aimed at the wrong people (we wouldn't be doing it, as we had a primary role, officially, as a repair facility and a secondary role as fighting soldiers). The sun was blazing, the flies were hovering and my bald-patch was beginning to hurt due to a lack of protection from the sun. As I had no method of protection other than my thick, black wool beret, I decided to sack the pointless training and head for some shade, rather than suffer heat stroke. Most of the rest of the unit stayed out in the heat, learning nothing but giving the impression that the unit really cared about soldiering. None of us were allowed to question the VIP.

Later that day, I decided to try my luck with the toilet facilities, which were more than a little crude. In place of the luxury of the toilet cubicles, we had an oilcan, with a hole cut out, surrounded by a very vague windbreak type of structure. There was talk of putting a bag in it and having to empty it after a few people had visited but this idea was quickly dismissed as unsanitary. Instead, we had the comparative luxury of one bag per terd. Unable to contain my delight; or the contents of my bowels any longer, I accepted the inevitable. Unfortunately, the inevitable also included the fact that we only had clear plastic bags, which made the whole experience just a little too graphic for my liking.

I fitted the plastic bag to the inside of the can and having dropped my trousers and sufficiently bared my backside to the world, I lowered myself onto it. I looked to the skies and asked the man upstairs to provide for me a firm delivery but not for the first time in recent weeks, I was badly forsaken. I didn't need a clear bag to see I had a dose of the runs, which I had been expecting sooner or later anyway, so the trauma wasn't too great, in truth. Following what had been deemed standard procedure; I bagged the whole mess up, tied a knot in it and threw it onto the heap for burning, job done. I also decided that, in future, I would try to find some black plastic bags.

# CHAPTER 13; NAMING THE LONER.

AS THE SUN rose, and I dreamt of sausage and eggs for breakfast, whilst eating my boil in the bag slop (we were on rations by this time), we were greeted with the unsavoury news that there was to be further NBC training that morning. Someone had managed to get their hands on a NAIAD or two, so the unit was officially fully prepared for any chemical warfare attack. In truth, the NAIAD is a twenty-five year old green box, which is heavy, fragile and may possibly give an alarm in the presence of some nerve agents. If it isn't serviced or maintained properly, or set up properly, it won't work at all. Still, box ticked in respect of chemical warfare protection.

Unsurprisingly, the unit NBC instructor, having swum against the tide for long enough, admitted that he hadn't got any servicing kits and that he couldn't really remember how to set it up either. Things weren't looking hopeful until the Section Artificer, who was rapidly showing himself to be the backbone of the unit, took over and, with my assistance, gave a reasonable demonstration of how to use the thing. Having said this, without any servicing kits, it was useless and I wouldn't feel safe relying on it even if we had them. After the demonstration, we threw it in the back of the lorry and forgot all about it, just like all the rest of the useless rubbish we had.

The necessity for NBC protection had increased overnight as we heard "intelligence" reports stating that we were well in range of practically everything Saddam had. (It was noted at the time that when such intelligence is delivered to the masses in such a fashion, it suggests that the person whose duty it was to disseminate the information wasn't actually listening to the details and just had a guess at it.) Further to this, we had previously been told that all his gun positions were dug in and had been for some time but it seemed that all of a sudden, Saddam's forces had become mobile. These few facts we were presented with suddenly seemed unreliable because they went against everything we had previously been told.

Somewhere, the intelligence people had got it wrong and we weren't particularly happy to find this out. In such situations, intelligence should surely be one of the most potent weapons available, however, in our case, there appeared to be no real effort to provide anything useful. It was also supposed, by the majority, that the information, in a valid, useable format, did actually exist. It was the Army's haphazard treatment of it, which was the problem.

That situation though, sat on a level with everything else, as even though we had given in our clothing sizes for ordering our desert combats and boots and had been told that these would arrive imminently, there was nothing forthcoming on that front. We still had no ammunition, which I still found hard to believe and there was certainly no sign of anything else useful either. The story was, as it was with everything we didn't have, that it was in a container, somewhere between Germany and Iraq. The story was beginning to wear a little thin by that point.

The war was going to happen any day and we were going to roll over the border on the first day. We would be the first British soft-skinned vehicles into Iraq because we were going in as one unit, which included us, whether we had a role, or not. There was the small matter of fifty thousand Americans going in before us but none of us had high hopes for their performance. Certainly, they had vast quantities of equipment, all of which was fully operational but we just weren't confident in their abilities as soldiers. The differences between the Americans and ourselves were certainly readily apparent, so much so that we could have been considered opposites.

The British Army has rules of engagement in war and in peace times. These are strict guidelines on when and how to open fire. Couple this with the fact that the British Army, collectively has been patrolling the streets of Northern Ireland, Bosnia and Kosovo for years and the likelihood of accidental deaths from friendly fire is greatly reduced. The Americans, with their shoot on sight policy, vast quantities of equipment and lack of experience and knowledge represent a big, trigger-happy accident, waiting to happen. It was rumoured that their rules of engagement start and end with the word "YeeHaa". No one felt genuinely safe when going in with them. After all, there is an unofficial suggestion that they killed twice as many Brits in the first Gulf war as the Iraqis did.

We were so close to going in that, even without ammunition, we knew the convoy order for the move into Iraq. I was surprised that the workshop ASM wasn't at the front. The standard British Army doctrine is to lead from the front and his duty was to lead our convoy into Iraq. I don't know whether it was because he had served twenty-one and a half years, or whether he didn't know how to read a map, if he was scared of hitting a land-mine or if he was just worried that the Americans might not recognise him in time but his duty was to lead and he chose not to. (I'm sure that there was official reasoning for this but official reasoning often differs from the truth) He was to be at the rear and probably out of a divine ruling, or just the fact that he was the only one capable, the Section Artificer was to be our leader instead, accompanied by his able sidekick, the Scandinavian.

He didn't seem nervous about this duty but I suddenly found that I had incurred an extra role because of this personnel change. Somehow, a man who left the Army two years ago and hadn't fired a rifle in three years was to be stood out of the cupola (a circular hole in the top of the cab), with the machine gun. Apparently, I was extremely calm, experienced and assured, so I was the best available person for the job. I wondered temporarily, if it was simply that I was more easily expendable than the rest but logic suggested that I had been chosen because I was the best available, the man they felt most capable of providing accurate fire under pressure . It had to be that because firstly, the whole convoy would face unnecessary risk and secondly, I was stepping in for one of the most able men at the unit. I knew then that the British Army was in its deepest crisis in history and I suddenly appeared to have a starring role.

I was immediately concerned about this. I didn't panic because it's something I just don't do. I appreciated the sentiment that I was always very calm and saw sense in their reasoning because panicking with a machine gun can be very dangerous. The slight hitch in the plan was that, despite the fact that they thought I was very experienced, I had never even laid a finger on a machine gun. I'd fired pistols and a few rifles but nothing, which could remove a man's head quite so easily. I expressed my concerns to my boss, the Section Artificer, who didn't look too worried.

"Don't worry, I'll run through it with you tomorrow. It'll only take ten minutes. I think you'll be alright." He said, calmly.

If this didn't fill me with confidence, I at least realised he had confidence in me, for some strange reason. I don't think it was in any way because of my abilities as a soldier. I think it was plainly down to the fact that he knew I wasn't a flapper. Flapping or panicking is something that some men do and some men don't. I don't, I never have. I have never possessed much in the way of soldiering ability and yet I have always found such bizarre responsibilities bestowed upon me because I am always calm, always. Where soldiering ability is plentiful in the Army, calmness is a much rarer commodity and this was the only thing of value I had to offer.

My relaxed outlook on life was soon in evidence again, when we were handed a surprise visit by the Commanding Officer of the regiment. He was accompanied by the usual entourage of the Regimental Sergeant Major, the Adjutant and some other buffoons (As a point of clarification, I would like to state that I do not exempt the Adjutant from being a buffoon, indeed, the majority thought so). Bringing up the rear, like an anxious, excitable lapdog; was One Pip Louis.

On the unexpected arrival of such an exalted super-being, it is common for the majority of the lower-ranked personnel to get a bit jumpy and nervous but for me, it really didn't matter. I have never been nervous about talking to people. A person's rank or status in life is unimportant to me as I always try to communicate on a level with everyone. I do not and will not adopt a "Three bags full, Sir" strategy when talking to anyone. I will not be a yes man and I will not give the answers expected of someone of my rank. I decided to try him with a bit of the truth, just to see how aware of it he really was. Nothing to lose, after all.

To my surprise, he had come for no reason other than to meet me. I was genuinely surprised by this but when he told me that I was the only reservist at the unit, it made sense. He seemed genuinely surprised that a reservist had been sent out to invade another country, possibly not quite as surprised as I was but there was no doubt that he sympathised with my position. I didn't ask for any sympathy, as my state of mind at that time was reasonably good at that time but when I offered the sentiment that "The blokes at work didn't think they would send a useless bastard like me to Iraq, whilst the regulars stayed in Germany", he could do nothing but agree.

He asked me how well I had done on the kit and equipment side of things and wasn't surprised that I had received almost nothing. Noticing the Jungle Boots I was wearing, he commented that I'd done better than most, to which I replied that I'd salvaged them from the loft at home and although the soles were splitting, they were more suitable than the ones I'd been issued. In fairness, he didn't seem to be too bad a bloke and I didn't feel the need to complain at length to him, as he seemed to understand just how poor the situation was.

I did tell him that I was worried about having to give a cover story if I was taken prisoner of war because surely no one would believe mine. I couldn't believe it myself, so they would probably assume I was some kind of special-forces deviant and give me the hardest buggering known to man. This, coupled with the fact that I have never quite been able to present myself as a "grey man", made me shudder at the prospect of being introduced to one of Saddam's Professional Rapists, who, apparently really did exist, if you believed everything you read in the newspapers.

One pip Louis looked shocked at my casual manner towards the CO, particularly when I jokingly told him to fuck off over the boots (he took this in good humour) but I had no reason to stand on ceremony. Neither was I deliberately disrespectful, as similarly, I had no need for that either. The Adjutant offered some vague quip, which made his chins wobble as he laughed but no one else seemed entertained by him. The CO, with far more dignity and decorum than he'd presented on the morning of his speech, left our little compound and carried on with his business. We too, got back to drinking our cups of tea.

That night, I decided I needed some thinking time, as it had been impossible to achieve anything akin to privacy since I arrived, as everything and everywhere was communal. The best place seemed to be lying down on the roof of the truck. Looking up at the night sky over the Gulf, it certainly was food for thought. The sky seemed to be so much clearer than our own and the stars much brighter. It was nice to take a little time to myself just to appreciate exactly where I was in the world. It certainly wasn't where I wanted to be but at least the stars were out and my mind was able to wander somewhere near to the relaxation I craved for a few minutes.

My therapeutic ramblings were suddenly disturbed by the whole vehicle being rocked and none too gently either. I couldn't seem to work out exactly what was causing it so I had to investigate. I stuck my head in through the back door of the wagon and seeing nothing to explain the situation, I got down from the roof and onto the floor. In the dark, it was difficult to see very far but I was sure that there were no tricky tricksters rocking the wagon deliberately. I wondered up to the cab, where, upon opening the door, I found one man, having a very different kind of private moment to mine. I saw no shame in his actions and we quickly agreed that such an action, from then on, should be known as "a Cabber."

# CHAPTER 14;
# CONTAGIOUS PANIC.

FOR ONCE, THE winds were almost non-existent and the sand wasn't blowing into our eyes. This gave rise to a feeling of relaxation and a sense of fairly well-being. The morning was warm but not yet unpleasantly hot and our section, those men who had performed no Optronics-related tasks in a week, were going about their daily routine of washing, eating and cleaning the rifle. This was the lead up to the war and although we still had no ammunition and none of the kit had turned up, we had settled into the soldiering routine.

There was little more to do other than maintain and repair our equipment and look after ourselves, a process firmly hampered by the lack of facilities at our disposal. The oilcans were still in use as toilets but the desert rose was beginning to wilt due to the heat. Morale was somewhere between average and low, which was about as good as it got. The Unnamed man was busy cleaning his rifle, without losing too many parts, the rest of us were eating and the Artificer was somewhere, sorting out something, which someone had messed up.

We had listened to George W. Bush battering on about some "sincere reasoning" for the war, on the radio. Indeed, we were all becoming tired of the endless debate about whether or not the UN weapon inspectors would be given more time, or whether the war should actually take place. It seemed that the second resolution, whether it was needed or not, would be a long time in coming and I personally just wanted the war to start because the quicker it started, the quicker it ended and the quicker we could all go home. Most were in agreement. We were also all agreed that the war was going ahead, whether anyone approved and regardless of UN resolutions. It didn't matter how much Jacques Chirac whinged, nothing was going to stop this war.

This was no great insight on our part, as the world's media knew that there was something like two hundred thousand troops sat just south of the Iraqi border. It seemed very unlikely that we were going to turn around and leave, without firing a shot. I wondered why the French and the German's carried on their protests. It had been obvious for weeks that America and Britain were going to start this war, in the name of democracy, whether the rest of the democratic world agreed or not. Only One Pip appeared to believe the news but then he was young and naïve, or "a fucking thick bastard" as my mate Dave called him.

In the relaxed mood, I was stripped down to my underpants, having a strip-wash over my bowl of cold water. Everyone was sat around, just passing the time until we went to war. Suddenly, very suddenly in fact, the peace was disturbed.

"GAS GAS GAS." Came a very loud shout from nearby.

Everyone responded, hurriedly turning around, looking to put on their respirator. I knew where mine was and it wasn't within reach. Everyone had masked and given the standard return shout of "GAS GAS GAS" by the time I'd stumbled onto the back of the wagon and picked mine up. I was far from panicking but my heart rate was higher than usual and it wasn't due to physical exertion. I pulled on the mask and exhaled as hard as I could, in the standard manner.

As I was undercover, I didn't bother with my suit. I decided against it, even though I had recently managed to swap my little suit with a little man, who had been issued with a big suit. It only protects from falling vapour and as such, is pretty irrelevant if you aren't out in the open. Nonetheless, there were some who, in the heat of the moment, decided to err well on the side of caution and put theirs on, in the back of the wagon. I just sat there, waiting and hoping that this hadn't been a real attack, or if it was, that it hadn't been so close. If it was in our vicinity, I knew that I would be having problems soon. I knew that if it were real, I would have managed to inhale enough of whatever it was, to kill me three or four times over. No one made any attempt to speak, so we were just left with the hissing of the respirator canisters as we breathed.

Most of the training with NBC protection, after the masking drills, is centered around the development of symptoms within yourself. These could be anything from sore eyes, to dizziness or shortness of breath in the first instance. Later symptoms are much more graphic and unpleasant and are all linked to a loss of control of the body's system's. It entered my mind, at that point, that there may well be other symptoms than those in the training manual because there are certainly other chemical agents. I gave it a couple of minutes and decided that I had developed no immediate symptoms, which was obviously a good thing.

The mood in the back of the wagon was anything other than calm. The reality of our situation had hit home to us, to me in particular. We were in a war situation. These weren't drills and getting it wrong could actually mean death. The Anthrax injection suddenly seemed a little less sinister than it had at Grantham and would have provided me with some peace of mind at that time. As it was, all I had was my ability to stay calm and it hadn't failed me, despite my blunder. Others weren't so calm but then in that situation, they had every reason not to be.

After ten sweaty anxious minutes, word came around that this was our very first false alarm. It wasn't a drill. This was simply caused by someone who was worried about the situation we were in and had instigated a large-scale panic throughout the unit. Either that or someone had decided to err on the side of caution and instigated a large-scale panic. Whichever it was, this signified the beginning of living in a chemical environment. Although we had been told to carry our protective equipment with us at all times, it now seemed more than just a silly statement. False alarm or not, this was real and people were rightfully becoming nervous.

The nervousness and tetchiness of the day passed over into the night's "Big pre-invasion briefing", which as ever was ably delivered by the OC workshops. The mutterings of discontent were clearly audible after his every utterance as it seemed that the unit, as a whole, had tired of bad intelligence and weak excuses for lack of equipment. It seemed though, that there was a plan and that we were definitely going in, at some point in the very near future. It also seemed to me to be very problematic and possibly being under a little more strain than the rest; I vented some part of my frustrations. I vented my frustrations at the OC, in a rather sudden fashion.

"Sir, I'm not being funny but I'll not be going into Iraq without any bullets." I rasped, to the amazement of the unit.

"Corporal Jones, what you're talking about is desertion." Came the reply, after a little pause.

"Well, what are you going to do, shoot me?" I replied, unable to resist a little irony.

"I'll get you some bullets, Corporal Jones, okay?"

"Thank you Sir." I replied, quietly.

I was surprised at the OC's response to this. It wasn't the Army way. Maybe it showed some humanity, beneath the façade of command. Maybe it just showed the strain we were under, the OC included. Either way, the unit seemed a little cheered at the prospect of ammunition, a point which was uppermost in everyone's mind. As the Geordie offered; "Thank fuck for that, if we had some coconuts and chocolate, we could have had mutiny on the fuckin' Bounty."

By way of explaining my own outburst, it is point that, on the face of it, it may seem like some attempt to cause disaffection within the ranks, however, from my perspective, it was more that I was in a position to speak up for the silent majority, without consequence. I only aired the concerns of the unit, in order that the matter be properly addressed. I still believe that, had the ammunition situation not been addressed (irrespective of my input), then we really would have been looking at mass desertion. Someone had to say it.

Several false alarms later and another day had passed. It now appeared that we had already had our last night where sleep was a possibility. Such was the tension that in the event of almost any unrecognised aircraft flying overhead, a false alarm was raised. It became quite ridiculous, to a point where I was having to mask up because someone else had panicked upon seeing something I had already seen and deemed safe. It is a point of note that, when seeing others masking up, it is imperative to do the same. That is alarm enough in itself.

At around midnight on the 16th of March (I deliberately made occasional reference to the date as it was easy to lose track), came our final Gas alert of the day. I didn't raise the alarm but I fully understand why someone did. To our North, which in our case meant the entirety of Iraq, there was an incredibly bright flash, so bright, in fact, that I suffered after-burn on the retina (Green or yellow blurs before the eye) for a few seconds afterwards. This was a massive explosion. It was miles away and was certainly in Iraq itself. From the time differential between the flash and the bang, I would have guessed that it was twenty miles and the size of the flash, from that distance meant that this really was a huge explosion.

Despite the distance and the obvious time between the flash and bang, someone gave a shout of GAS GAS GAS upon hearing it. It wasn't an entirely stupid thing to do but it did contradict the basics of NBC defence training. Nonetheless, general panic was resumed and many were seen charging around with masks on, diving under vehicles or just running somewhere, for some stupid reason. I responded by laying down under our wagon and waiting for the commotion to die down, which it eventually did. I was certainly surprised to witness such an explosion at that point because the war hadn't even started yet and wasn't absolutely certain to go ahead at all, officially.

The explosion, though huge, wasn't aimed at us but the general panic about chemical weapons made every explosion a point of worry. The entire unit was becoming very nervous and it became a vicious circle. We were forced to react to every explosion and although I would have preferred not to, it is difficult not to follow suit when you see fifty people hurriedly pulling on their respirators.

There were many theories about the nature of the explosion we'd witnessed. My belief was that, if it had come from the Iraqis, then there would have been more than one. I believe this simply because Iraq could only aim indiscriminately into the area where various regiments were placed somewhere to the South of their border. They would have had to cover a large geographical area, which meant that they would have had to launch several missiles, to hit a number of targets. This appeared to be just the one, albeit a big one, aimed at a specific target, with specific co-ordinates. One massive explosion, which appeared to be in Iraq and then nothing else to follow, appeared to me, to signify that this was the first American missile launched. It seemed too deliberate and precise to be anything else.

I cannot be sure that this was the case and remain open to suggestion as to the cause of the explosion but to me at least, this would appear the most logical conclusion. The notion that George W Bush was still publicly and politically pushing the case for war and discussing a second resolution and attempting to convince the United Nations of its worth did little to detract from my theory. He'd already sent a huge invasion force half the way around the world, to the border of Iraq before the negotiations were finished, so the American intention was clear. I am confident that the truth of this will never surface, as a simple statement of "I don't know" would seem to cover all bases, if the matter is ever raised. One look at the permanently glazed expression on Mr Bush's face would certainly make this statement all the more plausible. Such trivial matters are easily swept under the carpet.

# CHAPTER 15; ONE STEP FORWARD...

I WOULD HAVE fully expected our next move to be the most grievous one of a huge step forward into Iraq but it came as a surprise when, the following morning, we were told that we would be moving a few kilometres, about fifteen minutes in fact, down the road, away from Iraq. We weren't sure of the reasoning but it was suggested that we had ended up in the wrong place previously. It was also suggested that we moved away because we needed to use the radios, which meant that from that point of view also, we'd been in the wrong place.

We settled into what had become routine, that of parking the vehicle, digging lots of holes and "Disguising" the vehicles with cam-nets. It was much the same as our previous location but here, at least, we could actually use the phone. This was good because as the outbreak of war was imminent, it would have been nice to at least speak to the missus or my parents to let them know I was OK. For their part, they sat at home watching the news in a state of genuine disbelief that I was actually there.

Somewhere around midmorning, the section Artificer made a suggestion, which startled me, to a degree. Having checked that there were no other reservists at the unit and that we were to be the first British unit to enter Iraq, it would appear that I was going to be the first called up reservist into a combat zone for almost fifty years. Amazingly enough, my run of bad luck with the Army had continued to an extent where, even having left, they demanded more of me than they reasonably should. It seemed to me that no one had managed to fall quite as foul of the army system as I had and I hadn't done anything wrong at any time during my service. I couldn't believe that after the awful mis-management of my former career, they were prepared to inflict even more misery on me. I don't genuinely believe in bad luck but it seems I could have little influence on my own situation as it was well out of my hands.

There were many contributing factors to my predicament, if we briefly investigate the absolute causality of it. George Bush senior could have prevented it by finishing the job in the first place, but he didn't. His esteemed offspring may well not have vented the anger of his nation against the least popular child in the playground but he just couldn't help it. Tony Blair might have considered the wishes of his own county or the rest of the world when making his decision but that wasn't the case either. In his support for the US, he didn't necessarily have to commit more troops than his run-down, decimated Armed forces could spare but he had. The Ministry of defence could have sourced people from within the regular ranks of the Army for war, replacing their numbers second-rate soldiers such as myself for the more mundane duties in Europe but that was too complex for them to administer.

A good number of variables before the Army could even give consideration to calling me up it seemed, yet in sourcing people, the Army could have actually decided to ask the individual units just what they needed before randomly plucking people from the street and sending them to Iraq for weight of numbers but numbers it was. Further to this, if they really only needed weight of numbers for infantry tasks, they could have called up ex-infantry soldiers, whereas I was selected for a specialist role and then given an infantry-type role instead. The point was that few extra infantrymen were called up, yet this is what we were tasked to do.

The upshot of this was that there were many difficult decisions, made in haste, with little thought for the consequences, which contributed to my predicament. There were more factors too but my part in the whole sequence was that I signed on the line years earlier and I also had the decency to actually turn up. All those people made all those decisions, some of which were definitely wrong, some were wrong possibly only in my view and yet they wouldn't directly face the consequences because I was on the receiving end, not them.

Someone pushed the panic button and sent as many TA and reservists into a war-zone as possible, without thought for the consequences. They didn't consider that most of the units didn't really want or need them. They didn't consider the vast cost to the taxpayer to mobilise and equip men from the street. They didn't consider that the ability or motivation of these men may well be lacking. In fact, there was no consideration given to any relevant matter because it was simply a case of obtaining a few thousand men from the most convenient source. The financial or spiritual welfare of the individuals concerned wasn't even on the list.

It's easy to make snap decisions, if you don't have to live with the consequences. Whoever did make these decisions really ought to question their own morality on human rights grounds but unfortunately, such an autocratic system considers little other than "one's own opinions", so this operation would already have been pronounced a resounding success, in the typical

British military tradition. (Loads of boxes ticked) Furthermore, I would be prepared to bet that, upon pronouncing this debacle a resounding success, the officer-in-command of it got his well-deserved MBE. "Oh, it was nothing, your majesty…" Too fucking right it wasn't.

Another ill-considered point was that of how to deal with the sixteen hundred or so who hadn't turned up for mobilisation at Chilwell. It seemed that the threat of imprisonment on the grounds of desertion wasn't to be carried out. In fact, no legal action was to be taken against the people who just ignored their call-up papers because it was simply too much like hard work for the ministry of defence. I don't resent the individuals for not turning up, it just made me realise more and more that I shouldn't have turned up either. I wish them all the best of luck and only wish that I had been sensible enough to ignore my call-up papers because, as ever with the Army, there was a punishment for doing the decent thing and if enough people decide not to bother, then more often than not, they get away with it. The scant little bit of motivation I had drained away to nothing, at a point when I needed to be more motivated than ever. For once though, on the night's big pre-invasion briefing type gathering, there was some semblance of good news with which to cheer my troubled soul.

Almost pleasingly for my forthcoming jaunt into military history, it seemed that we were actually going to be able to defend ourselves, to an extent. It seemed that the great military think-tank had finally accepted that, to invade a country, we really did need some ammunition. Unfortunately, we, as the poor relations of world soldiering, looked like getting around thirty rounds per man. This was infinitely better than nothing but was probably only just enough to get us killed. At least, if we had no rounds, we could surrender en masse, I thought. The initial claim that we had some rounds was true in a sense but in reality, it was another false dawn. Furthermore, we hadn't actually seen them yet.

Thirty rounds per man was enough to defend ourselves in a fire-fight for about a minute or so, so it wasn't surprising, that like Oliver Twist, we wanted more. We wanted a good deal more too. We weren't just defending ourselves; we were supposed to be invading a country and that meant that we needed about ten times that amount. Unsurprisingly, the system, yet again failed to provide. I was really getting sick of hearing that everything was in a container on its way. Bullets in a container on a boat wouldn't help us. Things were looking a little bleak and not for the first time.

The strangest point about the war was that we, along with thousands of other British troops and many more thousands of American troops, were situated just south of the Iraqi border. In fact, Kuwait was filled to bursting with troops and military machinery. Every man and woman on the ground knew full well that the war was going to happen. All of the world's media also knew full well that it was going to happen and yet the world's leaders were still sat around the negotiating table deciding whether to go ahead.

It was quite obvious to anyone at home and everyone on the ground that this war had been set in stone for months. There was no debate. France, as always the petulant, argumentative child of world politics was complaining about American dictatorship. They insisted that the correct course of action was to give the UN weapons inspectors more time, although this course of action represented no course of action, in reality. Having said this, the only action the French have ever taken is industrial action. The French were firmly against invading Iraq, although their reasoning was at best unclear and at worst, a little dubious. Unfortunately, all they would achieve is to irritate the biggest bully in the playground.

The Germans, always so peaceful in their intent, would not hear of invading Iraq but then they too were only reverting to type. Their, arrogant yet intelligent child, with no real friends, would serve to compliment the petulance of the French but together, neither had the strength to challenge the biggest bully in the playground. All they could achieve was unpleasantness but then, the Germans wouldn't want to appear too aggressive, would they?

The Russians came lately into the debate but this lonely child, of infinite talent and mystery but without real means, could not genuinely offer to challenge the might of the biggest bully in the playground. They too, could only sit and sulk at the unfaltering intent and the irresistible force of the Americans. It seemed that, if it ever had been possible to overcome the biggest bully in the playground, then all the children must form an alliance but unfortunately, one fickle child put paid to that idea well before the debate was officially ended.

Britain, so recently a great empire, had become content to follow the playground's biggest bully around like a pet. Rather than stand in opposition to what was, in many opinions a blatant piece of dictatorship to the world, Britain saw fit to stand safely with the inevitable winner of this particular tussle. This seemingly rich and apparently powerful nation, with an apparently well-deserved reputation for decency and courage, had decided it could form a far stronger alliance with the Americans, than it ever could in opposing them. We had become the irritating kid who follows the playground bully around, mocking the weak but who, on his own, would dare to oppose no one. The British, in their weakness, might have caused this war because if they had shown genuine opposition to it and stood their ground, the Americans might just have listened to reason. As it was, the Americans would have their own way, in every single matter.

# CHAPTER 16;
# WAITING ON TENTERHOOKS.

WE SAT IN our location for a couple of days, with little noteworthy incident. Rounds had been acquired from outside the ordinary realms of the system (Stolen) but the details of this aren't important. We had a hundred rounds a man and suddenly, despite the total lack of almost everything else we'd been promised, we were ready to start a war. I was ready too, to a point. I wasn't trained and I didn't have any of the right equipment but I had some bullets and that was as much as I was going to get and I was getting fed up waiting. Everyone was fed up with waiting and morale was beginning to sag. It had never soared, incidentally. We all just wanted to get it over with because waiting for a war, which we knew was going to happen, was driving everyone mad.

I managed to get a hold of the welfare telephone after thirty or forty other people had had their turn and for once the battery wasn't flat and I could actually call the missus and, to an extent, put her mind at rest. There were certain things we were able to tell our families and certain things, like, our position and when we might decide to invade and the like, which we certainly couldn't.

The welfare telephone was an unsecured means of communication, which meant that its signal could easily be monitored by anyone in the area, hence the restriction on passage of information. We had been warned upon entry into theatre that any such breach of security would result in probable loss of rank and being instantly shipped back to the UK to be charged. This charge carried similarly for any use of mobile phones and for some strange reason, I did my best to adhere to this rule, rather than trying to get thrown out of theatre. (Never did quite work that one out)

I called the missus and with a relieved tone, she answered. She was obviously pleased to hear from me for the first time in over a week but likewise, she had one or two questions. Unsurprisingly, the Army welfare system had made no attempt to contact her in any way shape or form and as far as she was concerned, I might well have disappeared from the face of the earth. She wasn't living in the married quarters with all the other wives and nor did she have a TA unit to contact. There was no one to answer any of her questions but me and I hadn't been able to contact her.

It can't have been pleasant for her at home, watching the news and wondering exactly which part of it I would be involved in. The sudden and uncertain nature of my departure had compounded these problems in the extreme. Whilst I had been deliberately kept in the dark about my immediate future, she had received even less information than I had and was understandably worried. She didn't think I was a soldier either, it seemed.

I told her that I hadn't been able to contact her for a while because we had been on radio silence and as I said it, an extremely ignorant voice piped up that I wasn't supposed to tell anyone that. I don't listen to anyone else's phone conversations and I was very offended that he chose to listen in judgement over mine. The missus also asked if we were going to be the first in and I vaguely tried to clarify this enquiry by saying "First Brits". Apparently, according to One Pip Louis, this also constituted a breach of security. After attempting to pacify the missus further, I put the phone down and decided to face the music. I knew I had breached security in no way whatsoever but I knew that in his infinite ignorance, he wouldn't see it that way.

After five minutes or so, I was firstly accosted by the Scandinavian, who upon receipt of my explanation, looked confused and said nothing more of it. Around half an hour later, I was addressed by the section Artificer, who accepted my explanation in similar manner. Within the hour, I was also accosted by the over-promoted buffoon, who, surprisingly enough, managed to see my point without much fuss. I was surprised when about an hour later; One Pip Louis decided to take it upon himself to show me the error of my ways. The difference between our respective points of view was that he had been told his by someone else, whereas I fully understood mine.

He informed me that I had been careless with regard to security during a telephone conversation and that I could be charged and lose my rank and be kicked out of theatre for it. Why I didn't just accept the charge was beyond me but I felt I had to question this on moral grounds.

"In what way would you say that I compromised security Sir?" I asked, with as much of respectful tone as I could muster.

"You can't say that we were on radio silence."

"Why not? What on earth does that tell anyone?"

"Well, if they (Being the Iraqis) are monitoring our signals then they will know that we've been spoofing him for the last week."

"What on earth does that mean?" I asked, a little confused by his terminology.

"It means that we've been playing back some old transmissions to them whilst we've been on radio silence." I paused for a second or two, in order to digest this remarkable suggestion.

"Who the bloody hell's told you that load of crap? I'm sorry to shatter your illusions but I think that's just a bit ridiculous. Besides which, it doesn't really matter if they know that one unit in this area has been on radio silence, even if they are monitoring signals. It tells them absolutely nothing. It's an absolutely worthless piece of information, so I don't know why you've made such a fuss about it. What else was I supposed to have said?"

"You said that we were going to be the first Brits into Iraq."

"So they know that out of all the British regiments here, one regiment will be the first into Iraq?" I offered.

"Yes exactly." He replied, displaying the full extent of his wisdom on the matter.

"My point is that my missus isn't married to a squaddie. She hasn't been warned that this might happen and she hasn't been told anything about it. She has a lot of questions and I intend to answer her as best I can because she needs to know. Can't you understand the situation she's in?" I asked, becoming annoyed at the length of the conversation.

"Well, she should just accept it?" Came the wise verdict.

"Accept what? Accept that I've been dragged from the street and forcibly sent to war against my will and that I can't go home or I'd be shot for desertion, or that there's nothing she can do about it and no one's going to tell her anything? I thought that this war was about human rights, so why should she, or I just accept it? We're horrified when we watch the news and see Iraqis being forced to fight by Saddam and we don't accept that do we? She shouldn't accept this and I shouldn't because it's wrong and because the British Army as a regime is no better than the Iraqis, despite public appearances. It's wrong and she shouldn't accept it. She should question it because apparently we live in a democracy and she has a right to.

Further to that, I think she's old enough to decide what she should and shouldn't accept and you're in no place to speak because you've got no experience to speak of. All you've done is just acted on an opinion, which someone's forced into your head. You haven't questioned it or asked whether it makes sense, you've just accepted it and look where that's got you, making a fucking idiot out of yourself in front of me. Now, if you've nothing else to say, I think I'll be off." I concluded, to which, he responded only with silence. I walked away and left him digesting my perspective. He could have shouted at me to come back, if required. He didn't.

I hoped that it was food for thought because he needed to see life from another perspective, rather than just the military training manual. My attitude was beginning to suffer from the irritation at the ineptitude of the people commanding me. I never managed to be in the best of spirits but the waiting around and the pedantic attitude of the hierarchy was grinding me down. I was becoming tired of performing pointless tasks for useless people.

The "management" we were receiving was nothing other than instructions sourced straight from the training manual. We had to do everything by the book, even if it didn't need doing in the first place. I had found in the past, that during training exercises, pointless tasks were taken to the maximum. It was all part of the training and was perfectly acceptable, in a training environment. It seemed that some people thought we were still on exercise and that we needed to be found things to do, in order to prevent us resting. The unfortunate thing was, none of it was ever useful, or insightful, it was always just something to do. None of the hierarchy had the wisdom or the decency to realise this.

My attitude suffered to the point where I had even begun to ignore basic rules. Later, when on patrol, I genuinely couldn't be bothered to wear my helmet. It was uncomfortable in the heat and as it wasn't actually capable of stopping a bullet, I saw no point in wearing it. Of course that "choice" isn't the way with the Army and I soon found myself on the losing side of an attempt to argue my case. Of course, the fact that the helmet was just a useless embuggerance doesn't hold much sway when the Army training doctrine, the authority of all authorities, states that I should wear one. I got my ear bent for a while but to be fair, it was all just white noise by this point.

The seriousness of our situation and what seemed to be the confirmation that the war was officially going to start, came later on that night of the 20th March. From where we were positioned, we could see the main supply road, which led out of Iraq and suddenly, there appeared to be a huge amount of traffic on it. In the twilight of that day, a huge convoy of white four-wheel-drive vehicles was heading south.

We stood for a few minutes, unsure of exactly what we were watching but with all the flags and the symbols painted on the sides of the white vehicles, we knew that these were UN vehicles. From the length of the convoy, we could be almost certain that these vehicles belonged to the UN weapons inspections team and that they were very rapidly getting the fucking hell out of Iraq. Watching those vehicles speed away to the safety of southern Kuwait, I felt a slight chill at the prospect of having to drive the other way. I wished that I could have gone with them and I would have had every right to, had I been able to call myself a civilian but it seemed that "we soldiers" had to watch and listen, as the shit hit the fan and then follow it in. The irony of it was that they seemed to know that we were going to invade before we'd even had official confirmation.

## CHAPTER 17; WISH YOU WERE HERE?

A LITTLE AFTER our royal breakfast of boil in the bag slop and melted chocolate, we were called over for an intelligence brief. Fortunately, this wasn't to be conducted by the over-promoted buffoon. It was One Pip Louis' turn and he was at least generally capable of reproducing information for people to hear. His opinion wasn't worth its' weight in shit because he had no worthwhile life experience but he was, at least, reasonably able to communicate. We attended the briefing at the Control Point, (which was simply the back of another lorry) expectantly.

We were told that, using some strange new military tactic, the Americans had fired the first missiles of the war during the night. I'm no great military tactician of course but I thought that it might have been a good idea, when firing the first missiles of the war, to attempt to remove Iraq's main threat, namely artillery and missile launchers. I would have done this because there were thousands upon thousands of British and American troops well within striking distance of any retaliatory action from Iraq.

I would say that an attempt to avoid the war by a strategic hit on the Iraqi leader might have been a good idea a few weeks earlier when there were few troops sat in the area as potential targets. If you were to smoke out a wasp's nest, you wouldn't wait until people had gathered around it. Standing there, in the middle of the desert, knowing that the Americans had attempted and seemingly failed to prevent this war, I felt very uncomfortable at the prospect of the backlash.

There was mention of a possible injury to Saddam but the word "unconfirmed", seemed to just about sum the whole matter up. The war had started and the Americans had fired the first shot and managed to achieve absolutely nothing with it. It wasn't good and it wasn't a nice situation to be in but at least it had started, which meant that the end would come sooner. Apparently, we were still to stick with the "Shock and Awe" plan, even though the plan seemed to have gone awry at the launch of the first missile. It was time for chaos, it seemed.

Curiously, I found it surprising that the news that we were at war officially didn't seem to shock me. I think by that point, I'd decided I was as shocked as I was ever going to get and the news that we were at war was just added to the huge slippery pile of my problems. It didn't seem to change much because after we were told that we'd declared war, we went and sat down and had a cup of tea.

No one panicked about it until we heard the first explosion. It was absolutely huge and it sounded a little too close and was followed quickly by another similar sound. The general panic alarm was sounded. Even though no one had seen any smoke or flames or knew exactly where it had landed, the Gas alert was shouted within seconds and people looked scared. The drill of throwing on the mask and getting under cover seemed to be the most appropriate, so the unnamed man and I threw ourselves into the solid container box-body, on the back of a lorry. It was a well-covered area and felt safe. Unfortunately, when we closed the door behind us, it was pitch black too.

The unnamed man went through the almost automatic procedure of trying to put his suit on in the dark, whereas I decided against it. It wasn't part of the drill and there was little point as we were undercover. He knew that the suit was designed to protect the soldier from direct contact with hazardous vapours. Everyone knew that and although everyone got themselves well undercover, the donning of suits was still commonplace. He continued to struggle in the pitch-blackness whilst I sat and tried to listen to the sounds from outside. In locking ourselves into the darkness, we had removed ourselves completely from the decision making process and had to just wait until we were told to remove our masks.

The time ticked along for what I would guess to be around ten minutes before we heard anything significant. Someone banged on the side of the wagon and asked if anyone was in. We replied to the positive and then waited another five minutes or so before we heard someone shout that it was time to carry out unmasking drills. This consists of briefly sniffing the air, then waiting for a reaction and unmasking when all was found to be safe. This task took a few tense minutes before we were free to breathe in vast lung-fulls of dusty air.

After we were re-introduced to the sunshine, we were quickly summoned to the control point, for another briefing. This was to address the general panic we'd just experienced and to lay down some kind of standard procedure for such incidents. Such incidents, in my book, shouldn't have happened, as we weren't directly being bombarded and were not immediately downwind of any known explosion, yet we had to have drills for such incidents. Furthermore, I happen to know that the training manual also favoured my point of view on this matter.

One Pip Louis held the chair and with a shaky authority, he attempted to assert his will over the situation. This wasn't happening readily and a public argument soon commenced, which involved most of the hierarchy. The curiosity was that all the warrant officers and senior non-commissioned officers were arguing with One Pip Louis and yet he managed to have the final say, even though his plan was entirely nonsensical. From my previous point of view of being sat in the dark, I would have rather heard the all clear from a senior member of the workshop staff than just anyone.

His plan, the plan, which was officially implemented, was to control the situation from the control point (which was starting to look like a contradiction in terms) and send out a messenger to tell everyone that, under his absolute authority, it was safe. There were certain voices I would trust to tell me it was safe but the majority weren't in any position to tell. Certainly a young Second-Lieutenant, with six months experience shouldn't have had authority over five senior men with well over sixty years experience between them but that's how it was. Incidentally, there wasn't a plan B, if the Control Point was hit.

Unfortunately, we were at the mercy of the system again and the system dictated that, instead of the decision over whether the all clear could be given being made by an experienced senior man, with previous Gulf War experience, it would be made by someone who was far less qualified than me to judge. No one was happy with the situation and the little sub-groups, within five minutes of his final word, had decided that they would implement their own separate sub-policies.

I listened intently as the Over-promoted Buffoon, the section Artificer and the unit NBC instructor came out with their plan for dealing with such incidents and upon hearing it, I decided that I liked it even less than One-Pip Louis' plan. Their plan was to conduct matters from a more localised point of view and to ensure safety in the immediate area, which did actually make sense. The problem was that in order to achieve this, someone had to perform a sniff test.

A sniff test is when someone is designated to partially remove their respirator by pulling it slightly away from the face, just enough to sniff the air. The unfortunate individual is told that the area is presumed safe and when to carry out the procedure. The unfortunate individual also has a good chance of dying a very painful death if his superiors have made a mistake. That unfortunate individual, would in the first instance, be me and I didn't trust my superiors enough to follow that order. It seems that TA and reservist soldiers are infinitely more expendable than their regular Army counterparts and on these grounds alone, the decision was made.

"Yeah, there is such a thing as an acceptable loss in this situation." Offered the NBC instructor, who seemed to have forgotten most of his teachings.

"Well, I don't think I'll be carrying out any sniff tests unless I think it's safe because I don't trust any of you to make that decision for me, so it will be one I'll make myself." I replied.

"As NBC instructor, it's my responsibility to make those decisions and if I say you do a sniff test, you'll do one. It's as simple as that."

"No it's not. I'll use my own judgement in that situation, rather than listen to you. I think I know enough to make a reasonable decision for myself." I said, flatly.

"Are you qualified enough then?"

"Yes I am. I used to be an NBC instructor and I think my qualification's still valid, so I think I'll use my own judgement, rather than yours, thanks very much. I might even offer some helpful advice from time to time, if you're prepared to listen because you do seem to have forgotten one or two things. And I'll go a little further here, just to illustrate my stance because if you ever try forcing my hand on this one, I'll fucking knock you into next week. Have I made my point?"

The subject, from that moment, was closed. I had played my trump card and from that point, it seemed I would be more involved in the decision making process, than in the resulting action. I was quite relieved not be deemed part of the "acceptable losses" any longer, as the previous uncertainty had filled me with anything but confidence in the unit's handling of the NBC threat. I had been a good instructor in my time and had taught this subject so much, I could remember it backwards. It also seemed that I was the only one who felt certain about the drills and actions too. Maybe I had something useful to contribute to the unit at last. There were some, amongst the group who also considered that my firm stance was the right one to take and no-one offered my opponent any support.

As the day dragged on, there were several more loud explosions, some attributed to Scud missiles, some to terrorist attacks. None were confirmed as anything definite and confusion and panic seemed to be the order of the day. The war had started and although we were yet to be involved directly, it seemed to be going on all around us.

I took the opportunity, in the afternoon, to make what would be my last phone-call home for a while. Having had my mobile confiscated, I couldn't ring the missus at work because I couldn't remember the number. I could, however, remember my dad's number and it was there that I looked for temporary salvation. After a little buzzing and hissing, he answered the phone and his voice became a little shaky when he realised who it was.

I don't remember a word he said. I remember asking him to pass on a message to the missus in case I didn't speak to her again but the content of the conversation was a mystery. I was lost in my own little world. For four or five minutes, I felt like a six-year-old boy. I felt like he was with me and that somehow, I was safe. I felt protected by his words, in that, during my childhood, he provided the feeling of safety only a father could, the feeling I needed more than anything. For a short time, I wasn't in the worst place on Earth. I was at the sea-side, having an ice-cream, with my dad.

My illusion was promptly shattered by an enormous explosion and the, by now "usual" panic that followed. I think he heard the bang. The phone signal fluctuated briefly, before he asked; "What was that?" I could only answer "Don't worry, it's alright" to a question he hadn't asked. Neither he nor I knew when, or even if, we would speak again. This seemed a harsh reality for both of us.

# CHAPTER 18; GENUINELY UNFIT FOR SERVICE.

LATER THAT DAY, as daylight became dusk, it was time for us to move out of our location and take the road North, which meant that we were about to invade Iraq. We knew little about exactly who had already crossed the border but we were certainly getting in nice and early, particularly early for an Artillery regiment. The plan, scant though it was, was that we would be supporting the Americans, as they didn't have much in the way of Artillery. The British Artillery regiment was to give firing support to the American invasion force. At least we would be behind them.

In a blatant attempt to make my life even more stressful, there was a last minute change of plan. I had been practising with the machine gun (GPMG) since I learned of my role in this ill-conceived scheme and right at the last minute, it seemed that I was destined for another role. The unnamed man had put himself forward for the machine gun bit, probably because he genuinely wanted to be involved in the action. I didn't mind too much, as I wasn't particularly happy with the idea anyway.

Instead, it was decided that I would drive the old Bedford, whilst the unnamed man would have his head out of the cupola of the other wagon. With fifteen minutes to go before we were due to set off, I took charge of the vehicle. This creaking, thirty-five year old heap was to be my protective shell for the drive over the border, with the unnamed man giving covering fire, if required. I wasn't filled with confidence at either prospect.

I hadn't driven a Bedford for a few years but the crudeness and lack of comfort seemed to lurch instantly back into my mind. The vagueness of the brakes, if not reassuring, seemed at least familiar. The lack of power steering caused me to perspire under my body-armour as I tried to slowly manoeuvre the ageing heap into convoy position. I wasn't happy at the prospect of having to drive such an old shit-heap into Iraq but at least, if anyone was shooting, they would aim for the man with the machine gun first. I reckoned I could have fashioned a white hanky onto a stick before they aimed at me.

We rolled out into the blackness. We were in total blackout, which meant that we weren't even allowed to use the small convoy lights at the rear of each vehicle. These small, dim lights, situated underneath the rear of every vehicle in the British Army, are designed to be used when driving in convoys. They are there to enable the driver behind to follow the vehicle in front from the correct distance. They provide almost nothing in the way of illumination. We had been ordered to tape them up, which was ironic, considering that that would have been the exact correct time to use them, if they were ever to be of any use. Nonetheless, we ignored common sense, preferring to err too far on the side of caution and I tentatively followed the vehicle in front into the complete and utter darkness that is the early part of night in the Middle East.

The dust was everywhere and it was almost impossible to make out any image of the vehicle we were following. We were only really able to follow the dust plumes. It seemed like a good recipe for an accident and most of us expected to see one that night, such was the confidence in this latest directive from above. The convoy carried on, simply following orders from above, to drive towards Iraq, in the pitch darkness, without any form of illumination. From one point of view it made sense, in that our position couldn't possibly be compromised but from another, it seemed a bigger risk to drive around in the pitch-blackness. This was a stressful time and it wasn't just the heavy steering, which caused the sweat on my back.

We eventually made it to the road, which was as close to being a proper road as the Kuwaitis had in the north of the country. The convoy pulled on, without much incident and we began to crawl our way, at around thirty miles per hour, towards our destination, which was to be somewhere a little short of the Iraqi border. As my nerves began to settle, due to the prospect of some vague visibility, our plans began to take approximately the shape of a pear. At the first instance, we were unaware of its' exact consequence but there was a definite hissing on my side of the vehicle. Driving along, I took a vague guess that the antiquated nature of the compressor and braking system had decided, at this most inopportune time, to show its' true colours.

Ten minutes later and I decided to offer my sincere apologies to the brakes and compressor and just pronounced myself to be thoroughly pissed off at the prospect of a flat tyre. The wagon lolled and lurched around for a few yards as I pulled it over to the side of the road, in order to allow the rest of the convoy to pass, which they duly did, leaving just the unnamed and myself, alone, in the blackness, just a few kilometres short of the Iraqi border. I have always said that I believe in absolute causality over luck, either good or bad but with the Army, it seemed I was just plagued with bad luck.

Cursing my decision to take over the vehicle at such short notice, without attempting to locate any of its equipment, I made the first moves towards changing the wheel. Firstly, I decided to locate the wheel brace, as this is used to lower the spare from the underside of the vehicle body, as well as its' most obvious use. That was when I hit the first snag. It wasn't in the tool bin at the rear of the wagon. (Tool bin, just consider that for a moment. Somewhat bizarrely, I'd often found the vehicle's tools to be here during my service.) I asked the unnamed, who didn't really even bother to shrug. He didn't know and was never likely to. I did manage to find the bottle-jack but no rod to drive it.

I asked the unnamed if he knew the whereabouts of any of the equipment on the wagon as it was officially his, as he'd signed for it and all of its' equipment. Unsurprisingly, he didn't know. I couldn't even think where it was and I could remember that the wheel-nuts on one side of the vehicle had left-handed threads but I couldn't remember which side. I knew that the wheel-nuts would be tight and that if I ever did find that fucking wheel-brace, I didn't know which way to turn it. I cursed my lack of preparation and I cursed my lack of knowledge of the vehicle I was driving. This mess was my fault because I had forgotten one of the oldest lessons in the Army training manual. I should have taken the few minutes I had with the vehicle to ask these questions or to look for the tools but I hadn't. It is said, within military circles, that prior planning and preparation prevents piss-poor performance and I certainly couldn't argue with that.

With a little frustration, a little irritation and a pinch of absolute fear thrown in, I sat down in the dirt at the side of the vehicle. It was plain to see that neither the vehicle nor its' driver were of particular value to the war effort. We did make the effort to protect ourselves in as much as we pointed our weapons out into the pitch darkness. Some sort of night vision capability would have been a bonus but such things are the stuff of dreams, when it comes to general availability in the British Army.

Eventually, after a rather dark and nervous hour or so, the recovery vehicle arrived. I think they were expecting to have to tow us all the way because of some major mechanical defect and the gruff Jock mechanic looked more than a little disgruntled to have to assist two halfwits with the very simple task of changing a wheel. He turned the air blue with a few sentences that consisted of at least fifty percent expletives in his response to our predicament. I could offer little in disagreement, as my excuse of not knowing where the wheel-brace was looked more than lame. Oddly though, he seemed to prefer to vent his frustrations in the unnamed man's direction, as it was his vehicle.

I think that, at that exact moment, I couldn't have felt like a bigger arsehole than I did. I had totally under-performed, even for an ex-soldier with little taste for the event. I only hoped that, when we'd finished lugging the wheels around and got back on our way, things would improve. With a little bit of forward planning, the OC turned up in his Land rover. He seemed quite calm about the situation. But then, contrary to the Army's school of thought, shouting never solved anything. With a little more sweaty effort, the two arseholes got back into the old heap and followed the OC into the darkness.

The darkness on its' own was very impressive. I could barely see the vehicle in front and when we finally arrived at a left-hand junction, in the middle of nowhere, I was pleased to be able to stop, if only for a minute. The OC's driver, a chubby little man, with strange curly blonde hair, ran from his Landrover, to give us a message. We were expecting some great insight into the forthcoming events of the evening.

"Right, follow that vehicle down there." He said, pointing to the junction.

Still quite literally in the dark, we did as we were told and headed off down the road. The strange thing about the road was, in the middle of the desert, with shit and dust all around, in a country where the roads are certainly not of the highest standard, that it was the most perfectly constructed, immaculate road in the history of road building. It made little sense but this road, which was only a few minutes drive from the border, had been very recently and very splendidly built. We followed "that vehicle" for about fifteen dark and confusing minutes until we saw a few more vehicles parked on each side of the road. Another few yards and there was another gaggle, then a regiment and eventually, after driving past what looked like the Army's entire rolling stock, we arrived at our own gaggle of vehicles.

Before we could actually manage to pull off the road, we were told of our immediate plans. "Get digging" was the general scheme of things. I was quite used to digging and similarly, very tired of digging. In fact, I was exhausted by the events of the evening but a war waits for no man, so digging it was. Every man needs a good trench to lye in. Wearily, I got to my shovel and started to fling the soft sand all around. I must have been digging for a minute, when the next unfortunate load of shit hurtled my way. Just call me lucky.

"Can you go back and pick a trailer up?" Asked the Artificer Sergeant Major.

"What?" I asked, surprised and confused at just how such a thing had been left behind.

"Sixteen kilometres back from the junction, there's a trailer been left by a broken down vehicle. This lad's going with you and he knows where it is. Can you nip back and pick it up?"

"Yeah, I've got nothing better to do." I replied, upon seeing that my guide for this little, non-digging jaunt was to be the Geordie.

I needed little encouragement to ditch the digging gear and get back in the cab. I was tired of driving and I wasn't entirely happy at the prospect of heading off into the night with just the Geordie for protection but at least I wouldn't have to dig for a while. We crammed all of our gear, which included webbing, helmets and rifles into the cab, which was already stuffed, and set off.

Almost immediately, as I attempted to turn the vehicle around, I began having problems. It was probably the bad luck thing again. The Bedford, tired old heap that it is, has a turning circle so large that it isn't allowed to travel on the M25. Encouraged to turn around in the one move, I was soon in soft sand, belly down and going nowhere. Worse still, I couldn't get four-wheel drive because the selector was having none of it. The wagon, according to the Geordie, was "Fucking crap" although a man more used to driving it might have succeeded where I failed. I gave up when the stench of the clutch became overpowering. If the British war-fighting effort had been solely represented by my vehicle, and me, we would have driven in under the white flag, assuming we hadn't already broken down.

There was plenty of shouting and anger at the situation, most of which faded immediately into white noise. People who specialise in driving Army vehicles offered their suggestions at what I should have done, other "experts" mocked, some sneered and a sensible few generally accepted that soft sand wasn't particularly good for driving on. I wasn't really listening because none of it actually mattered. Life, for me, is about what is, not what if and the what is, in that instance, had already happened. The blame culture surfaced for a while. I was indifferent to it. Eventually, I got towed out. I knew from the moment I got stuck that I would have to be towed out. Finding a solution rather than a culprit, might have been the better course of action in such times.

Happily, the Geordie and I got underway and once we were away from the shouting and all the ridiculous orders and the general bullshit, we were able to relax. There may have been the threat of capture or the odd stray bullet but at least we were able to think for ourselves and have a decent conversation, without people butting in. As far as invading Iraq was concerned, I put it to the back of my mind. I was never really bothered about it anyway.

We drove for a while before we came back to the junction, which marked the end of the immaculate road. Apparently, the trailer was sixteen kilometres or so back from the junction, so I set the trip counter and blinked into the blackness. There wasn't much to see as we drove along the road, through featureless terrain, away from Iraq. It might have been a nice idea to keep on driving all the way to Kuwait but they would have missed the vehicle eventually.

At around five kilometres short of our supposed destination, we were halted at what looked like a roadblock. Fortunately, it looked like a British roadblock and we were soon greeted by a rather polite young marine, who informed us that we were just waiting for some helicopters to ferry some troops over the border. Apparently, it would only take half an hour and we would be on our way. He said it like it was an everyday occurrence and nothing much to comment on. These people were being thrown down on Iraqi soil (sand), which was something of an unknown quantity and I didn't envy them one bit.

We sat watching the helicopters take off and land and fly noisily overhead for a while, before the young lad came back, with further news of the delay. Apparently someone somewhere had a problem and it was going to take a while, so we might as well get some sleep. To us, this seemed like good news, as we were in need of a bit and we thought little about the nature of the problem.

When daylight broke, several hours later, no one came to tell us anything. The roadblock was moved and the half dozen or so vehicles, which were waiting either way, set off about their business. We drove to the set distance of sixteen kilometres and as far as ten beyond that but the trailer, in the dawn light, couldn't be seen anywhere. We drove around for a while but if it were there, it would have been quite easy to spot, we thought. Mildly annoyed but compensated by the amount of sleep we'd been afforded, we set off back, empty-handed, so to speak. When we explained the situation upon our return to our convoy, it was greeted with "Oh right". Never did find out what happened to it.

## CHAPTER 19; A WELCOME INVASION?

THE NEWS FROM the radio that eight people had been killed in a helicopter crash provided a particularly unpleasant explanation of the delays of the previous night. It wasn't good news for anyone and it wasn't altogether pleasant to think that this incident had, at the time, provided us with a most welcome respite. We had no way of knowing at the time and had appreciated the rest, rather than showing concern for the reason behind it. As it was, news of the first deaths of the conflict was a heavy blow to everyone's morale. It seemed to be such a waste but we didn't have time to dwell on such matters.

After digging more trenches and spending more time running around for the ever demanding Control Point, they decided that it was finally time for the big one, that being, the trip across the border. The Control Point (splendidly managed by One Pip Louis), after tying up far too much manpower for hours, came to the decision at two-thirty in the afternoon. It was a sweltering afternoon and the fifteen minutes notice to move scenario did little for anyone's motivation.

It goes with the general confusion of war that such entities as the Control Point are at odds with the entire situation. In such inexperienced hands, the Control Point became simply a point of annoyance. Nothing was planned, everything was rushed, all the information withheld until the last minute and some of the strangest decisions ever conceived were made. They simply listened to the radio and made a snap judgement on what to do next. Such an example was the fact that, at two-thirty in the afternoon, we were given fifteen minutes notice to move.

Every man on the ground knew full well that we wouldn't drive into Iraq in broad daylight yet that was what we were told was going to happen. If we were to drive into Iraq, then surely a little more than fifteen minutes would have been nice but the heavy-handed, small-minded approach seemed to overpower all other opinions. We were told that we would be setting off for the border at a quarter to Three in the afternoon. I even think he genuinely believed it. At least, he seemed to when I asked him about it.

Common sense was and always has been a much-undervalued commodity and a little wouldn't have gone amiss in this situation.

The section Artificer then struck a mighty blow against morale, when he gave the briefing on what we should do if and when we were contacted. The thought of having to jump out of the vehicle into a hail of incoming fire certainly did little for my state of mind but then, a fibreglass cab would provide little in the way of protection. Apparently, the safest place was on the road, behind the wheels but with greatly insufficient ammunition, this seemed likely to provide only a temporary respite. I just hoped that we didn't have to jump out of the vehicles because I really didn't fancy running around Iraq with piles of kit strapped to me and bullets flying everywhere. At least if bullets were flying, it would be easier to respond when under mechanical propulsion. Everything after that part of the briefing was prisoner of war drills and I really couldn't see an upside to that. It would be an understatement to say that I didn't fancy driving into Iraq much.

At around seven o'clock, it began to get dark and, still sitting in the cab, in the exact same location; we knew that the move to Iraq was imminent. The urgency of earlier had evaporated in the desert sun though and it seemed that, sooner or later, we would be piling into Iraq, in a most haphazard fashion. We had to wait for a battery of guns to go in before us and they had had no plans to move all day apparently. Maybe it would have been a good idea to ask them when we were going because they seemed to actually know something about the natural order of things. One Pip Louis certainly didn't.

We sat in the cab, the unnamed man and I, in the darkness, again with all lights blacked out, waiting for the guns to go past. We sat for a while, waiting for our signal to set off, in total darkness, in an attempt to disguise our position. Unfortunately, the press had other ideas and it seemed that there was a constant stream of their vehicles driving up and down the road beside us, with their lights on full beam. This did us few favours as the Iraqis, if they were watching, would have been able to identify each and every very vehicle easily by its' shape, as we were perfectly silhouetted in their lights.

This was a great point of annoyance for us. That I wasn't up to scratch, as far as war fighting was concerned, was beyond doubt but I, at least, had an appreciation for standard military practice. It seemed that no one had told these civilians that with their bright presence, they were jeopardising the entire war effort. If we were being targeted from a distance and the Artillery that the Americans were relying upon had been wiped out, it would have been a very high price to pay for a few photos and an exclusive story. At that time, we would have been best served to shoot all the press people to prevent them from causing us further danger. At that time I realised that I wasn't a civilian in every sense of the word. I don't know who was governing the press activities during that time but I feel strongly that someone ought to have told them that the British Army generally operate in the dark, which means no headlights and that they were to adhere to this, just as we had to.

At slightly before eleven o'clock, the guns went past and within minutes, we were following behind. The eight hours that we had been made to wait in the cab by One Pip faded quickly into memory as we rolled forward into the darkness. It was another black night over Iraq and visibility was minimal. The unnamed was driving and I was occupying the gun position out of the top of the cab. It seemed that after the events of the night before, I wasn't to drive into Iraq, which in some ways, was fortunate. It did seem though, that good-fortune only ever extended so far in this scenario. I never worked out whether this was punishment or reward.

The goggles I'd acquired afforded little more vision than the driver, who was squinting for all he was worth beneath me. Within minutes of setting off, a little confusion had set in and the vehicle in front, a Land rover, had sped away from us. We couldn't see anything but a few yards of road in front of us yet we had to make best speed along it. It was difficult, to say the least and the unnamed was feeling the pressure.

"I can't see a fucking thing in front of us." He complained.

"Neither can I mate. Get your foot down." I offered.

He duly did and we sped even faster into the blackness, not actually knowing if we were going the right way and only guessing that we were following the rest of the convoy. The plan had lasted about five minutes before it had gone to pot and fifteen minutes later, we still were speeding blindly towards Iraq, unsure of whether we were actually doing the right thing. Neither one of us could make out any vehicles in front and there was no way of seeing behind us to see if anyone was actually following us.

I think we both became gripped by fear, as the situation became clearer. Looking ahead, there was the Iraqi border. In the pitch-blackness, the only light visible anywhere were the burning oil fields before us. The total blackness, with the red flames on the horizon gave Iraq the most sinister appearance of anywhere I could ever imagine. Tolkein, in his description of the evil land of Mordor couldn't have been far wide of the mark. Whatever the public face Iraq presented, its appearance by night was frightening. There seemed to be no other British vehicles between us and Iraq and we couldn't see or hear any thing behind. After fifteen minutes of driving at full speed, which might have been just about enough to get us into Iraq, or thereabouts, I was contemplating telling the unnamed to stop and turn us around. I wouldn't have minded driving back down to one of the base-camps and looking an idiot but before I could make a decision, our minds were made up for us.

We slowed down, as we saw a Land Rover halted in front of us. Looking off to the side, there were quite a few vehicles hidden under cam-nets. Their shapes were well disguised and, at that moment, we couldn't be exactly sure of their origin. The unnamed questioned the nationality of the vehicles to our right. I offered nothing much by way of an answer. The one thing we were certain of was that the rest of the convoy had disappeared. They couldn't be going along this route as we had been driving too fast and for too long not to find them. Somehow, somewhere, the rest of the convoy had taken a wrong turn. To this point, the invasion of Iraq wasn't going quite as well as it might have but then, I didn't mind waiting.

Fortunately, we were soon greeted by the section Artificer, who, despite the vast confusion, knew exactly where we were on the map. He also knew exactly where we should have turned but then, he had been in that neck of the woods before and there's certainly no substitute for experience. Looking behind us, several more vehicles had arrived and we were suddenly cosy in the knowledge that the vehicles immediately to our right were also British. All we needed to do was to find the entrance to Iraq, although I didn't expect it to be signposted.

Our remnant of the convoy turned itself around and headed back up the road, towards where we should have turned. This was no small task in the dark, in vehicles with the largest turning circles in the world but after a minute or two, we were on our way, away from Iraq, albeit briefly.

After an hour or so, we came across some of the rest of our convoy, who had been sat waiting for us for a while. Apparently, by this time, they knew where they were going too, so our chances of actually finding Iraq were beginning to look quite promising. Onward we drove, into the night, before we arrived at a series of lights. They stood like dim lampposts, marking out the beginning of the exclusion zone between Kuwait and Iraq. Until that moment, I didn't even know that there was an exclusion zone but the dusty track, which rolled away before us seemed to be the road through it.

For the unnamed and myself, in our ignorance, it was something of a false dawn. We both assumed that this was Iraq and timed ourselves at zero one-twenty hours (Zulu), which was three hours behind local time. For some reason, the British Army had decided to operate on a time-zone which meant that we got up at three o'clock in the morning, when it first came light. It made no sense to me but then I came across little that did, so I went along with it. This time though, was not the time of our entry into Iraq but our entry into the part the Americans had decided was theirs. They had certainly parked enough vehicles there to call it their own driveway. Doubtless, the surface sand was already stuck together with chewing gum by the time we drove past.

A couple of hours later and we arrived at a large berm, with one small break in it. Looking down the road, we saw that the other half of our convoy was already there and facing in the opposite direction to us. Their route was a mystery and to any watching Iraqis it may have looked a little strange but at least we were there. This was the abandoned UN gate into Iraq. There were a few old signs denoting United Nations rules and a couple of old huts, which had fallen into disrepair but mainly, the place was inhabited by stray dogs. These were dirty, flea-bitten mangy things that looked like they would be only too happy to bite your leg, or any other part of the anatomy. There were no endearing images to be had here. I am a cat person. I always have been and always will be. I do not like dogs, particularly, dirty, aggressive-looking ones. I wasn't cheered by their presence in any way.

The two separate convoys formed again into one and we set off through the breach, into Iraq. I thought that it might have felt like some kind of auspicious moment but at ten past three (Zulu), the unnamed and I entered Iraq, in the dawn light. It looked a lot less threatening in the light and as we cleared the breach, we were greeted by the image of a country, which, looked to have been ravaged by years of fighting.

There were buildings, long since deserted and forgotten about. The roads were in a state of total disrepair and anything, which had, at one time, represented civilisation, looked to have been thrown to the ground and smashed. By night, Iraq looked an image of menace and evil. By day, it just looked like a burnt-out, deserted shit-hole. In this first, deserted little town we drove through, the dogs had taken over and decided to live like, well, dogs.

The first Iraqi people we saw looked only too pleased to see us. There weren't many around but then it was early morning and there was a war on, apparently, although we could have been forgiven for thinking that this was anything but. Most of them waved and smiled, some clapped, a few cheered. We did our best to wave back. The military term for this practise is "Hearts and Minds" but then, there isn't a military term for simply being civil. I'll smile all day as long as they're not shooting at me.

Having been surprised by the Greeks throwing pieces of pavement at us on our way to an awful six month tour of Kosovo a few years earlier, I was nonetheless surprised to see the Iraqis seemingly thanking us for invading, or should I say liberating their country. The Greeks were none too pleased to be used as a NATO staging post, given NATO's lack of support in their hour of need and made their feelings firmly known to us but the Iraqis were a little confusing in their intent. It was a point that we all waved back but the right hand was never far from the trigger, whatever local customs might dictate. At least we knew the Greeks hated us and we knew why. We hadn't a clue what the Iraqis thought.

# CHAPTER 20;
# BEST LAID PLANS...

WE TURNED DOWN a narrow dirt track and in three rows; the convoy came to a halt at our destination. As far as destinations go, it was as bland and featureless as any of our previous locations but this one, significantly, arse twitchingly, was in Iraq. I waited in my position, out of the top of the cab, where I could see for miles in front of me and equally far to the sides. I felt comfortable with this idea, as I didn't want to be surprised by anyone's sudden arrival.

Unfortunately, I was ordered to step down from my vantage point and told that I should be lying on the ground, giving cover, as that was standard practice. Standard practice when on foot patrol yes but in vehicles, in an area that hadn't been cleared of mines, to my knowledge, which was surrounded by berms on all sides, it was plain stupid. Obviously, after a brief common-sense based protest, I went with the stupidity, which had brought me this far, and laid down, in the dirt, beside the wagon, pointing my rifle into the berm, which was about twenty yards away. That was also as far as the eye could see from this point, which wasn't helpful.

I may have been a civilian who had been forced to act like a soldier but this act of "by the book" thoughtlessness might well have jeopardised our lives. There was nothing we could do about the lack of mine clearance but to order everyone to simply lye down, with their weapon pointing away from the vehicles, as the foot-soldiering textbook denotes was quite pathetic. It was symbolic of trained engineers attempting to fill the void of a complete lack of infantry know-how. We were, quite simply, playing at it, without any appreciation of the point of our actions. My mate Dave muttered his opinion… "For fuck's sake, ten thousand Iraqis could jump over that berm, and we'd be fuckin' dead before we'd even seen 'em comin'. Fucking useless cunts." Several nervous heads nodded into the sand.

Certainly, I felt a little ridiculous as the local goat-herder, with herd, strolled past, with flip-flops and tea towel in place, in complete silence. We just laid there, in silence, wondering just what the bloody hell we were doing. If anyone were to attack us at that point, we would have been wiped out within seconds. I know little of the art of soldiering but I was embarrassed by the chronic lack of intelligence involved in our "all around defence" strategy. At least half of the people in the convoy were unable to see more than twenty yards in front of them. The whole lot of us deserved to be wiped out there and then yet most of the men on the ground knew better and were generally capable soldiers. These orders were becoming increasingly difficult to follow, as the incompetence of command became more and more apparent.

After a few minutes, it was wisely judged to be time to completely abandon the all around defence we'd set up and stand up and have a casual walk around, in the area, which hadn't been cleared of land-mines. There were a few mutterings of discontent at the nature of our arrival and few renditions of circus music at the poor quality of our part in the invasion. Morale was low, people were tired and once we'd moved into our positions in the location, it was time to get digging again.

We were starting to become schooled in the art of digging huge trenches and, with so much practice; the task was becoming ever easier. We even managed to have a laugh and a giggle whilst we shifted three tons of loose earth out of the ground. We dug out a toilet hole and a desert rose. Such was our enthusiasm for the endless digging that we also dug a huge hole for burning the rubbish and all this in the searing heat of mid-morning. I think it was the chain-gang mentality that kept our spirits up. Either that, or morale had hit its' lowest possible point and could help but rise on the rebound. I couldn't really understand it but somehow, we became cheerful, simply by digging huge holes. Maybe we were all showing the first signs of madness.

After a couple of hours of digging, it was time to rig up the vehicles and get all the equipment set up, on the off-chance that the workshops had some repair work coming in. We hadn't repaired anything for days but knowing that this was the last task before we could sit down and have a cup of tea motivated everyone, regardless of its' pointless nature. We duly completed it and switched on the kettle. Thoughts turned to a huge mug-full and a bag of warm slop, which, even though mildly unpleasant, would fill a gap.

The plan was that we would stay at that location for around six days. At least that was the official word and most of the hierarchy appeared to believe it. I didn't. Neither did the rest of the men on the ground. We knew that the guns would be moving continuously towards Basra and possibly beyond, so surely we would have to move with them, which meant that we wouldn't be staying anywhere for six days. All the plans said that it was a mobile campaign; so being static seemed to go against the grain. I reckoned I was on to something here and thought it best that the point was discussed.

I raised the question with the over-promoted buffoon and the absolute certainty of his answer should have prompted my suspicions. I did, for a few minutes at least; take comfort in his words and the thought of a few days break from digging and a bit of rest and routine really appealed to me. When the kettle boiled, I made a cuppa for the group and we relaxed for a minute. That was when it all went perfectly and somewhat predictably pear-shaped.

There were always rumours about when and where we were to move and I became tired of hearing them. I couldn't influence matters, so I didn't concern myself with them. Rumours are, however, a sign of discontent and the Army almost runs on them. This latest rumour, unbelievable though it was, was that we were to be setting off in ten minutes and that we didn't even have time to finish our tea. We scoffed at it, as we should have at such a ridiculous suggestion.

By the time I'd thoroughly burned my lip attempting to hastily guzzle the tea, which was far too hot; the official word had been sent that we were moving and that the last five minutes were included in the previous ten minutes. The much needed and well-deserved tea was thrown over the shoulder as we hurriedly set about packing away all of our equipment. I don't know where the five minutes went but the equipment was packed quickly enough and we were then told it was time to get down in the dirt again and try our, by now famous, all around defence manoeuvre. Cue lots of discontented mutterings.

We were all a little confused by the general panic of our imminent departure and some were more than a little annoyed that all our hours of dedicated civil engineering were to be wasted. For me, it wasn't really a case of being annoyed at having to do anything in particular. I was distraught at the prospect of being involved in the war in any capacity. It didn't matter what we did on a daily basis. Hurriedly, we jumped onto our respective vehicles and the convoy set off again, to where, we didn't know.

The drive, in its entirety, lasted all of fifteen minutes. We simply went back to the road and headed a little further up it, stopping at yet another bland, featureless shit-hole, which looked remarkably similar to the rest of Iraq. Almost automatically, we went into the routine of getting all of the equipment set up and then digging some holes. It wasn't fun but it passed a couple of hours away, which was about all we could hope to do. The process of setting up a harbour area and then packing up and leaving within a day or two had become routine. We were used to it, just like we were becoming used to feeling dirty, rationing water and shitting in a bag.

As we sat down, to partake in a very well earned and much appreciated cup of tea, "I'm drinking this fucker if it kills me". The Geordie popped his head around the door. He had some reasonably interesting news for us. By default, he had managed to get a lot of the shitty jobs, and had been on the recce party (an advance party, who assess the area for safety, prior to our departure, allegedly) for the previous location and knew the exact reason for our hasty departure. Apparently, despite the thoroughness of the earlier recce, which had been carried out by the over-promoted buffoon, we had managed to set ourselves up just a few hundred metres away from a division of Iraqi infantry, who were accompanied by a few tanks. He comforted us with the news that they were now about four miles away. This still didn't seem far enough for me.

I wasn't disappointed that we'd decided to run, rather than fight. We had no armoured vehicles and barely enough ammunition to defend ourselves, let alone attack anyone. All we could do was drive away, as quickly as possible. If the British Army had such a thing as an invasion force (and it didn't), then this was its' soft underbelly. We didn't have the manpower or the collective expertise to attack anyone. We were, quite simply a soft target. To use another well-suited footballing analogy, we were shit and we knew we were.

Not long after we had settled in to our new temporary home, the Iraqi night was upon us again. As was the norm, we were in total blackout, which meant that there were plenty of opportunities to stumble around on the uneven ground, bruising knees and shins etc. I partook in this activity liberally, falling over a couple of times before I eventually came to rest on the back of the wagon. I took five minutes to relax and to reflect on my situation, whilst things were calm. For a while, it was peaceful. On the horizon, with its' oil fires burning, Iraq seemed as sinister as it had appeared from the outside, yet looking up at the night sky, I felt as calm as I had felt since my hurried deployment.

I lay down and tried my hardest to imagine that I was somewhere else, anywhere else, in fact, just somewhere a little more pleasant than Iraq. My thoughts strayed away from my situation to home and to any other less important matter that I could think of. I think, during that brief period of relaxation, I managed a fairly inauspicious first for the British Army. To my knowledge, that was the first time any British soldier had masturbated on Iraqi soil during this conflict. I wasn't proud but such actions are born out of desperation, at least that's my excuse anyway. I made a mental note not to call Guinness. It's also worthy of note that you can't really make a mess in a desert.

My respite was only a brief one as, within minutes, there was a scene of confusion and general panic within our area. In the darkness, which had, to that point, concealed our whereabouts quite well, there was a sudden instance of bright lights. The commotion was obvious and quite chaotic as the dirty old pick up truck drove straight through our position, with its' lights on full beam. We ran to stop it and to tell the driver to turn off his lights immediately. This wasn't done with anything like a civil tone and offence was quickly taken. I didn't blame him. He was just driving to his house and we had, rather inconsiderately, parked our entourage in his way.

This point wasn't easily made in the first instance, as a man speaking exclusively Arabic tried to explain to six soldiers (who might well have been of less than average intelligence) exactly what he was doing. Misunderstandings are easily achieved in such a charged atmosphere and it wasn't long before the general consensus was to send for seniority. No one could make head or tail of the situation, so the easy way out was to pass responsibility up the ladder. That was where it all went totally shit-shaped.

Someone shouted for the over-promoted buffoon to come and attempt to sort the situation out. He wouldn't have been my first or second choice but at least the matter was out of my hands. The unfortunate problem with shouting names in the dark is that sometimes, things can be misheard. Stepping forward, out of the back of the Control point, was One Pip Louis. He couldn't have arrived at a worse moment. On hearing the shout, he immediately misheard it as a shout for Gas Gas Gas. This wasn't ideal.

Within a few seconds, he had his mask on. He then proceeded, as he should have (had this been any sort of genuine alert), to inform everyone else of the situation, as loudly as he could. If the Iraqi man was struggling to understand us before, he would have been even more confused when the six men who had been remonstrating with him suddenly pulled on gas masks and hurriedly crawled under the nearest vehicle. Confusion reigned supreme and we really were suffering from the effects of it.

Underneath my wagon, we didn't know what was going on, or why the alarm had been raised. We had only heard One Pip Louis and responded accordingly. I still don't know quite how we managed to cram ourselves under the vehicle but the Iraqi man just stood there, out on his own, thoroughly confused by our actions. I would be surprised if he were at all impressed by the British Army, in that instance. Nonetheless, a couple of minutes later, after the area was declared clear, we all got to our feet and made light of it. For his part, he turned off his lights and set off in darkness, so the message did get through, although I don't know how.

The area fell again into a calm silence. There were the background noises, which we were rapidly becoming accustomed to. These consisted of lots of loud explosions, the odd bit of machine gun fire in the distance and the dogs barking. There were a lot of dogs barking, some close, some far away. None welcome, in my book. The background noises, despite their obvious volume, didn't really interfere much with my relaxed state of mind. I would imagine that my situation was similar to that of someone living near an airport. I certainly didn't like the noise but when I became used to it, it wasn't so bad.

Dave and I retired for the night. For the first time in a while, I hadn't been stung for any pointless duties, so a night's sleep, or at least, an attempt at one, looked to be on the cards. The unnamed was on radio duty, so for once, we had a little room. We unfurled the sleeping bags and gave it our best shot. The background noises continued, as they inevitably would but sleep was soon upon us and for once, it looked like we may actually get a few hours in. This situation could never last, of course.

It might have been around one in the morning when the balloon went up. The increasingly over-familiar Gas Gas Gas shout went out and hazily, lazily, we responded. It didn't take overly long for either of us to respond, despite our relaxed state. It became second nature to sleep with all the necessary kit and equipment to hand and I awoke with my respirator pouch in my left hand and my rifle in my right. Calmly, I pulled the thing over my face and shut my eyes again. Outside the confines of our wagon, things weren't quite going so smoothly.

There was quite a commotion and a little shouting, accompanied by a female voice. I didn't gather who it was but she sounded desperate. The tears were quite obviously flowing as we managed to deduce that she had forgotten where she'd left her respirator. There was the ever helpful mention of "Where did you last see it?" but this offered little in the way of comfort in what must have been a nightmarish experience. She continued this frantic search for a few minutes, in the knowledge that no one had a spare and that everyone was using their own. We just laid back and listened to the show playing out. There was nothing we could do to help. If this was a real attack, then unfortunately, it was her problem and the consequences would be hers alone. Sympathy was useless.

## CHAPTER 21; UNEASY LIKE SUNDAY MORNING.

WE AWOKE THE following morning, to the news that it had been an eventful night. There were some stories breaking among the newspapers and some coming over the radio. Most came by word of mouth. Things were not going well, it seemed. We were told that, just a little way down the road, two Land Rovers had been stolen by the local militia. To make matters worse, there were two soldiers still missing with the vehicles. In the attack, another soldier had been badly wounded and another had had his legs blown off by a rocket-propelled grenade. This had happened about half a mile down the road from where we were. The details were hazy, to say the least but the general idea was that we were somewhere between a rock and a hard place.

Further details about six or seven American marines being taken prisoner of war emerged via the world service. Selfishly, we were considerably less concerned with this because it wasn't in our immediate vicinity. The notion of being taken prisoner of war looked less and less attractive but this was happening twenty or thirty miles away, so it wasn't a particular concern to us. There was a rumour, or it may just have been propaganda, that Saddam Hussein was offering a personal reward of ten thousand dollars for any American or British soldiers taken prisoner. I was surprised to hear that Saddam was dealing in dollars, rather than currency featuring his own head but the idea did fall in with the general picture painted of him in the press at least. I wondered if there was any genuine substance in this story.

We knew little of the actuality but there was plenty of rumour and speculation to make up for our lack of knowledge. As I went on duty that morning, for the full twenty-four hours of guard, the mood was more subdued than it ever was for any duty I'd ever started. Of the six of us, most were more than a little apprehensive at the increasingly real prospect of having to defend ourselves from attack. It was worthy of note that among this group, I was perceived to be the experienced man.

It is a strange point but one that must be made that when I was in the regular Army, there were always far too many duties and far too many people employed on them. Duties are a source of adverse morale in the regular Army as there are never enough bodies to cope with a seemingly unnecessary workload. Most of the time this is a perfectly acceptable statement and the reality is that most guard duties in the Army are a complete waste of time, other than presenting the stiff regimental hierarchy with endless opportunities to dish out a bollocking. The difference was, that this, all of a sudden, wasn't most of the time and six men, standing behind a berm would offer only weak resistance in the face of a genuine attack.

The six of us, two TA, one reservist and three regular soldiers (one of whom wasn't the brightest) all felt a little isolated, in our little outpost, at the corner of our area. True enough, we were only fifty yards from the vehicles and the rest of the unit but the difference between them, washing, shaving and eating and us, lying down in the dirt, looking out over the barrel of a machine gun, was considerable.

If we were attacked (and this did appear to be a distinct possibility), then we would most likely die instantly. We would be the focal point of any attack and our life expectancy, in such a situation, would be barely above ten seconds. I personally resented the enforced risking of my life, not just because of the suspect reasoning behind the war but because we really shouldn't have been put in that situation. Despite the berm built up before us, we were offered almost no protection from any attack. We had no armoured vehicles, little ammunition and scant soldiering know-how. We shouldn't have been in that situation because our unit (workshops) didn't even need to be there. There was a very realistic possibility of suffering the most painful and most pointless death in the history of war fighting.

The day passed uneasily and uneventfully into the night. This, in itself was a relief. It seemed every minute spent was a minute closer to getting home alive. The darkness brought with it new uncertainty, as this seemed to be the darkest of nights and there were many stories of many scary people about. I've never been a wishful thinker but I really did just want to close my eyes and hope that I went away. "I wish I could do a fuckin' Rentaghost", Offered the Geordie, holding his nose. The night enveloped us with such a thick, foreboding blackness that a man could have walked to within five yards of us unnoticed. We had nothing in the way of a night-vision capability and the over-reliance on the very tired and nervous mark-one eyeball was dubious to say the least. Hallucinations, caused by sleep depravation were also becoming a problem. "Twitchy" best described our collective state of mind.

We "guarded" our area in pairs, to enable the rest of the guard shift to get some sleep and to perform some unnecessary tasks detailed by the Control point. Two people, in the dark, in the middle of nowhere, with apparently three hundred armed civilian militia on the rampage, in the local area, weren't much better than nothing. The story was that these were the same people who attacked and stole the British army vehicles the previous night. They weren't after any particular military objectives. They simply wanted to kill and maim as many people as possible. We weren't sure whether this was a certainty, or whether it was more propaganda, to maintain the evil image of the Iraqi regime. It really didn't matter. The feeling of absolute, arse tingling, terror was much the same either way. There had been briefings of what we were supposed to do, in the event of various situations but these offered little comfort. Most of the actions involved great risk to life. Sadly, none of them involved doing a runner.

When I was on guard, with The Geordie, we were confronted by our first strange incident of the night. A few hundred metres in front of our position was the main supply road, which led, albeit some distance away, to Baghdad. There were hundreds of military vehicles, mainly American, passing up it every day. The vast majority of these were in convoy (behind the Coca-Cola wagon) heading to Baghdad, so it was an oddity when a vehicle strayed from this pattern.

One vehicle, on its' own had strayed from this pattern and had left the road and was turning towards us. From the light provided by other vehicles, we were able to make out its' shape – a Land Rover. It stopped a little distance away from the road, with its' lights pointing directly into our area. This wasn't helpful, as we were unable to see the vehicle any longer but they would be able to see us, in every minute detail. Everyone passing up the road would also be able to see us, due to the light of this Land Rover.

Such an action, by a soldier in a British vehicle would have been deemed a monumental error. Our problem was that we knew there were two British Army Land-Rovers missing and this behaviour was certainly well removed from British Army practice. We hoped that it didn't add up to the conclusion we had already jumped to but sitting there, with his lights aimed directly into our area was hardly the friendliest of actions, if this were friendly. We could do little but watch and hope that this was simply a very stupid man. If it were anything else, we would surely know about it soon enough.

It stayed there for quite some time. No one was sure exactly what was going on but no one was comfortable with the vehicle's presence. A number of people came to offer their opinions but nothing more sensible than our first suggestion arose. We waited for any sign of life, or any approaching action. There was nothing. The vehicle just turned around and drove away up to the road. We were still dubious as to their intent but we said nothing further of it.

After an agonisingly slow couple of hours on the gun-post, The Geordie and I were allowed to get some well-earned rest. It wasn't sleep by anyone's definition but it was certainly appreciated. Just the notion of laying down in the sleeping bag, out under the stars, with only the stray dogs for company seemed a far safer and calmer practice than standing out to be shot at. We settled into our positions, on the ground and made best attempts to sleep.

That particular pleasure lasted about ten minutes. The over-promoted buffoon was soon onto the idea that we had relaxed for a minute and had found us some unlikely task, with which to occupy our freshly idle hands. At least that was the way it always seemed with the buffoon. Quick as a flash, we were out of the sleeping bags and ready for action, or rather, we gave that impression. Actually, we were both "Fuckin shagged".

Apparently the ASM wanted three volunteers for a mercy mission deep into the unsecured territory near Basra. By some small coincidence, we were two of those. The plot was that, as our vehicles were only supposed to go out in twos and he needed to go out, we would need to follow behind his vehicle to provide armed support in case of attack. Of all the things I'd always wanted, this certainly wasn't one.

"Alright then sir, are we going to be going anywhere near where those two Land-Rovers were attacked last night?" I enquired.

"Yes, we most certainly are. We'll be going right along that same road." He replied cheerfully.

"Alright then sir, are we going to be going anywhere near that thing?" I asked, pointing to what was almost certainly an Iraqi missile launcher, which was throwing missiles by the dozen towards Basra.

"Yes. We've got to drive right past there. Don't worry though, they'll not be able to hit us with that." He replied, again with a fair degree of cheer.

"Alright then but I would imagine that with that missile launcher, there might just be one or two armed men, who might well not take too kindly to us driving past."

"Corporal Jones" (Lance-Corporals and full Corporals are addressed in the same way in the Army) "I feel you that are worrying too much." Came the by now annoyingly cheerful retort.

"Maybe sir but then, we are in Iraq and there is a war on and that fucking thing is chucking missiles all over the place. Do you think I'm wrong to worry a little bit sir?" I offered, quite calmly.

"Jonah, it'll be alright. We'll just nip straight past and they'll be none the wiser."

With that pearl of wisdom, the ASM went into the control point to acquire a map and a few other bits and pieces we needed. The Geordie and I had a minute or two to reflect on this latest task allocation and neither of us were too comfortable at the prospect of driving through Iraq in the middle of a very dark, scary night. We didn't know what was waiting for us out there but we had an inkling, from the radio, that it might not be pleasant. We were unenthused, to say the least.

"Youth, do I worry too much about this stuff?" I asked.

"Jonesy man, howay, it's like you fuckin' said. We're in Iraq and there is a fuckin' war on like. I don't fancy this much myself." He offered, in his usual articulate manner.

"Yeah but the thing is, we're going to do it. We've been told to. We don't fucking agree with it. The papers and military history are full of stories where little jaunts like this fucking go wrong and I really don't feel up to it, yet we've been fucking ordered to do it and that's that. There's no fucking getting out of it. We can't just say; " No, that's a fucking stupid idea, get fucked you useless cunts." but why not? We're not going to fucking down tools and tell them to fuck off. We're going to do this to the best of our fucking abilities, even though we both know it's completely fucking wrong and stupid and we don't want to. We are a pair of fucking idiots man."

"Aye, right we are son but we are going to do it though aren't we?"

"Yeah. I suppose so."

"Did you know how many times you said fucking just then? It was a lot, even by Army standards. Howay, let's chuck this tackle in the back of the Rover." He concluded.

"Alright. I just get annoyed with the inevitability of it, you know?"

"Aye. There's fuck all you can do about the inevitability though. It's fuckin' inevitable." Declared the greatest mind in the North East.

"Yeah, I suppose so. It just confuses me a bit that when we first turned up, they didn't fucking want us for anything. I kind of expected that we wouldn't be that involved in all this useless caper."

"Aye. It is a bit fuckin' strange like, when you think about it."

We loaded up the Rover and the Geordie volunteered to drive, which meant that the other young lad and I were to hang out of the back, ready to be shot at. I was in acceptance of the situation by the time we set off but I wasn't relaxed in any way. It was a very tense time as we set off out of our area and pulled onto the dusty road, away from relative safety and into the dark and dusty night.

My goggles weren't doing much to deflect the dust from my eyes and visibility was becoming more and more difficult, the further we went. I couldn't see more than thirty yards in the few vague lights, which were scattered around the area. I was afraid to blink, as I didn't want to take my eyes away from the surrounding area for a minute. We were only too aware of the events of the previous night, along the same road. This made us all overly tense but also made sure that we were well alert, should anything happen.

We drove along the road, which was barely more than a well-worn dirt track, through a dusty plain. Every corner seemed to offer a lovely little hiding place for any would-be ambushers and I found myself continuously staring into each one as we drove by. It felt as though the whole of the outside world was about to jump out and attack us. We felt like three little men in a flimsy little vehicle, in the middle of a big-nasty war-zone. Fear was certainly upon us from the outset.

At what I would guess to be somewhere near our halfway point, we stumbled upon a conundrum. We turned up a narrow and very bumpy dirt track, which was shrouded on both sides by thick trees and bushes. We couldn't see much at first but when the bushes gave way to smaller vegetation and eventually a berm, we saw it.

On the other side of the berm on our left, which was no more than eight feet high, there was a Russian-spec, Iraqi missile launcher and it was in use. The track we were on formed a channel, between the berm on our left and another on our right, which seemed quiet and insignificant in comparison. The missiles were being launched no more than a hundred yards away from us, directly to our left and they were going towards Basra, by the dozen. Although the ASM's vehicle carried on away into the dust, The Geordie brought the vehicle, to a halt, for just a second.

"Fancy it youth?" I offered.

"Nah, let's fuck off."

That was just about as long as we had to make up our minds. We were as sure as we could ever be, even in the supreme confusion that is untrained soldiers at war that this was exactly what we thought it was. We also knew that we had to keep up with the ASM or face being lost, as we had no map or directions but in that second; it seemed to me that we had a duty. We all knew that we hadn't the equipment, or the know-how but this was an opportunity to remove a major piece of Iraqi machinery. Even if the term wasn't meant in the purest sense, we were all British soldiers and we had a duty to attempt to disable this piece of equipment.

None of us wanted the duty. It was just something that we had. As British soldiers, we had a responsibility to take any such opportunities, which came our way, whether we were equipped or not. Whether we wanted to or not, whether we thought it was safe or not. Thankfully, in some respects, the decision was made for us, all in a second, as the ASM carried straight on past it, seeming not to notice its presence. I'd never stop wondering what might have happened had we engaged them but given our level of expertise, I may well not have lived to tell the tale. A point worth knowing was that these men have been at war for years and there's never, ever been a substitute for experience. Perhaps the ASM realised that too. Perhaps he just thought it wasn't an advantage worth dying for. Failure to carry out one's duties is a difficult thing to comprehend.

After forty tense and uncomfortable minutes, we arrived at what must have been our destination. It wasn't any particular place, as it was just as bland and featureless as the rest of Iraq but there were a few British Army vehicles parked up, which was all the welcome we needed. All I wanted to know was what was so important that it couldn't wait until daylight.

The answer turned up, in the shape of an Army vehicle. It was an eight-ton lorry. There was nothing special about it and no important task for it to perform. It had to go back with us simply because it was a lorry. All the other vehicles in that particular position were armoured, leaving this vehicle and its' crew as the only soft target. There had been numerous incidents of machine-gun fire in the area hence it was deemed unsafe for soft-skinned vehicles, which of course, made me all the more pleased to be there. They weren't allowed to drive back as a single vehicle, so we were summoned to escort them back. We were forced to risk our lives to minimise the risk to theirs. No one explained exactly why they couldn't have been escorted back to us by one of their armoured vehicles. I just knew that that wasn't how the Army worked.

The prospect of driving back through an area where we could be easily attacked appealed to me only slightly more than staying in an area, which had been attacked numerous times, so we hurriedly jumped aboard. The Geordie was feeling a little groggy from the lack of sleep but said he would be all right to drive, so we set off back along the dusty dirt track, into the darkness.

The return journey was marginally less tense than the outward one but was made slightly more perilous by The Geordie's complete inability to keep his eyes open. We weren't able to pull over and change drivers for fear of losing our escort, so it was a case of trying to talk to him to keep him awake. Remembering to do this, whilst keeping my eyes open for any sign of ambush was difficult but I was quickly reminded when the vehicle suddenly mounted the embankment, or veered off to one side all of a sudden. There were plenty of stupid ways to die in Iraq and a road accident looked a good bet, particularly when "The unknown Geordie stuntman" as he was suddenly christened, managed to swerve over a lump and drive the Land-Rover on two wheels for about twenty metres, before finally righting it. He followed this with the cheerful question; "Did you notice a little lapse in concentration there?" Lots of relieved laughter saw us complete this bumpy ride without so much as a scratch. Another day passed without dying. Things were looking up.

## CHAPTER 22; RELAXATION IS PRICELESS.

THE FOLLOWING MORNING brought with it an end to my guard duty. I'd managed all of half an hours "sleep", which was just enough to make me realise how tired I was. It had been a fortnight since I'd had a proper night's sleep but in the previous three nights I had only managed any sleep at all in one of them. As I trudged back to the wagon, the prospect of relaxation brought with it the true depth of my tiredness. I was shattered and my body was desperate for a bit of a shut-down.

As much as I was desperate to simply lie down and pass out, there were a few tasks I needed to complete first. It is easy to be lazy in the field but that is where problems can start. I needed to make some attempt at cleaning my body and to have a shave and clean my teeth then there was the prospect of eating. Apparently, I was supposed to clean my rifle first, if you stick to the military doctrine but then the military doctrine also states that a dirty rifle will only fire a few times. I decided that they hadn't issued me with enough ammunition to warrant this and set about other, more important matters.

I decided that the best policy was to strip off and try to clean myself up with the bowl, on the tailboard of the wagon. This was a very public practice but naked carcasses are commonplace in such situations. I cleaned my teeth, washed as much of my body as I could and had a shave, all in the same water, which was a murky brown by the time I'd finished. Wearing just my underwear, I discarded the water in a purposely dug hole and went about sorting out food and a hot drink.

It's fair to say that I relaxed almost completely and I slowly began to get dressed after my breakfast and mug of tea. I was in no particular hurry to do this and was getting into the practice of sitting down between putting on each item of clothing. I had a t-shirt and trousers but no socks or boots on as I sat down for the final time. For me, this was the moment that I had been waiting for. It was time for some sleep. I slumped in the back of the wagon, ready to close my eyes and forget my precise location for a while.

The machine gun fire, whizzing a few feet over our heads was an unwelcome interruption to my rest. We couldn't tell exactly where it came from but it was pretty close, which unfortunately meant that we had to respond, whether we had boots on or not. The rest of the unit looked to be responding by sprinting about a hundred yards or so towards the furthest berm, which was apparently the direction of the supposed incoming fire. I saw no sense in covering a hundred yards of open ground just to take cover but it is a thing in the Army that it usually pays to do exactly what everyone else does, whether it makes sense at the time or not.

As I attempted to grab my various pieces of kit and equipment, whilst trying to pull on my boots and guess exactly what was going on, I noticed that I was lagging behind almost everyone. It seemed that everyone else, probably by virtue of the fact that they were already wearing boots, was streaking away from me and I was bringing up the rear.

When I breathlessly arrived at the far berm, having managed to almost dress myself, it seemed that the threat, or rather, the source of the noise had disappeared. There was nothing but complete silence; overlaid by my extremely heavy breathing and a general look of confused panic on the faces of all involved. I wasn't confused. Neither was I panicking. I was too tired to manage either. All I did was simply trail behind everyone else, in a kind of calmly exhausted manner.

The situation, though potentially perilous, wasn't exhilarating in any way. I felt no rush of excitement, as I had become used to responding with a frantic haste to most of the intrusive sounds we heard. I guessed that the machine gun fire, though quite close, wasn't aimed deliberately at us. It couldn't have been because we were all in soft-skinned vehicles in flat terrain. Anyone who was trying to hit us would have done so with ease. I had little doubt in my mind that we hadn't been contacted at all. We were overreacting yet again. I wasn't particularly critical of this action because it's always better to err on the side of caution in such situations. Unfortunately, this over-reaction had been a little more physically strenuous than usual.

I was a little critical of the method of pepper potting back to the "safety" of our vehicles. The soldiering textbook states that when retreating under fire, it is necessary to pull back alternately, with half of your number providing cover, whilst the other half moves. This process is repeated until your unit has retreated to a sufficient safe distance to enable a normal relaxed posture. The problem was, if we had been contacted, then we were retreating from reasonable cover into danger. If we hadn't been contacted, then it was perfectly safe to stand up and have a smoke exactly where we were. We managed a hybrid of not being exactly sure whether we were and not exactly retreating to safety. Furthermore, the practice of pepper potting; i.e. up and running, then down and aiming, was a very physically demanding activity. Such things aren't always welcomed when it's hot and it doesn't need to be done. I couldn't tell whether I was feeling irritation or just a pain in my arse.

With such obvious activity in our area and further information we received via the radios, we could gather that the Americans had achieved little more than simply bypassing any Iraqi resistance, en route to Baghdad. We were in an area the Americans had supposedly cleared but the problems we and every other British unit came across suggested otherwise. The general consensus on the ground was that "The fucking yanks have only bothered their arses to do half a job again." It was a sore point with most of us that although the Americans made most of the headlines and called it their coalition, they left us with most of the dirty work. If they had settled for a less rapid method of progressing through Iraq, ensuring that they wiped out any opposition as they went, the casualties for the coalition could have been greatly reduced. As it was, we could only make the best of what they had left us and what they had left us, was a bit of a mess.

It was a point of vast irritation with most of us that on that day, we received the first of our out of date newspapers. It was four or five days old, when we saw it but the difference between the newspaper stories and the truth was vast. Everything we knew or came across, or had been told, had been awfully misrepresented in the papers. My particular irritation that day was with some Colonel or other, who was singing the praises of the Army's fantastic E-mail letter writing service.

It was apparently faultless and all the troops were delighted with the fantastic service they were providing. I don't remember anyone asking my opinion. At least fifty percent of my mail went missing. Most other people had problems with overdue or lost mail but simply having a common surname presents a huge problem in the Armed forces, it seems. It may be a trivial point but letters are a powerful aid to boosting morale. Any message from home, no matter how short or simple, counts for something, when everything seems so bleak. Most of mine didn't arrive. The Geordie also agreed that it was "wank".

The next morning, I awoke to the cheery surprise that I had been visited by several mosquitoes, during the night, doubtless seeking respite from the heavy overnight rain. There must have been a few of them because I had twenty-one bites on my forehead alone and they were itching quite furiously. Some men attract women, some attract money and some attract a lot of good fortune. Apparently, I attract mosquitoes. I always have and unfortunately, I always will. I certainly was annoyed that I wasn't given any mosquito repellent when I asked but then, if I knew where I was going, I would have taken my own anyway. I doubted that there were any mosquitoes in my bathroom cabinet at home, at that time.

Seeking salvation from my newly found habit of head scratching, I headed for the medical wagon, in hope of some cream or anything to relieve the itching. On my way, I was accosted by the over-promoted buffoon, who wanted to know why I wasn't wearing my helmet. I put across my case as best I could and unsurprisingly, it wasn't good enough for the buffoon. Regimented and systematic, without the influence of judgement, was always the way with him.

"Obviously, at the first hint of any noise or anything, I'll put the damn thing on but I can't wear it much because this sweaty dirty pad on the front will make them worse and they'll take months to heal and probably cause scarring." I offered, trying not to sound too definite about my stance.

"Unfortunately, there's a war on and you've got to wear your helmet all the time, whether you like it or not because it can prevent your head from being blown off." He replied.

"Well, I think we both know that the thing's pretty useless when it comes to actually stopping any rounds and it won't do me much good if someone shoots at me really but I can't wear it because it doesn't make medical sense. Everyone knows it's fucking useless and I don't see any point in wearing something useless, if it's going to cause me problems."

"I'm telling you to wear it, so wear it." A rather thoughtless response, I thought.

"Yeah, fair enough, I'll put it on, all the way over there, then when they tell me not to wear it, I'll stop wearing it. Bit daft this, innit?" I offered, pointing towards the medical wagon.

He could do little other than to allow me to go to the medical wagon, reluctantly wearing my helmet and then to allow them to arbitrate in the matter. Knowing what I did about hygiene and treatment of bites, I felt quite confident that my point of view would be shared by anyone with any common sense. Fortunately, in most cases, the medics are a reasonable bet for locating some common sense, but there are exceptions. I approached the rear of the wagon and spoke to someone in the back, who didn't look to be busy.

"Hello mate, I've got a load of bites on my forehead and they're itching like fuck. Can I get some cream or something please?"

"No because we haven't got much. Why don't you just scratch them?" Came the less than helpful response. Such a response would not have been thrown at a senior man.

"Because scratching them could cause infection and further discomfort and scarring. I really would like some cream, or something, if it's not too much trouble."

"Sorry, I don't know where it is." Was the un-cooperative and seemingly final reply.

"Is there anyone else around who I might speak with?"

"Yeah, next wagon along."

"Good, 'cos you're a useless, bone-idle cunt." I replied flatly.

I stepped into the tent at the back of the next vehicle, to be greeted by an altogether better response. It looked to be something similar to a treatment room, only smaller, dirtier and vastly less well equipped. Nonetheless, it was pleasing to be greeted by someone who looked at least slightly interested in performing their duty. I saw no reason whatsoever for anyone to be less motivated than myself and was surprised to have just encountered someone. I, at least, performed most of the tasks asked of me, with a degree of diligence.

"Hello mate, I've been bitten to fuck on my forehead. Might you have anything which would provide me relief from this furious itching sensation?" I offered, as cordially as I possibly could.

"Let's have a look." (On inspection) "Fucking hell, there are some greedy mosquitoes about this place. They've given you a good going over. I'll get you some cream."

"Marvellous, thank you very much." I said, perhaps a little too gratefully.

"Oh and try not to wear your helmet unless you really need to because it'll cause irritation. Just rub this in as and when you need it and you'll probably be alright in a day or two."

"Yeah, there's a bit of a problem with that because, as much as I don't want to wear it, I keep being told to."

"Who by?" He asked.

"I'll give you one guess." I replied, to which he guessed correctly.

"That man is such a knob. If he carries on with it, just send him to me and I'll refer him to the Chief Medical Officer." Came the assured final word.

I skipped merrily out into the open air, bare-headed and walked calmly back towards my own wagon. On my way, I bumped into the Geordie, who was looking quite pleased with himself.

"How's things young man?" I asked.

"Oh fuckin' tip-top mate. I've managed to find a use for all that treacle pudding we had left over from the ration packs." He exclaimed, joyfully.

"You should have said. I've been throwing mine away."

"Yeah, so has everyone else mostly but that's about to stop because it's suddenly become a very important piece of equipment, has the rat-pack treacle pudding."

"I'm staggered. Do tell." I offered, picking up the heavy sarcasm in his voice.

"Well, you know that no-one, except you, for some reason, has managed to get any Kevlar plates for their body armour?" He began, patting the newly solid part of his set.

"Fuck me. It's true. It will stop a bullet." I replied, patting the solidly-packed treacle puddings in the front of his armour."

"Aye, it's a bit heavier than Kevlar but I feel safe in the knowledge that rat-pack treacle pudding is the hardest substance known to man." He declared triumphantly.

"In all seriousness mate, it just might make enough of a difference. I've got to admit, it actually could be actually useful. It might just save your life."

"Well, we won't see any plates will we? I've looked at the Chocolate pudding but that's not as hard. It's pretty tough but I reckon the treacle's tougher."

"You can actually eat the Chocolate pudding as well."

"Aye but it's a bit chewy. Only if I was really desperate would I stoop so low." He concluded.

Just as we were revelling in our own stupidity, the war made its' best effort to get our minds back on the job. One-Pip-Louis was stood on the back of the Control Point, frantically shouting that we had a problem. The problem, in its' simplest terms, was that our unit, in its cosy, lorry-bound slumber, was about to be attacked by an Iraqi tank, which was steadily rolling down the road towards us. We'd had better news. Within seconds, the unit task force, which consisted of everyone who wasn't hiding in the back of their wagons, was ready to attack this most unwelcome visitor. Despite my earlier stance over the discomfort of the helmet, I readily accepted that this was just one such time when all reasoning went to pot. I fastened the damn thing onto my head, in readiness.

Regardless of any particular rank, The Geordie took command, assisted by myself. Everyone else appeared to be in a flap. I couldn't see the point of that. One-Pip gave us the approximate direction of its advance and instructed us that we would need an anti-tank missile. That was as far as his leadership abilities went. It was a good job he spoke up, or we might just have tried to take out a tank with a knife and fork. Perhaps he thought so. Furthermore, it was noted that it was "us" that needed the anti-tank missile and "us" didn't include him. Twat.

Under The Geordie's command and my further delegation, we advanced through the mud, roughly in the direction of the tank. We probably appeared as an untrained rabble, which wasn't far from the truth but in such situations, all the training in the world is worthless, if you can't keep a calm head and a clear mind.

Two such people were myself and fortunately, The Geordie. Despite the frantic nature of our deployment, I found myself to be thinking quickly and clearly. I knew exactly what we were going to attempt to do and I was going to give it my best shot. The other option was to sit back and wait for the bang, which I just wasn't prepared to do. It has to be said though, that although I noted that I was particularly relaxed with my impending doom, I noticed that the Geordie seemed to be finding it even easier.

He was directing people left, right and centre, all correctly and all just a little bit quicker than I could think to do it myself. People were responding positively too, which is always a good sign. The nature of our potential task meant that success was less likely than death but with The Geordie, we sensed that we might just squeeze through. I felt oddly relaxed about the whole idea but if I was cool, he was ice and a slice.

Our advance was trudging slowly through the mud into cover at the far end of our area and there was still no sign of our potential killer. This was good because it meant that upon its' arrival, we would be ready, or at least, we would be in position. We waited, partly excited, partly curious, everyone focussed. I took a mental note of my situation in life because I felt as though a life changing moment was about to happen. We lay there, in the mud, in silence, not moving an inch, waiting to be attacked and most likely killed. I can't say what went through anyone else's mind at that time but mine was nothing more than focussed on the job at hand. I don't really know why. The prospect of my imminent death wasn't an issue.

Fortunately, that was the last we ever heard of that particular tank. One-Pip said that he'd just heard on the radio that it had been destroyed, by the Scots Dragoons, a quarter of a mile down the road. None of us were actually sure if this was true, or if it was simply a cover for a bad misunderstanding of a previous message. Wearily, like men who had just returned from their impending doom, for what seemed like a dubious reprieve, we got to our feet and tried our best to wipe most of the mud off, offering forth our frustrations at the confusion of war.

After we had been made to unload our weapons under expert supervision (By One-Pip) we returned to the slumber from which we'd so recently risen. I began to pick some of the mud from my rifle, which as ever with the SA80, was filthy from the minute I tried to actually use it. The thing picks up dirt almost magnetically and stores it safely in all the little nooks and crannies which make it impossible to keep clean. It is the bane of a British soldier's life and I decided that it would be easier to let the mud dry before I tried to clean it. I set off back towards the relative comfort of the wagon.

I set it down on the back of the tailboard and removed my boots, so as not to bring too much filth into the back of the wagon. I took my shirt and trousers off in the doorway and promised to wash them as soon as I saw sufficient water to do so. A piece of good fortune for me was that I had been issued with a complete set of new kit before deployment, so it was pleasing to be able to ditch my filth in favour of an immaculate new set.

I put on my new trousers and relaxed in the back of the wagon. After the mayhem we'd just experienced, it was nice to sit for a minute, in the peace and quiet, which the Iraqis now afforded us. As ever, my mind reverted to priority one, which wasn't cleaning my filthy rifle, as the military doctrine states but making a cup of tea, which had always seemed all the more important.

I was soon joined by Dave and the unnamed, who both looked anything but refreshed by the morning's rigorous exercise regime. Tea was the one thing on their minds too; so it was that we sat down to partake in a nice, warm mug-full. The kettle boiled and we brewed up and sat down in the back of the wagon. Conversation was firmly fixed on the previous scenario and the hope that we might not experience much activity for the remainder of the day. I went to take a drink of my tea, almost overwhelmed by the relaxation it was about to afford me.

As I put the mug to my lip, my senses were jolted, by an exceptionally loud explosion. I had heard quite a few by that point but that ranked among the loudest. The normal panic didn't immediately ensue as we were becoming used to loud explosions and no one had felt the force of the blast, or seen the fireball. We decided that it was nothing to panic about and returned to our peaceful pursuit.

Within a few seconds, we heard another explosion, the magnitude of which far outweighed any I'd heard before, even more than the previous one. This one was no more than twenty seconds after the first and was much closer. The wagon rocked and shook with the force of the blast. The sand, hitting the side of the wagon also did little to inspire confidence.

"Fucking hell. They're getting closer." Said the unnamed, more than a little startled.

"That's got to be Iraqi Artillery, finding their range." Said Dave, decidedly worried.

"Fuckin' Hell, Dave, that sounds like an alarmingly accurate guess. We'd best drink up now boys." I offered, to which, the response was the forceful downing of the slightly too hot tea.

We sat and listened for a few seconds, as the general panic commenced outside. There was obviously the gas alarm and a few cries of "Incoming", which to me seemed a statement of the obvious but nothing in terms of real action. In truth, there isn't much you can do when you're being bombarded by artillery. Dave, the unnamed and I, after donning the respirators, did the only thing we could do. Simultaneously, without a spoken word, we all looked upwards and asked the man upstairs to blow the next one off course. We waited for some sign of his intervention.

The seconds passed into minutes, with all three of us sat there, not speaking. The only sound was the laboured breathing through the filters of the masks. Nothing happened. There was no further explosion. With each passing second, the world seemed a calmer place. A few more minutes and the respirators were removed. It seemed that this wasn't our turn. The entirety of our future was completely out of our hands, yet a little glance skywards confirmed that we had all discovered a new faith.

# CHAPTER 23; THE STENCH OF WAR.

THE FOLLOWING MORNING was something similar to the previous morning. It is a point with the Army that routine is paramount in everything they do and most mornings began in a similar fashion. After we'd done the usual tasks, played out to the usual accompaniment of a couple of explosions and fairly distant machine-gun fire, it was time to sort out the rest of the taskings for the day, which wouldn't be much. I hadn't seen a spanner for countless days and whatever workload we would incur, would only be incurred after the main event, which was the war itself. So there still appeared no point in the unit being there.

Having nothing to do, for a short period of time, can be a blessing but when there is absolutely nothing to occupy your time, for hours on end, even the briefest of tasks becomes a burden. I decided that I needed to break the monotony of endlessly sitting on my arse and went in search of suitable employment. There wasn't much around but after a while, I found my mate Dave, who appeared to have happened across something. So it was that I decided to tag along. It wasn't that my presence was required at the unit in any case.

We obviously had a cup of tea first and generally made our best attempt to move the morning on into the afternoon. Dave's employment on his call-up, which differed to mine, was recovery of vehicles. He was paired with another friend of mine, who was also TA, namely Mike, who had a particularly impressive moustache. We hadn't seen much of him since our mobilisation but it was noted that he had worked hard on his suntan during his busy schedule and was several shades darker than Dave or myself. It was also a point worthy of note that neither Dave nor Mike took their job, or the war particularly seriously. Theirs was a refreshing attitude as they simply giggled along with the whole silly scheme, whereas I only giggled at some of it.

The detail of another silly scheme was about to unfold for them as a messenger arrived from the Control Point, confirming their day's employment. Apparently, there was a broken down lorry out and about somewhere in the desert and if it wasn't too much trouble, would they return it from whence it came? They agreed that they would and suggested that as I was at a loose end, I might come along for assistance (even though I'd already decided to). I hadn't done much recovery work before and as the company was more than agreeable; I went along, mainly for the ride but partially for a bit of a change.

The ride wasn't a long one and within an hour of passing the all-the-fucking-same scenery, we, or rather Dave, using the GPS, found the vehicle quite easily. Apparently, according to the driver, the vehicle was "Fucked", which, according to most Army drivers, is the problem when most vehicles break down. From my previous experience in the Army, I knew that this term could encompass everything from a blown brake-light bulb to a complete write off of the vehicle. Usually, the person operating the vehicle doesn't care much. It isn't their vehicle and they don't have to pay for repairs. They just want to get home. Being the qualified man, Dave decided that he should have a look before anyone decided that the lorry was "Fucked".

He got the driver to jack the cab up, away from the engine and went to have a look around and a bit of a tinker, to see if there was anything he could do at the roadside. He said he didn't need assistance, so Mike and I had a look around the immediate area, which appeared to be a smaller version of our own harbour-area. As with most soldiers in wartime, we were on the look out for anything worth stealing. Such is the state of play with the British Army's stores set up that most useful items have to be acquired from elsewhere.

There had been a few Americans in the area recently and these people, who are usually overburdened with supplies and equipment, are known to liberally distribute useful things all over the place. Unfortunately, the Magpie-like nature of the British soldiers in the area had already engulfed the entire surplus and all that was left was stories of the things they'd acquired. Undaunted, we returned to Dave, who confirmed that driver's worst suspicions when he said that the vehicle would have to be towed, as he was unable to repair it where it was.

He asked me for a little assistance underneath the vehicle, as the prop-shaft needed to be disconnected, before the vehicle could be towed. I was only too happy to oblige and rolled underneath into the dirt, to help in any way possible, not having done this job before. That was when we heard the footsteps. Initially, we couldn't be sure exactly which direction they came from but as they got closer, we saw that they came from our left and they were heading straight for the vehicle. We didn't know who or why, at this time.

Privacy, in such an environment, is obviously a scarce commodity and these footsteps were in search of just such a thing. When the footsteps found what would have appeared to be a fairly private place, they stopped, right next to the vehicle. Dave and myself casually raised an eyebrow, as the boots turned away from the vehicle, giving a possible indication of what was about to happen. Just a couple of feet behind Dave's head, the combat trousers fell to the ground, around the top of the boots. They were quickly followed by a pair of grubby pink knickers, which went a long way towards confirming our suspicions that this was a female. This said, we weren't quite certain, at this point. Confirmation would be along shortly, though perhaps not in the manner we expected.

The unfortunate problem, for women in particular, when living in field conditions is how to keep smelling fresh. With a shortage of water and no particular facilities available, it was fair to say that most people had a bit of a whiff about their general person. Genitalia are a particular problem, when it comes to hygiene and although we all made our best efforts, most of us were probably a little less than fresh in that area.

This woman stank. I don't wish to lay the blame entirely at her feet (Or to have anything to do with her feet, for that matter) but the smell she gave off was unbearable. Neither of us was more than a few feet away and we had to cover our mouths and noses, partly to block the smell and partly just to mask the sounds of our laughter. The seconds passed very slowly as she dribbled urine into a cut off plastic bottle. When it was half full of the deep yellow fluid, she deemed that sufficient and without any real effort to wipe away any residue, she pulled up her grubby knickers and her combat trousers and went about her business, none the wiser as to our presence. After a few seconds silent restraint, Dave and I howled. Mike was a few yards away urinating behind a tree and missed the entire episode. He was gutted because, as he said, he hadn't had a sniff of it for weeks. Although we never even saw her face, we had managed more than just a sniff, we assured him.

With giggles abounding, we hooked up the vehicle and set off back to our destination. Mike turned on the radio and it wasn't long before we were listening to yet another one of Tony Blair's morality-laden speeches. The chosen subject for this dose of bullshit was whether or not Britain should send further reinforcements to Iraq, as America had donated yet another hundred thousand or so godforsaken souls to the cause. His answer, unsurprisingly, was that he was perfectly satisfied with the personnel he already had in the area.

He made no mention of the fact that in sending persons such as me straight into a war-zone, he had scraped the bottom of the military barrel, before the war even kicked off. There were no reinforcements to be sourced from anywhere. They didn't exist. It appeared to me that America genuinely believed that, as Britain had volunteered to assist with this crusade "Against terrorism" we probably had available military manpower to commit to such a cause. This was just another detail that our beloved Tony had forgotten to mention. None of us chose to comment over Tony's words because none of us needed to. His voice sounded quite shaky over the radio but then he was apparently under quite a lot of pressure. I really felt for him, as he had to paper over quite a few big cracks with little glue and thin paper but then, at least he had a bed to sleep in at night, that's if he could sleep.

# CHAPTER 24; NO MORE MORALE.

ANOTHER IRAQ MORNING brought with it strange tidings. Arriving on the back of a Four-ton Bedford were more personnel. These weren't the reinforcements that we weren't expecting and Tony said weren't coming. They were just more TA men who had been called up and then thrown into the wilderness. They had all been to a couple of units in the area before, only to be told they weren't needed. It seemed that the task was to find them a place in theatre, rather than simply to them back home.

These were ten men. Ten more people to feed, house and clothe. Ten people who were costing the British taxpayer a thousand pounds or more each per week and were serving absolutely no purpose whatsoever. I could see no merits as to their continued presence in the area and plenty of reasons to send them back home but the Army just don't do things like that. Maybe sending them back would be like admitting they had made a mistake. I couldn't think of any other consequences. Needless to say, they were to stay in theatre, for the foreseeable future.

As all seemed quiet on all fronts, we set about doing that which we had come to excel at, namely, drinking tea and reading old newspapers. The newspapers were something of a curiosity to me because it seemed that they were only interested in headline news and scandal. They weren't too bothered about the truth. The falseness of it all really was quite insulting to the troops on the ground. It was a cause of great irritation amongst the ranks and it's fair to say that the inaccuracies and lies did very much affect the morale of the soldiers on the ground.

A picture in the daily mail showed a "British soldier" wearing a respirator and rubber gloves, without an NBC suit, holding his rifle. The caption underneath read; "Ready for action…". I'm sure the public believed it but this must have just been a mock-up, taken well away from the operational theatre because this man wasn't even in a dress state which actually existed in any Army training doctrine. No one would put the gloves on before the chemical suit itself, because the gloves were supposed to go over the suit.

There was a more obvious problem with the picture though, was that the man was holding the rifle in a left-handed posture.

The SA80 cannot be operated in this way. It is a right-handed weapon, which would eject red-hot brass into the face of who-ever fired it left-handed. Every single soldier in the British Army is well aware of this, which probably meant that this was just a news reporter in fancy dress. It was clear that who-ever wrote the corresponding article knew little about the subject matter but it was printed anyway. The problem I and most of my colleagues had with this was that it gave the general public a totally false image of the Armed forces.

There were many sarcastic well wishers towards a young lad who was set to make his debut for England at rugby union. He had been in the Army but had decided to leave mid-way through his officer training to concentrate on his rugby career. Most were miffed by his absence from the conflict. I doubted that they would be even the least bit interested in his absence, were they not present in the Gulf. I couldn't bring myself to resent his position. I would say good luck to anyone who managed to get out of it. I put the newspaper to one side because it just seemed to be a source of aggravation for everyone, as lies often are.

We were briefed by One-Pip of a new and altogether more intimidating threat to our safety, not that there weren't enough of those already. In his superbly communicative style, he informed us to be on our guard because they were using strap-ons. The subsequent inquisition found that this was not a type of sex-aid, as first suggested but a strap on bomb. The cunning plan was for them (The less sensible of the Iraqis, we assumed) to run as close as possible and then pull the plug, blowing up themselves and anyone in the immediate vicinity.

I for one, wasn't particularly pleased with this development. I had a lot of moral issues with the war. I didn't believe for one minute that there was justification to invade Iraq. I didn't believe that the cause of the conflict was worth the life of one British soldier and I personally didn't feel any particular need or desire to kill anyone (Save for a few moments with One-pip and the Buffoon), or I hadn't until that point.

My stance on killing Iraqis had suddenly become unclear, even to myself. I had maintained throughout that I had no wish to kill anyone and that we had no real reason to kill anyone. However, I had to consider that a suicide bomber, who simply wishes to die and to kill and maim as many people as possible in the process, does not represent a reasonable military entity, i.e. a war-fighting soldier. Suddenly, I was reluctant to kill people who actually really wanted to die. It seemed that in this situation, I stood corrected.

Another oddity was that these people wanted to die purely for religious reasons. My understanding of religion, scant though it is, seems to imply goodwill to all men and common decency and all such similar standards. I couldn't quite understand how killing and maiming other men fitted into the religious side of things. I have never had any genuine religious beliefs and prefer to stand by proper human values of honesty and decency.

It seems that some religions are not concerned with these or other human qualities though. To me, it seemed that the great evils of this conflict were our invasion, in the name of God and democracy, although obviously driven mainly by economic reasoning, and the malevolent Iraqi response, in the name of Allah. And there we had it, money and religion, the two causes of every single war in the history of mankind. For anyone to suggest otherwise is a misquotation of the truth.

Morale, at this point, was beginning to scrape new depths. Until that point, I had reluctantly accepted the situation I was in. I wasn't happy but I'd decided that there was nothing much I could do about it, so I went along with it. I think I began to think about a possible way out of the war at that time because it seemed that no matter what punishment was thrown in my direction, it would be better than being blown up by an Iraqi lunatic. I knew full well that if such an incident were to occur, we had barely any protection against it. Suddenly, any Iraqi civilians wondering around in the area were considered a threat. It seemed to me that everyone was nervous enough already but war doesn't take into account people's feelings.

Our first such potential punter arrived in the mid-morning sun, looking scruffy and dishevelled, which seemed to be the Iraqi national dress. The Geordie and I muttered uncomfortable nothings as he got out of his battered pick up and walked briskly towards us. He did nothing to suggest that he might be a threat in any way but then I wouldn't have expected a warning. As he came closer, it seemed that there was a decision to make, which seemed an awkward one.

The Geordie made it, and as usual, he was a few seconds before me. At what he hoped was something like a safe distance, he stopped the man by cocking his rifle and pointing it directly at him. To me, this seemed a little over aggressive at the time but if he was a suicide bomber, I wouldn't have been able to apologise for my lack of judgement afterwards. In hindsight, The Geordie had interpreted the situation perfectly. We could have no contact with the Iraqis and we couldn't allow them to come anywhere near us. We had to treat everyone as a potential threat. The Geordie did and he did it well too.

"Stop there. Don't take another fucking step towards me you cunt." Offered the British Army's chief public relations officer.

The man tried to say something in response but nothing he could say would be of any use. There was simply no way of communicating or interacting with him at all. All we could do was to tell him, in no uncertain terms, to turn around and leave. Steve presented his case firmly.

"I don't give a fuck what you want. Just get back in your fucking van and fuck off…Now." The volume and tone were rising all the way.

Despite the language gap, the man seemed to get the message and decided it would be in his best interests to try somewhere else. The Geordie looked pleased with himself. The job was done. I had to concede that despite his chubby appearance, he was pretty effective in the field. With this action, he set a precedent, which became a standard practice from that moment on. The public relations could be handled by someone else, who wasn't at risk of being blown up.

The rest of the day passed uneventfully for us but the stark truth of our situation was being played out on the radio. Five American marines had been killed by a suicide bomber in a taxi, a couple of miles away. Apparently, the vehicle had arrived fairly innocuously, innocently enough for all five to gather around the vehicle and attempt to communicate with its driver. At the time, it probably didn't seem like a mistake and on another day, with another vehicle, it wouldn't have been.

Similarly, an officer of the Black Watch had suffered an unfortunate fate. A rocket-propelled grenade had struck him just as he emerged from the hatch of his armoured vehicle, killing him instantly. This man may well have been one of the most highly skilled military personnel in the area, serving with a unit of considerable war-fighting repute. Were it not for such an episode of bad timing and pure misfortune, he still might be.

That was the nature of our employment. It didn't matter how good or bad you were as a soldier, you just had to be unlucky, or make the slightest error of judgement or timing and that was that. Every death we heard about was simply a case of wrong place, wrong time, so much so, it seemed that it was barely influenced by the individual at all. It seemed that luck, the fictitious entity we like to blame for many things, influenced matters of life and death in war.

I made best attempts to get some sleep that night. It was quiet, with the exception of the dogs barking occasionally but it wasn't the noise that was keeping me awake. I had allowed myself to start thinking about home and to consider possible methods of returning home sooner than the Army planned for me. Rather than accepting the situation, I had begun to look for a way out. My mind had given itself over to wishful thinking and wishful thinking only ever leads to disappointment. At that time, I wished, more than anything else, to feel as safe and secure as I had when I was a child with my parents. I'm not ashamed to say that I wanted my mother, as ridiculous as that may seem. It's difficult to overcome the wants of the mind in these quiet moments. Quiet moments which would not have occurred, had the Army actually found a role for me, besides that of simple cannon-fodder.

# CHAPTER 25; THE FINAL STRAW.

ANOTHER EARLY MORNING briefing brought with the familiar feeling of resignation. I don't think it made me any uneasier because the mind will only accept so much stress and I had reached my absolute maximum some weeks earlier. It was nonetheless, an unpleasant notion on behalf of the Iraqi Army. Some of Saddam's troops had apparently been ordered to shoot from behind the white flag of surrender, we were told. We were also told that they had developed a habit of shooting from behind women and children. Such a practice was unpleasant, even by the standards of war and these are usually quite low.

I wasn't sure exactly where the truth lay in the matter. From the Iraqi point of view, it not only provided the obvious ploy but also prevented any Iraqis from surrendering, as this requires trust on both parties. To administer the surrender of troops would be difficult enough but this new twist rendered it nigh on impossible and the Iraqis wouldn't dare surrender, for fear of being shot. If this was the case, then it was nothing short of a brilliant piece of military strategy on the part of the Iraqis.

On the other hand, it gave the Americans license to shoot at surrendering troops and the implication of such treachery also further soiled the reputation of the Iraqi regime. It was difficult to see where this episode had originated. It may well have been based on the truth, or it might have developed from a cover story, devised by members of coalition forces, who had mistakenly fired upon surrendering troops.

This supposition I do not base on any fact presented but simply on a basic evaluation of the psyche of the combat soldier. It can be difficult to judge, in the chaos that is armed combat, exactly who should be shot and who not. I felt that perhaps some stressed, tired and scared individuals had found difficulty with this and perhaps had to explain their actions to someone. Would these soldiers, faced with possible murder charges over an easily justifiable killing, necessarily tell the truth? I doubted it. It seemed that, there and then the truth was an irrelevance but then, it always has been in times of war. Maybe it came down from the hierarchy who didn't want the hassle and expense of more prisoners of war. Plenty of motivation for dishonesty on both sides, it seemed. In fact, overall, there were far too many shades of grey in this conflict and I was becoming confused as to exactly what I agreed and disagreed with.

Something I definitely disagreed with was an occurrence, which took place around midday. It was, for all intents and purposes, none of my business. Maybe if I hadn't been aware of it, it would never have mattered so much to me. As it was, this was the act, which tipped me well and truly over the edge. To that point, my mind had, intermittently, strayed towards thoughts of an escape route but if I hadn't seen someone else taking one, I would never have tried myself.

Not for the first time in recent weeks, I was taken by surprise. True enough, it seemed as though the worst of the war was behind us. The Americans had entered Baghdad, despite "Information" to the contrary and the main thrust of the invasion was slowing. The war wasn't quite over but it was beginning to calm down, to an extent. Even so, I was surprised to find that they were sending someone home. This one man was being allowed to leave the war-zone, simply because he was leaving the Army. I wasn't sure if he had completed twenty-two years service or he had just come to his senses but the truth of it was that this man was being allowed home and I wasn't. This man, who was part of the unit, who had a role at the unit and who was needed by the unit, was being sent home. This man, who was in permanent employment with the Army and was until that point, financially dependant upon the Army was being allowed to leave. His box was well and truly ticked, it seemed.

I, however, was staying. I had no job within the unit and they openly admitted that there was no manning requirement for me. I wasn't (or hadn't been) dependant upon the Army to pay my mortgage and I certainly wasn't a willing volunteer, yet I was staying. It wasn't because they needed me. They actually needed the man who was being sent home. It was simply the system, which stipulated that I should be there and he shouldn't. As ever, there was no room for judgement, or logical reasoning. They were quite prepared to be a man short in one area and hold on to a surplus in another, purely because the system stated that this should be the case.

To me, it came as a surprise that anyone was allowed home at all. Until that point, I had been told that people weren't even being allowed home to attend the funerals of their nearest and dearest and knew of one individual who had accepted this without question. It was certainly a surprise that, right out of the blue, they were allowing someone home and if they could allow him to go, then I saw no reason why I should stay.

I hadn't participated in one trade-related activity for weeks and the grounds for my recall had been my trade capacity, nothing else. I was forced into being a soldier but the man they sent home surely had far greater soldiering knowledge and experience than I did. There was no logical reason for me to stay. I spoke with several people on the matter, to assess if I had simply lost the plot but it seemed I hadn't. They all agreed that I was right and yet it seemed there was little I could do about it. It seemed that, yet again stupidity had won the day in the British Army.

I had little time to ponder my view in the matter as we were told, in the usual abrupt and very sudden manner, that we were leaving for pastures invariably Browner. I tried to summon some enthusiasm from somewhere but I was struggling to find any. We needed to rush in order get all of our equipment packed for the move, despite the fact that we were almost certain to be waiting for at least a couple of hours before we set off. My problem was that I didn't want to go there and similarly, I didn't want to stay where I was.

Making excuses for my feelings was easy. I disagreed with the war before it began. I disagreed with my call-up and I disagreed with the way it had been handled and my treatment since. Furthermore, I had no military career to protect and no incentive to perform to anything like the best of my abilities. Nonetheless, my once robust state of mind was beginning to crumble into the Iraqi dust. The simple point of my enforced presence in Iraq was driving me in a different direction to the entirety of the war effort and this wasn't a good situation. If only they could have kept me busy. If only they needed me at all.

With or without my drive and ambition, we eventually set off for our next destination. Unlike all of our previous stop-offs, this new location was to be something distinctively different. We were going to Basra airport. The city had been secured, to an extent, two days earlier and we were moving in to occupy our little corner of it. The one thing I was pleased about was that I knew that there were thousands of British troops already there. This would be a position of relative safety.

We arrived at the airport to find that it was even more secure than we had expected. There was a high and solid perimeter fence on all sides, which may not stop armour but would certainly give away any attempt to arrive on the quiet. The nicety of it was that our position was nearly a kilometre inside the fence, which was good because it meant that we were only at risk of attack from rocket-propelled grenades, which were known to be largely inaccurate and from sniper fire, which hadn't been common in that area. The place was almost comfortable, relatively speaking.

Unsurprisingly, although there were facilities such as running water, inside the airport, we never got a look in. There is a pecking order in the Army and usually the serious combat regiments have first pick over everything. Their senior officers are generally first to lay their grubby mitts on a few little trophies and to bag the prime real estate positions. An artillery regiment comes well down the order and we personnel attached to the Artillery, well we don't usually get considered at all.

Not that this was a particular concern of mine. I didn't care about running water, or the war or anything other than how the hell I was going to get out of Iraq. It wasn't just a case that I had had enough. It was that I believed I had no duty to stay there and that I should have had a right to go home. The first night at Basra airport was when I first thought of desertion. It seemed a little tricky, as I had to get back to Kuwait first, which meant travelling through Iraq for a good few miles. Such was my soldiering ability that I would have surely got lost and died of dehydration, somewhere in the desert, if I managed to avoid getting shot. I am quite confident that I could get home un-aided from anywhere in Europe but this place was different. This was a prison without walls.

The prison mentality seemed to be the theme of the evening as the Optronics section made an impressively manful effort at digging a huge trench. As the Section Artificer pointed out, it was hard work but not as hard as trying to dig one with your bare hands when Artillery shells are landing all around. We needed little motivation as we grafted on into the night with pick and shovel swinging. At around two o'clock in the morning, we agreed that the hole was sufficiently large and deep to afford us all some sort of protection and decided to give our aching bodies some rest.

There wasn't much chance of sleep that night though. There were tanks driving all over the area, sometimes stopping to fire, sometimes just thundering straight past. The Patriot missile battery did their best to match the noise, though God only knows what they were firing at. Each thundering blast brought about a vague consciousness and an instinctive grab for the respirator pouch, which was always close at hand, as the mind constantly raced from sleep to awakened panic and then back to sleep within a minute. The dogs were quiet in comparison but we knew they were still around. I wondered if they'd been deafened by the noise.

# CHAPTER 26; ENOUGH IS ENOUGH.

THE MORNING CAME, seemingly minutes after the evening. It wasn't welcomed by me. The short bout of unconsciousness had afforded me a fairly convincing dream of home. This wasn't my first and these had started to happen more and more often. Opening my eyes, I awoke back into the nightmare. I wasn't in the best of moods and didn't feel particularly like co-operating or following orders, not least when they were nonsensical, which seemed to include the majority. The step by step, textbook method of soldiering employed by the Royal Electrical and Mechanical Engineers was a poor substitute for genuine soldiering ability and it was grating on the nerves of a very tired and frustrated man.

The Scandinavian, my immediate superior, quite rightly took exception to my attitude and made his feelings known in an abrupt and forthright manner. He was completely correct in his actions but he was bollocking a man who just didn't belong in the Army anymore. I wasn't an asset to the cause and I wasn't prepared to try to be. It wasn't my cause and it never had been. I'd stopped trying to motivate myself because this cause wasn't worth the effort and I didn't owe anything to my country. As unfortunate as it was on the people around me, I'd run out of steam and, although I'm sure I did have plenty to offer, I wasn't offering it anymore.

I felt that there was a debt owed here alright. Rightly or wrongly, I felt that my country perhaps owed me a little slice of human rights, with a sprinkling of common decency. Apparently, we pay taxes in Britain to afford a standard of living for everyone and I felt that this ought to include me. I wanted my life back and I was going to get it. It's been said by a great number, for many years that no one ever beats the Army system but the only motivation I could find, was to have a go.

I apologised to the Scandinavian and to all others present. They were all decent men who deserved better than I'd given them. I did feel that I'd let them down but it wasn't fair on them to have me around any longer and I wasn't going to cause them any further problems. I explained that it would be better for all parties if I left. There was no anger and no resentment on a personal level. They all just agreed that I was right to try because I felt so strongly about it. The Artificer suggested that beating the system would be difficult. I asked what other options I had.

I went to speak with the OC. He had always been a reasonable man and in truth, wasn't responsible for much of the stupidity. I knew he would listen to me but then, I didn't see any other option for him. I wasn't aggressive or impolite. I had no complaint against the man. I had a genuine complaint against the government, against Tony Blair and against the Army in general but not him.

"Sir, I don't want to be an arsehole but I've got a problem and in five minutes time, you'll probably think I'm an arsehole." Was how I began, to which, he was all ears. "I've got a real problem with this war and I genuinely believe that I really shouldn't be here. I disagree with the reasoning behind the war and I disagree with almost every order I've been given. I find it difficult to respect the authority of people who are senior to me and I've become reluctant to follow orders. I just think that the whole thing is an absolute load of shit and that I should never have been involved in the first place.

I knew when I signed up for the Army that I could get called up as a reservist after I left but at that time, the reservist's role wasn't what it is now. As you know, that was re-negotiated after I joined. I left the Army because I was spending far too much time on overseas tours and this is my third in four years. Everyone in the Army is supposed to get two years off between tours but I've not even had that and I'm not even in the Army. I got stung when I was in and now I'm being punished again after I've got out.

I have been bullied into coming here because my only other options were to accept the punishments the Army had lined up for me had I refused to come. I turned up at RTMC when I had to and got sent out here, which was a bit of a shock but you know, as well as I do, I haven't got a job here. The unit doesn't need me. You know yourself that you never needed anyone from my particular trade group and you never asked for anyone. This unit sent a man home yesterday who did have a role and a specific job within the unit. I don't see the justification for keeping me here. In plain logical terms, all I am here is another mouth to feed, which is just a waste of taxpayer's money. I have got a job to go to at home and all I want to do is to go home and work for a living and I'm being denied that right because of a contract I signed seven years ago, the nature of which, the Army has re-negotiated without my consent, not that they needed it.

I can't do anything about it. The Army have got me over a barrel and there's nothing I can do. I accept that but unfortunately you can take a horse to water but you can't make it drink. There is absolutely no point in me being here. In fact I am detrimental to the cause. There are young lads who come to me complaining about how bad it is in the Army and how much they want to leave. I don't offer them any discouragement. I think it is crap. I left for the same reason. I'm not helping anyone here and it's not doing me any good either. I can accept that the stupid, shitty pathetic system, which everyone adheres to states that I've got to stay but there's no point in you keeping me here. You would benefit from getting rid of me sir and I'm asking you how this can be done."

In truth, he looked a little stunned by my argument. I knew from his face that he couldn't bring himself to disagree with me in any way. I was right and I knew it and now he knew it. I didn't know what was coming next but I knew that I'd managed to turn an important cog in the wheel. I left the OC, with him having promised he would give the matter some thought for a while and get back to me. I had no reason to disbelieve him.

I returned to the Optronics section and explained my chosen course of action. It wasn't a normal thing for soldiers to do but it made sense to me and I didn't really consider myself a soldier anyway. No one knew what might happen to me but it was quite obvious that something was going to. I found time for a cup of tea whilst I turned it over in my mind. There wasn't much else to do other than thinking. I'd tested the system. All I could do was sit around and wait for the system to respond.

It wasn't long before I got my short and very sharp answer. One Pip arrived and informed me that I needed to pack all of my kit as I was leaving the unit. I asked where. He didn't know. I was confused but it seemed that I was on my way somewhere. Apparently, I had ten minutes. This didn't seem like long but most of my kit was always packed anyway. It seemed that the powers that be within the unit didn't approve of someone such as me voicing their opinion but then, the rigid Army system doesn't allow for creative thinking in the ranks. It never has. I feared I had managed to make matters worse for myself, though I had earlier suspected that that was impossible.

One Pip tried to convince me that I ought to change my mind and stay at the unit. He said that I was an asset to the cause in that I could help and advise the "Less switched on members of the unit". I replied that I had been recalled as a Lance-Corporal Electronics Technician, which is what I represented on paper, not a solution to the problems caused by government enforced tick-box training methods and an "All welcome" recruitment policy. I said that in my current state of mind, I wouldn't be an asset to anyone, as I couldn't possibly work for the British Army any longer because I disagreed with everything it did and everything it stood for. That was the first time in my life I have ever been genuinely able to say that I was ashamed to be British.

It was also the first time in my life that I had refused to serve the Army. There had been a great many tasks, which I'd reluctantly completed but I had never flatly refused to serve. I had always had a healthy respect for authority and generally done everything asked of me. It was a line I hadn't crossed before and it pushed me into uncertain territory. I packed the rest of my kit and said the briefest of goodbyes to the people who had come to be friends. These men, who I had let down badly, bore me no malice, nor I them. I knew that I was partly indebted to them for my physical well being but that had very suddenly become a thing of the past.

The Regimental Quartermaster told me to get into the back of the Land Rover. Ordinarily, I would have been in the front but he made it clear that I was to be treated like shit on his boot. I had no personal grievance with him but it seemed he wasn't prepared to tolerate my little spat and I was due to receive some kind of punishment for my troubles. It has been the way with the British Army for years to punish people who complain or show reluctance to abide by the system.

In this instance, I had to concede that the system was all they had and my problems couldn't be allowed to jeopardise that. For the unit, it was better that I was removed straight away. It didn't matter to them where I went, as long as I was away from the unit. It was curious to me though, that they went about it in such an unpleasant fashion, when it had been my suggestion all along. There was little I could do other than to get into the back of the Land Rover, which was already packed with kit and attempt to make myself comfortable.

The vehicle set off, driven by someone I hadn't seen before, following the quartermaster's vehicle to a destination I hadn't been informed about. I knew this wasn't standard practice, which was a cause of concern because that meant anything could happen. We travelled for five minutes or so before stopping for the Quartermaster to pick up someone else I hadn't seen previously, an Artillery officer, no less. I was surprised when he came over and spoke to me directly but apparently I was suddenly his problem.

"Corporal Jones?" He asked.

"Sir." I confirmed.

"Right, you'll be following the Quartermaster's vehicle. You're coming with me." He stated.

"Where to Sir?" I asked, trying not to sound too agitated.

"We're going to get you a flight home." He replied.

If I hadn't already been slumped in the back of the vehicle, I would have fallen over with shock. I couldn't believe that the net result of telling the Army where to get off was going to get me exactly what I wanted. I didn't want to count any un-hatched chickens but he sounded sure of himself and they had agreed that they had no use for me, so why not? I did find it sadly ironic that in all my years of slogging my guts out for the Army, all I got was more work and more duties and when I refused, it seemed I would be rewarded. I only hoped that the system agreed.

## CHAPTER 27; A REMARKABLY DIFFERENT WAR.

I FOUND THAT my new temporary home was to be with the Clerks, assisting them with their duties (whatever they were) until my flight was due. I wasn't quite sure when that would be but I was told that it would definitely be within a week, because someone had passed through the same process only a day before. At that point, a week suddenly seemed like a long time but my mind was filled with hope that somehow, the Army had managed to make a common sense decision about the necessity of my presence in Iraq.

The unit concurred, as it had from the outset, that there was no manning requirement for someone of my former trade group and that it would be in everyone's best interests if I were sent home. A little voice in my mind kept reminding me that I had never had such good fortune with the armed forces before but then I had never refused to serve either. Uncertain territory yes, but surely, whether I would face punitive action or not, there was no point in keeping a man who refused to serve.

My duty, I later found, until my flight came through, was to consist of helping the Clerks out with a few clerical duties, a bit of hard labour and helping to sort out the mail. I was quite pleased with this situation because I saw the mail as the one worthwhile job in theatre, as it is absolutely crucial to morale and morale is a difficult thing to maintain. We were also some way back from anything like front line action. This was the tranquil world of the rear echelon.

I immediately took on board that the Clerks had experienced a completely different environment from us. I noticed that their efforts were mainly concentrated towards performing their duties, rather than trying to act like the soldiers they weren't. There simply wasn't the stress and tension that I'd been used to. In bluntest terms, the Clerks didn't give a toss about the war. They were completely relaxed about it. None of them seemed to be as closely attached to their respirator as I was either.

I managed to find myself some kind of sleeping position in a corner of their tent and it seemed that they had plenty of spare rations, so life could have been a lot worse. I also noticed, there and then, that I stank. Compared to everyone else at the front line, I was ordinarily smelly but compared to the Clerks, who regularly had the time and the facilities for showers and washing clothes, I was absolutely howling. It wasn't just my body either. My clothes just weren't as clean as theirs. I simply hadn't been able to keep myself as clean as these people and to me at least, it quickly became obvious.

Within a day or two, I'd settled into my new roles of postman and general dogsbody quite well. My morale was reasonably high and I'd managed to upgrade my personal hygiene standards to a more acceptable level. I'd even had a shower, which was surprisingly refreshing, after weeks of strip washing. I had relaxed enough to detach myself from my respirator pouch, which said something about the difference in conditions.

Sorting the mail meant we always got first pick of the newspapers, which were still a few days old but to us represented fresh news. There was a story about how American special-forces had rescued a surprisingly attractive blonde haired girl who had been taken prisoner of war a few days earlier. I wondered if she would have been rescued had she been pig-ugly, or had she been a man. To me, it seemed not but it did seem like a perfectly good opportunity to make a film, billed as "Based on a true story". I doubted it would be long before the sexed-up scripts and six-figure cash offers would be falling on her doormat.

Apparently, her convoy had been ambushed and she had single-handedly accounted for twenty-odd dead Iraqis, until such a point as she ran out of ammunition. Oddly, after killing who knows how many Iraqis, they decided to take her prisoner. Most soldiers, having engaged the enemy in such a fire-fight, tend not to be taken prisoner of war. They tend to die, however, it was stated, in black and white before me, that after killing so many Iraqis, the few she left alive had spared this young woman's life, for some odd reason. I wondered exactly which pieces of the page I was reading were true. Certainly, if it was true in its entirety, then it was the only genuine truth reported from the whole conflict. Perhaps I was becoming overly cynical in my appreciation of such matters.

After three or four days of assisting the Clerks with their donkey-work and sorting the mail, the senior warrant officer, known to most as the Wee Man, informed me that he was quite pleased with my work levels and that he was confused as to why the Quartermaster had informed him that I was a total wanker and that I wasn't to be given an easy time. I was equally confused, as I had never actually spoken to the Quartermaster or interacted with him in any way. Maybe he was a sound judge of character and just wanted to share his opinions. Maybe he resented my outburst of a few days earlier. I suspected the latter.

The Wee Man though, had been nothing if not pleasant towards me. In fact, it was fair to say that the Clerks were a sociable group and that I was probably more in tune with their approach to the war than anyone else's, as they just got on with the work, which needed doing, rather than finding ridiculous military-style tasks for everyone. It seemed so much more of a common sense world than the workshop, who were simply tradesmen masquerading as a fighting unit.

That morning brought with it some bad news. In fairness, I had half-expected it but having been reassured of the opposite several times, by a number of people, it came as a shock. I wasn't going to get a flight home. The British Army, having sent me out to Iraq, were going to find a use for me and I was going to have to wait there until they found me a job with another unit. They didn't know how long this would take but I was assured that there was no way I would be allowed home. After all, they said, I was an asset. I pointed out that I wasn't genuinely their asset to hang on to. As far as I was concerned, I should only ever have been their asset for as long as they needed me and it seemed that they never had, officially or otherwise.

My mind was reeling from the shock of having been promised a flight home then denied such a prize. It wasn't something I could take easily and I found the anger starting to simmer within. Until then, the relaxed and friendly atmosphere and the promise of a flight home had tempered my anger at the situation I was in but when it was taken away in such an abrupt manner, I began to wobble. I knew that I just couldn't sit around and wait to be re-deployed somewhere else in Iraq. I couldn't waste the time waiting and I couldn't waste the time getting out of whatever unit they sent me to. Having been assured that I was going home, I couldn't re-adjust my mind-set to accept staying for as long as the Army saw fit.

Apparently, most units in the area had already been asked if they needed someone of my trade and had replied negatively. There were a few more to be asked but if they all said no, then I would have to wait until something happened to someone at a particular unit and they requested a replacement. I was told that this wouldn't be long because people were being sent home all the time. I didn't appreciate the pun and informed them that this wouldn't be happening because I wasn't having any of it. It seemed that it was time to try the system again.

# CHAPTER 28; NOT QUITE INSANE.

THE FIELD HOSPITAL was a couple of miles walk away from the Clerk's tented HQ but even in the searing mid-morning heat, I could see the benefits of walking there alone. I needed time to gather my thoughts and to assess exactly what I was going to say before I got there. It seemed that the reasonable, sensible approach had got me nowhere, so it was time to take medical advice in the matter. After twenty-five minutes sweaty strolling, I arrived.

"I'd like to see the Psychiatrist please." I said at the reception desk in the front tent.

"Right, okay. What's it concerning?" Came the reply.

"It's concerning what would appear to be my mental health, or what bit of it I've got left." I stated.

"Okay, take a seat. He'll be here in a minute or two."

I took a seat on one of the benches at the front of the field hospital complex. The field hospital, which was no over-statement of its stature, was a huge complex of tents, all connected together and lined inside, to give the impression, at least from the inside that you were actually in a building. Certainly, it appeared that there was an impressively long corridor behind the reception tent. I wouldn't be venturing down there though.

The Psychiatrist appeared, a tall bald Captain, with a moustache and a fairly relaxed manner. He gestured for me to follow him back out of the reception area and into his little hut, which was a small, domed inflatable tent, just to the side of the reception area. Inside, it almost looked like a small, octagonal surgery, with windows and a desk. The desk wasn't inflatable.

He took some details from me and asked me a few formal questions before asking me to get down the nitty-gritty of my problem. I did nothing other than to tell him the truth. I hadn't lied to anyone about anything until that point and I wasn't about to start. Besides which, I genuinely had problems, not least containing my anger, which was threatening to boil over at any moment. I started from the beginning and took him right up to where we were, which seemed to be on the verge of madness. He listened, thought for a few seconds and then formulated a response.

"So, what you're telling me is, you were called up by the British Army, which you've already left because, it would seem to you at least, that they used and abused you, then on your return, after barely any training and being misled into thinking you were going to Germany, they flew you out here. You expected that, as you were called up under threat of prosecution, you would be needed out here and you were annoyed to find that you simply aren't and never have been. You feel that, in turning up at RTMC Chilwell, you did the decent and honest thing because you could have thrown the papers in the bin or lied at the medical or got out of it in other ways and you expected to be treated with the same decency by the Army, in return.

You disagreed with the war even before it started and you feel that you and indeed the rest of the country have been misled as to the reasons behind it by the government. You feel a lot of resentment towards the government and you don't wish to be representative of their political stance in any way. You feel that your life isn't valued by the Army, in as much as they genuinely don't care a toss what happens to you, as long as they have another bum on another seat and you are annoyed that the Army system doesn't allow for anyone to make a common sense judgement over whether you go home or stay here. You feel that, in keeping you here, the British Army and/or the British government are denying you your basic human rights and quite hypocritically, implying that this war is a human rights issue.

You are in fact, being kept here, completely against your will and for no sensible reason whatsoever, other than the Army system stipulating that you must stay and you feel that you owe nothing to your country as you have already served and left the Army with a glowing reference and generally done your bit. You now feel exceptionally frustrated and angry towards the powers that be within the Army because you are being kept from your life at home and you are achieving absolutely nothing out here because, as your unit has agreed, there is no need for you to be in this operational theatre at all.

You are becoming increasingly desperate to return home and are now reluctant to co-operate with the Army's wishes. You have reached a point where you are genuinely considering desertion or inflicting some kind of injury upon yourself, in order to facilitate a return home. You feel that you have been bullied by the system and now you have drawn the line and you have said that if you are not allowed to leave theatre, you will take matters into your own hands. You have said that you are no longer able to behave reasonably towards such an unreasonable regime. You also say that, as a result of all this, you are exceptionally angry, though this anger would not appear to be directed at anyone within this vicinity. Does that about sum up your state of mind?"

"Well, I'd say that's pretty much it. I don't genuinely think that I'll injure myself or anyone else but there is a realistic possibility that I will do a bunk if I'm not sent home. This is nothing other than a complete waste of my life. My time's valuable to me, if no one else and if I'm doing nothing other than sitting on my arse here, then I might as well go home because I'm actually quite an important figure in the life I've left behind. As for the anger, I don't feel any anger towards you or anyone around here because the unit accept that they don't need me and they didn't ask for me anyway. They're perfectly happy for me to go."

"So, your anger is aimed more towards the higher authorities that have caused your situation, like the American and British governments and whoever has stipulated that you can't go home."

"Yeah. It keeps me awake at night but I don't find that I'm snapping at people or wanting to hit anyone. I haven't refused to do anything I've been asked out here because I don't see the point in that. If someone wants me to do something then it's fair enough, I'll do it. It's on a larger scale that I don't wish to co-operate."

"You're happy to work whilst you're here, as long you're allowed to go home then, is that it?"

"I'm not one for being idle, it just makes the days go slower. I like to be busy. In fact that's part of the problem. I just think that I've been nothing but reasonable, honest and decent about the whole thing and the Army have been exactly the opposite. They're treating me now as though I'm actually a regular soldier again, as though I'm theirs and they'll keep me as long as they want me but they don't pay my mortgage. I don't owe them anything and for the Army as a whole, I am reluctant to do anything more."

"Okay, well listening to you, I can tell you that firstly, we both know that you're perfectly sane and very lucid about the whole thing. You aren't depressed but you do have the potential to be a problem because the root cause of your anger is your presence here. Your anger won't go away until you are allowed to leave because you feel so strongly about it. The problem with your anger is that it is a very logically centred anger, in as much as you're angry towards people like the Prime Minister or whoever made the decision to call you up, rather than anyone you can see or meet. Unfortunately, it means that you are unlikely to release this anger properly because you won't come face to face with its focal point.

It doesn't matter whether I agree with your point of view because it is how you feel and you're very angry about it. As it happens, I can see that you're a common sense man, from a common sense world and this grates with you and has done for some time. I would say that if you weren't at least a little bit upset by what the Army has done to you then you would probably have to come and speak to someone like me for a reality check.

I can't pronounce you to be mentally ill, or depressed because you aren't.

If you had tried to convince me that you were, even falsely, then it might have got you home eventually but it isn't worth the stigma against your name as far as future employment is concerned. I will however, recommend that you are sent home on the earliest available flight because, as I said, although you aren't a problem now, potentially, you could be. Logically speaking, as you haven't got a job in theatre and you are so reluctant to stay here, they ought to send you home. As you say, all you're doing here is costing the taxpayer money, whilst you could be back in England, earning a living and contributing to society. To keep you out here would simply be to break you just for the sake of proving how high and mighty the Army are and with you not actually being in the Army, I don't see that you're theirs to break."

"No but then I shouldn't have been sent here in the first place."

"No, quite obviously not but all I can do is recommend that in my professional medical opinion, you should be removed from theatre, at the earliest available opportunity. I'll put it in writing and then there's no debate about it and they should process your flight application. I don't see why not, although, as you know, if there is a complete wanker in the system somewhere, then this bit of paper won't get you anywhere, even with my qualified, professional opinion scrawled on it."

"I suppose we'll have to wait and see." I concluded.

I thanked him for his help, not just because he had tried to grant my wish but because he had genuinely listened to my point of view and given me a common sense answer in return. Amidst all the blatant stupidity of the Army, my conversation with the Psychiatrist was a breath of sweet-smelling, common sense filled fresh-air and it tempered my anger, to a degree.

I returned to the Clerk's tent and submitted my medically approved application for a flight home. Everyone appeared hopeful that this approach would bear fruit. Certainly, it added substantial weight to my cause. Although I was hopeful of success, in the back of my mind, I knew that my presence within the Army had consistently brought about ill fortune. I knew I couldn't trust them to look after my best interests. They never had.

The Regimental Admin Officer informed me that if I went home in a couple of days, I would be returning just a day too soon to qualify for a medal. Apparently, Royal recognition of our efforts was something we should all aspire to. I have never viewed the royal family as aspirational figures. I may be nothing more than a working-man, with a capable mind but my ancestry doesn't consist of murderers, thieves, cowards and tyrants. Neither do I present an entirely false public image. At that time, I couldn't see any worth in any medal and I wasn't concerned with acquiring one. The public façade of people like Prince Philip, wearing a couple of dozen medals on his chest, de-values any achievement by anyone else, in any case. He, like me, is nobody's hero. He, like me, didn't deserve a medal.

## CHAPTER 29; PART OF THE PUBLIC IMAGE.

AS A SPARE man, who was waiting for a flight, or for further employment, I was to be found tasks, to prevent inactivity. I didn't mind this too much and was only too willing to pitch in, so when I was tasked to drive the unit press officer around until my flight came through, it didn't seem like too much of a hardship and I was almost enthusiastic at the prospect of influencing the world's perception of current events, in my own little way. At least I wouldn't be sat idle.

We were to meet the press team and escort them and the Commanding Officer of the regiment, up to Basra Airport. I was surprised to be going back to what had, six days earlier, represented a front line position. I was also surprised to return to the place, which I had been forcibly ejected from, six days earlier. At least it gave me an opportunity to catch up with people who, by that point, seemed like friends from distant memory.

The press team were there to film the guns firing on a position to the North of Basra. It was unclear exactly what the position was and it was a surprise to me that the press hadn't already shot endless footage of the guns firing. After all, guns firing looked pretty much the same, wherever they were. It was whatever they were aiming at that was made to look different.

They did their bit of asking stupid questions and suggesting angles to shoot from. They also did the habitual press thing of attempting to conduct the war solely for media purposes. The Commanding Officer informed them that they couldn't just fire a few shells, just for the camera. It was apparent that the press were at least mentally detached from the war and had the singular interest of finding out snippets of information, rather than actually achieving an appreciation for the situation they were in.

It was also plain to see that the Second in Command of the regiment was enjoying his few minutes of fame and doing his best to pander to the needs of the press. Maintaining the public image seemed to be one of the main aims of the entire war. To me, it all just seemed like a tissue of lies, deliberately designed to mislead the public into thinking the Armed forces were happily functioning splendidly in fighting the forces of evil, which of course, they were (Pause for thought).

As ever, the press were shielded from the reality of the war and a more acceptable face was presented to them, with one of the gun crews cheerfully posing for photos. It was all good, clean, wholesome fun, at least on the outside. I made no effort to speak with the press, as I have never been one to suffer fools gladly and their behaviour, in such an environment, was a cause of irritation to me and, as such, I avoided them for the rest of the day.

We were due to return to our original location, which was about an hour's drive, before dark. We had to return before dark because Iraq is a very unforgiving and confusing place by night. There are no streetlights, or even streets, for that matter, and navigation becomes almost impossible. It is also a point that there are various holes in the dirt-track roads and sometimes large, oil filled ditches running alongside. These are the hazards presented by driving through Iraq at night, without lights. Further to those hazards, there was still a war going on, apparently and there had been numerous reports of rocket-propelled grenade attacks along that particular stretch of road.

At an hour and a half before dusk, I reminded the press officer, who was chatting with friends over a coffee, that we ought to be leaving sooner, rather than later, as I had never driven that route before and didn't fancy taking a wrong turn in the dark. My suggestion was greeted with the usual response that a senior officer would give to a junior non-commissioned officer; blatant disregard. It is a situation, which annoys me tremendously that opinions in the Army only ever carry as much weight as the rank of the people who give them. The intelligence and sense behind the opinion is of little importance. I didn't want to be stuck in the middle of Iraq at night. I saw no need to risk this situation and I simply wished to avoid it. I also didn't want to have to say; "I told you so".

So it was then, that when we set off, much later than we should have and in fading light, that we found the landscape looked a little different in the dark and were soon unable to locate our destination. We knew where it was; to within mile or so but there were no signposts, no gateposts and no distinguishing features visible in the dark. I tried not to show my annoyance at the situation we'd been placed in, entirely because of the stupidity and arrogance of one man. I also tried not to show my annoyance at the fact that he'd left his GPS behind and didn't have a map. In my own mind, I exonerated myself from any blame because I had acted entirely under his instruction all day and had never professed to know the way.

After driving for an hour and a half, I finally managed to persuade the useless bastard that we were lost and that we had to turn around and head back to the Airport. The Airport had a metalled road leading to it and a fence surrounding it and a few lights around it. An airport was easier to find in the dark than a featureless piece of desert, without markings. It seemed that this common sense suggestion didn't sit quite so well with the old war-dog, who insisted that we would find it and that he simply never accepted defeat, never.

As there were only two of us in the vicinity, I toyed with the idea of simply punching him a few times until he saw my point of view but he had a pistol, which was far easier to use in a Land-Rover than a rifle, so violence wasn't a constructive option. I was beginning to tire of thinking constructively, however. The arrogant twat was grinding me down.

Eventually, after three or four u-turns and experiencing several large holes in the road and worryingly motionless minutes of quiet contemplation, I managed to persuade him that I might well have a point and that there were several reports of Militia activity in the area and that we shouldn't be there, as his insistence on finding the invisible destination was endangering our lives. Just as I reached the very end of my tether, the great man gave in and accepted defeat, though I doubt it was really for the first time. All that was left to do was to find our way back to the Airport, in the dark, without headlights and hopefully, without being ambushed, tortured or killed. At this time, the prospect of a senseless death, caused entirely by one man's lack of judgement, did little to lift my spirits.

I was reasonably tense, as I had been driving to his instructions in the dark for far too long. He was very tense because he was lost and hadn't got a clue how to get back to the Airport. He knew it was entirely of his own doing because he knew I had made wiser suggestions than the course of action taken in several instances. He was also a fairly tense and excitable individual, who was made more so because my once polite and respectful tone had changed slightly and he knew of my visit to the psychiatrist. He also knew that I didn't suffer fools gladly because I had already given him an explanation for my bluntness.

Driving along the road was difficult enough, without his constant suggestions (orders) that I should drive more to the left, or more to the right, or slower, or in another direction. "No sir, not that direction because I now have one wheel hanging over the edge of a thirty foot drop. Thanks to your instructions" I replied, with deliberate calmness as I suddenly brought the vehicle to a halt, on the edge of a cliff. I didn't hear his response. All I could hear was my heart thumping and the blood rushing around my ears. After a few peaceful seconds, I suggested that I knew how to (fucking) drive (you cunt) Sir. I reversed the vehicle and we set off again in almost blissful silence.

The road was lumpy and bumpy but we were on the right track. I deduced this by the fact that we had caught up with a Land Rover in front, which could only be heading to one place, we hoped. We followed it along the track for a mile or so before I noticed some movement off to the right of the track. The vehicle in front didn't offer to stop and it appeared that they hadn't noticed the vague signs of movement, heading in their direction.

A second later and I realised exactly what I was looking at and that an armoured vehicle, which was about to cross our track, might well not be able to see a blacked-out Land-Rover passing before it. I ignored the voice urging me to carry on at speed. Contravening all rules on tactical practice, I flashed my headlights. Amid a cloud of dust and noise, the armoured vehicle stopped abruptly, about five feet away from the Land Rover we were following. I waved acknowledgement as we drove past but I doubt that they saw that either. It was, after all, a very dark night and visibility was very poor. Twenty five tonnes of armoured vehicle running into a land-rover would have hurt quite I bit, I thought.

We arrived back at the Airport, much to the surprise of the people we'd left a couple of hours or so earlier. The press officer spoke of our situation, without apportioning blame in the matter and requested a place to sleep for himself and his driver. At that precise moment, I resented being referred to as some kind of servant by a man who was vastly mentally inferior to me. That resentment passed into annoyance as the press officer was fed and watered, while I was told that it was now my duty to patrol around the perimeter fence, without refreshment. That'll be the class system again. That'll be the hierarchy, removed from reality, constantly wondering why people are leaving the Army in droves. Quite how I managed to be put forward for duty was still a bit of a surprise, however.

Apparently, they were a man short, so after my first cigarette in four years and a quick slurp of stolen tea, I was off patrolling around the fence, with some young man, who I hadn't been previously acquainted with. It wasn't much of a duty, in truth. Whether it was mine to do or not, it was only a case of strolling around, checking the security of the fence and that there were no unwanted visitors. Had there been any such unwanted visitors then it would have been an entirely different duty. As it was, it was quiet, at least on the ground.

The sudden deafening roar, which shattered the peace, belonged to an FA18 Hornet, my more interested friend informed me. I didn't feel particularly threatened by this and after the initial surge of noise, was quite calm as it passed overhead…until it dropped it's payload right in the middle of five thousand British troops. The explosion was huge and the bang was deafening. It was quite numbing to experience such an explosion at such close proximity. In fact, it was almost a pleasure to witness and feel something so powerful, so vividly but I never quite allowed myself to enjoy the moment.

The air escaping from the blast area caused a gale force wind, which almost blew us over on its own. My eyes were slightly shocked by the brightness and there was bright green after-burn to be had on either retina. It was a second or two before my mind began to function on normal levels, rather than just sit there, in awe of the incident we'd just witnessed. My hands automatically pulled the respirator onto my face, as the Gas shout went up. The entire area suddenly rose from its' slumber in a curious panic but all they were greeted with was the sound of the aircraft, rapidly disappearing into the distance.

Dazed, confused and more than slightly surprised, we righted ourselves from the finger-nail deep trenches we'd instantly dug for ourselves and sat, breathing deeply into the respirator filter, which were hissing a little more loudly than normal, perhaps due to a slightly increased heart-rate. I remember thinking it odd, that all we would do at that time was simply stand up and carry on strolling around. In truth, there wasn't much else we could do but I couldn't help but be amazed at how similar the place was before and after this incident. It made a bit of a crater but most of the sand, having been thrown a hundred feet in the air; just fell back into the hole.

I had heard stories of American spec missiles, which were so ferocious that, if dropped on sand, they would create so much heat that the sand would be instantly fused into a large lake of glass. In fact, this appeared not to be the case and the sand appeared to have done exactly what you would expect sand to do. There wasn't much of an effect and it hadn't hit anyone, so it seemed to be of little consequence. I think my teeth felt a little loose from the vibrations and my ears were ringing to the point of deafness, unless I was just surprised by the immediate silence.

The odd comparison, I found myself thinking, was that if such a thing had happened over an inhabited area of England, then it would have been a major international incident, that lived in the memory for years. Here, it was simply something that happened before our eyes. It was just part of the day's events. I didn't even pause to think that we were walking in that direction and would have been under the exact spot, a couple of minutes later. I did have a slight feeling that perhaps, I'd been lucky that day. It was the first time in a while that my mind had considered such a notion.

The official verdict of this incident never reached the newspapers. My learned friend assured me that this certainly was the aircraft type he'd stated and I knew full well that there were no Iraqi aircraft flying in the area yet I found it difficult to believe that we had just been bombed, and very impressively bombed at that, by one of our own coalition. There was never any official verdict on this incident. It wasn't noted and officially, it didn't happen. Officially, my ears were still ringing two days later from an incident, which never actually took place.

It seemed very calm after that brief piece of noise and movement, everyone was under-cover, wearing respirators, some calm, and some worried. I found myself, as usual, to be quite calm. I knew that if this was a chemical warhead then I might be in for a few problems, like my face falling off or the immediate lack of bowel control or whatever but I also knew that it was too late to do anything about it. In my own mind, I also supposed that just because the Americans stated officially that they hadn't used chemical warheads, it didn't mean that this was true. Nagging doubts aplenty. Perhaps I was a little paranoid. Perhaps I was right in believing no-one. I entertained both possibilities.

The delay between the explosion and the all clear was no longer than a fairly cautious one. The threat was quickly cleared and I deduced, from that, that the warhead had been of a conventional type. At least, I felt fine an hour later, when I was finally able to get my head down. Due to my exhausted state, I did actually sleep that night, for the first time in days and awoke, the following morning, feeling surprisingly refreshed.

## CHAPTER 30; JUST A NORMAL MORNING.

BREAKFAST WITH THE Regimental Sergeant Major would be a rarity for any junior-ranking soldier but for a man who had left the Army two years previously and so recently and forcibly ejected from the regiment upon his return, it seemed most odd that I would be chatting to him over my boil in the bag slop. It was also a surprise that he knew exactly who I was and was well aware of my situation. He even understood my point of view, which as RSM, he didn't need to tell me.

It isn't the RSM's job to be popular and most of them are among the least popular people at any unit. It's probably fair to say that a popular RSM isn't a good one and this one had been spoken of in a negative light on several occasions. The odd thing was, as much as I hated the Army and everything about it, I found the RSM to be amongst the more sensible people I came across. He seemed genuinely down to earth and could quite easily understand anyone's reasons for leaving the Army. It has never been within the remit of any RSM I have ever known to show understanding. He wasn't even worried about having breakfast with a man who had been thrown out of the unit and welcomed my point of view. Apparently, it takes all sorts, he said. I'm sure he was able to resume the role as and when he needed to but for a few minutes, I saw the man behind it and was pleasantly surprised.

After that surprisingly refreshing conversation, we were summoned to escort the press team on urgent business. Ever the sceptic, I guessed that this would have been something trivial. Nonetheless, I was soon involved and we were soon on our way to somewhere deep in the back of dusty beyond. If I liked surprises, I might have enjoyed my time in Iraq a little more, I supposed. As the story went, something major had been discovered when one of the gun batteries had moved into a new location earlier that morning.

We arrived at the front of what appeared to be a reasonably modern-looking (By Iraqi standards) warehouse, which appeared to have been built and then instantly allowed to fall into a state of disrepair over the next few years. Its contents were a mystery but we were told that only two people had set foot in the building before it had been closed, awaiting press attention. We weren't told exactly what it was and the press team seemed strangely reluctant to open the door and take a look inside. I thought this unusual by their normally inquisitive standards but couldn't see the point of dwelling on it as I pulled at the door and stepped inside.

Initially, I was greeted by the sight of a huge stack of oblong-shaped plywood boxes. From the doorway, it certainly appeared that this was nothing more on the inside, than the normal warehouse it appeared to be on the outside. It was then that I noticed that one of the cluster of white Hessian sacks over to my left was open. All I could see protruding from it was the sole of a shoe, or, more accurately, the sole of a military boot. There were a lot of these sacks, I would guess at somewhere between two and three hundred. Some of them had been placed in the plywood coffins, which were open on the floor but most appeared to be waiting to be placed into the huge pile of coffins before me.

Surprisingly for a building full of human remains, there was little in the way of a smell. Looking further inside one of the bags showed that the remains inside, complete with the equipment their previous owner had died with, had finished decomposing years previously. I could only speculate as to the age of the remains but whatever terrible fate these men had suffered, had been suffered probably more than a decade before, at my estimation.

Although it seemed that the majority of these men had met with a very unfortunate end, I felt sure that it hadn't happened within that particular building. If it had, it hadn't been carried out by the same people, who looked to be half way through attempting to give a reasonable burial to all the remains, before all the latest trouble started. It appeared that when these men had been killed, their remains had either been ignored, or deliberately treated with disrespect by the people who killed them.

I didn't feel ill, or scared at the thought of the things I saw, I simply felt a close affinity with the men whose remains lay in bags before me. From the bags, which were mostly open, it became clear that these were all soldiers. These were probably all just unimportant men, who had been dragged into some conflict, be it the Iran/Iraq war or the previous gulf war and killed for the sake of killing. These men weren't afforded one ounce of respect or human decency in the last minutes of their lives and were probably slaughtered casually by people who claimed to act in the name of their own God. These seemingly unimportant bags of bones had been, in previous years, my precise opposite numbers. They had been men like me, men who didn't matter to the people in charge, men who were expendable.

One of the press team began to rummage around in one of the bags. I told him to stop. I explained that in such a country, bacteria peculiar to the strain we regularly come into contact with is plentiful, particularly in such a place as this. He didn't know any better and he probably wouldn't have understood my point of view that we had no right to inspect these people, or to treat them like a commodity. Whatever violence they had suffered and however disrespectfully their remains had been treated previously, they weren't ours to tamper with. As it was, he did as he was told which was good because otherwise, I might have found him a sack of his own.

I was genuinely saddened by the predicament of these long dead soldiers because it seemed to me that for their lack of significance, these men might well have been allowed to live, without any adverse consequence but whether they had asked for mercy or not, it hadn't been forthcoming. I don't believe that we had discovered the site of these atrocities but we had found these remains before they were buried. I do believe that someone was attempting to bury these people, as there were certainly enough coffins. I only hope it was out of respect, by an entirely separate party to those who killed them.

In the building next door, there were files, which obviously related to the remains in the bags. Some contained pictures but these weren't of the passport variety. These were old and faded snaps of men who had been terribly beaten, or shot in the face. One appeared to have suffered acid burns. It wasn't a pleasant collection and not one I would wish to see again, though I doubt I will forget those faces in a hurry. These images were kept for someone's pleasure, or perhaps for pride in their achievement. I suppose we're all good at something.

The press did their thing of filming the senior officer giving his verdict and taking a few pictures of the less pleasant artefacts, then asking lots of silly and irrelevant questions. They took notes all the time and listened to the suggestion that we had found evidence of Saddam's evil regime. It was evidence of evil certainly and it was probably indirectly linked to Saddam but this evil had taken place years before and was no indication of the current political climate in Iraq. Nonetheless, the press took their notes, as they listened to the "informed" opinions of Army officers.

The building was sealed, pending war-crimes investigations, immediately after our little tour. I hoped they came to the same conclusion as I did, that this was a crime long since passed and of no relevance to this particular conflict. I also hoped that the news would reflect a similar picture but it didn't seem likely. The press were too hungry for headlines vilifying Saddam Hussein to stop and think about reality.

A quick surprise came to my ears that very afternoon. I wasn't expecting the news to break quite so fast but there were reports of the discovery of an execution centre, crammed with dead bodies on the outskirts of Basra. This year's calendar was on the wall of the purpose-built torture chambers in the building next to where the bodies were discovered. It was certainly evidence of the brutality of Saddam's evil regime, the report said.

I hadn't seen anything, which vaguely resembled a purpose-built torture chamber, though I am no expert in construction engineering, or torture, for that matter. I didn't notice this year's calendar anywhere either and to me, it looked like we had simply discovered someone's attempts to give a proper burial to some bodies, rather than the discovery of an evil still in practice but the radio report gave a wholeheartedly different impression. I couldn't believe my ears but I was further amazed when someone sitting next to me chose to believe the impression given over the radio, rather than my impression of the place.

Maybe not everyone needed to be as sceptical as myself and some chose to believe the radio but, to my knowledge, no one from the radio station had even set foot in Iraq at that point, yet they seemed to be the authoritative voice in the matter. The press had obviously just written whatever they were told and the radio had reported similarly, based upon their information. It seemed that the use of sensible judgement was forbidden at all times and the public version was straying ever further from the truth, just as it was directed to do.

# CHAPTER 31; AN INCREDIBLY UNFAIR DEAL.

TIME WAS PASSING ever slower for me, as I bided my time, as usefully as I could, whilst waiting for a flight. I was assured that my application was going through and that there were no problems and that although, as ever with the Army, it was a slow process and I must of course be patient, I would be allowed to go home. Five days had passed since I saw the Psychiatrist, which made ten, in total since I was first promised a flight home.

I had made best efforts to keep myself busy, despite my reluctance to involve myself with anything military. It seemed that I had acquired a reputation as something of a useful man to have around, as I had been called upon to repair a few air-conditioning units and service a few generators and been only too willing to help. These duties weren't too far removed from the actual reason I was re-called though, so I had to be careful not to prove myself too useful, as the Chief Clerk had already begun to joke about them not being able to manage without me when I went. The joke didn't sit too well with me and I assured him that I was perfectly capable of proving myself to be entirely worthless to the cause, should the need arise. Neither of us found much humour in this quip.

That day brought with it a rush of anticipation. It wasn't anything to do with my eagerly anticipated flight home but news that we were no longer to be on radio silence. The conflict had subsided, almost down to peacekeeping levels and this meant an end to tactical operations, not that the clerks had practiced much of this anyway. It also meant that I would be allowed to make a phone-call home, for the first time in almost five weeks.

Although the public statement, issued by the ministry of defence, said that every soldier is allowed twenty minutes to phone home every week, this understandably doesn't apply during radio silence. Most of the units involved in the fighting were on radio silence for a good length of time during the conflict, which meant that the people who were most at risk had the least contact with their families, those who's plight the Army didn't consider.

I was sure that it hadn't been a pleasant time for the missus, who was probably more worried than most, due to the sudden and secretive nature of my deployment and complete lack of knowledge of all matters military. There were perfectly sensible reasons for being on radio silence and I didn't wish to challenge these. I simply resented the lies, which the Army told the newspapers about everyone contacting their families on a regular basis. I had been assured, however, that the regiment had been in regular contact with her, as it had with all the wives, to inform her, as best they could, of the goings on in Iraq. Perhaps I should have had more faith in the Army to do this but I simply doubted their ability to get even this simple task right.

After waiting for as long as I could possibly stand for the phone to charge itself up, I yielded to my overwhelming inner pressures and decide to call the missus. I felt strangely nervous about speaking to her, probably because, a man who had become used to the sounds of gunfire and explosions might just find speaking to a civilian woman on the other side of the world a little odd, I reasoned, though I wasn't really sure. I dialled the number and waited for a response. A voice from what felt like a former life answered.

"Hello." She said.

"It's me." I replied, slightly un-informatively.

"Who?"

"You remember, that bloke you used to live with before I got dragged into this stupid mess."

She sounded quite shocked. Maybe from watching too much television, or just from hopeful expectation, I had expected the phone to snatched up in anticipation of my call. Life wasn't about to imitate art here, it seemed but I would have at least expected her to recognise my voice. It was a very deflating feeling and in truth, it was probably a good job I was on the other side of the world because, although I have never acted violently towards a woman, I found this disappointment alarmingly hard to take, crushing even and was instantly agitated.

"Sorry, I didn't recognise your voice." Came the overly apologetic reply.

"Who were you expecting?" Was my far from reasonable demand.

"Well, I've been having a few phone calls because I'm trying to sell your car, so I've been expecting calls about that. We haven't got any money because they've messed your pay up and we haven't been paid a penny and you said that if there were any financial problems, then I was to sell your car." She explained, pacifying me in one sense, antagonising me in another.

"Have you tried ringing them?" I asked, more than a little surprised at the tangent the conversation was taking.

"Yeah but they won't discuss it with me because I'm not your wife, so you've got to sort it out from that end, they tell me."

"Fantastic. I don't think I'll be able to. Anyway, how's things? Are you alright?" I asked, awkwardly.

"Well, not brilliant, no. Your mum's been looking after me. She's tried to sort your wages out too but they just keep lying to her and fobbing her off. How is it out there?"

"Shit, not to be too polite about it. I've never known such a pathetic load of shit in all my life. I've been trying to get a flight home for nearly a fortnight but there's no one around who's got the guts or the decency to actually make a decision to send home a man who they accept they don't need. I don't know when I'll get back to you but I've managed to remove myself from the place where most of the bother is at least, so there's not much to worry about. It's just a case of when these bunch of twats let me go home really."

The rest of the conversation was punctuated with awkward silences. In hindsight, it wasn't surprising because we were living in different worlds but at the time, I felt disappointed, like I'd just spoken to a distant stranger, when I expected overwhelming familiarity. It wasn't pleasant but at least my family would know that I was alive and well. I was freshly angered about my commitment to the Army though. It seemed that they were only too keen to make sure I upheld my end of the deal but it seemed that in their commitment to me, the contract, as ever, wasn't worth the paper it was printed on.

The problem was, it was their contract and their terms and they still weren't able to keep to it. In my eyes, any official duty I had to the Army was a thing of the past because my contract must surely be null and void because they had breached it so many times. The missus hadn't received so much as a phone-call or a sheet of paper from the Army explaining my whereabouts or the nature of my employment either. It's an odd situation to find yourself constantly seething, at no-one in particular.

There wasn't much I could do from my end. All I could really do was hope it got sorted out, which it clearly wouldn't. It seemed unfair that the Army should jeopardise my financial stability in such a way. It also seemed unfair that they would refuse to discuss it with the missus, as we had joint bank accounts and she had access to every penny I have ever had, or hadn't, in this case. She would also soon have access to the debts, which would quickly pile up, but no access to the money I was due, with which to pay them. All I could produce was anger and more anger. I didn't think I could be made any more desperate, or any more frustrated.

That particular cause for annoyance came only a few minutes before the next, which was when the announcement was made about the flights. I was told that I wouldn't be allowed home because it would send out the wrong message to other people in my position. Apparently, if I was allowed home, then other people might notice and get itchy feet and they couldn't allow that to happen because it would destroy the morale of the men left in theatre. Unfortunately, they had already allowed it to happen. They had allowed it to happen to me and it had destroyed my morale completely.

I was gutted. It seemed that there was no end to the unreasonable measures, which the Army would take, or maybe it was just that I was unlucky. The thing about it that really did piss me off was that "people in my position" surely meant other people who weren't needed by their units. I couldn't see the point of keeping them. Surely the units were the best people to decide who they kept and who left and surely the people who weren't needed by the units should be allowed to leave.

Further to that bombshell, was the next, which went; if I was allowed back early, I was still on a six-month call-up, on the Queen's authority, which meant that they wouldn't revoke it and that I would have to be re-deployed to another operational theatre, probably Kosovo. The reason I was given for this was that the Army was vastly undermanned and that the regular soldiers would get upset at the amount of time they were having to spend overseas and a lot of them would decide to leave the Army due to this and they couldn't allow that to happen, could they? Except that they already had and unsurprisingly, it had happened to me. Maybe I was just unlucky.

My thoughts began to turn once again towards desertion. The Army, for all their arrogance, their bullying and their unfair tactics were deserving of having to explain to the general public why a reservist had deserted. The problem was, I just couldn't. The fact that I had recently found out that I had no means of buying a flight ticket, should I even make it to an airport, may have been a contributory factor in my decision but the simple truth was, I couldn't face the consequences.

It wouldn't just affect me either. I would have been thrown in a military prison, I would guess for a period of around six months, during which, I would have lost my home, my job and any future prospects of employment and it wasn't fair to inflict that situation on the missus because she had been put through enough by the Army already. The fact was that the Army had won because I didn't have any other option than to accept the shit they threw in my direction and it had been more than plentiful. As everyone told me, you can't beat the system.

The reason for not being able to beat the system is simple. The system has the authority of the Queen behind it and between the Queen and myself were rank upon rank of people who were afraid to make a decision, or challenge the system in any way. The system survives due to the spineless nature of the people who administer it and not because it is some all-conquering and infallible masterpiece.

As it is, the unchallengeable Royal Decree over armed forces employment has been in force since well before Britain came under democratic rule. This unchallengeable authority was instilled by the monarch of the time, who ruled the entirety Britain by Royal dictatorship. The army is run under the Queen's regulations and although I doubt she personally has much input, its authority is in her name and carries the same authority, which is unchallengeable by any entity in the land, even to this day. This same authority dates back to a time when women could be legally raped, if the King decreed it necessary. It is the authority of a dictatorship regime and as such, is entirely at odds with democracy. George W Bush, when dictating to the world his intention to invade Iraq, stated that a dictatorship regime is not acceptable in today's world. I'm sure the irony wouldn't be lost on a man of such obvious wit.

The Army argue that the same system of carrying out orders to the letter, no matter how remote their origin, has won countless wars and battles over the years. I personally believe that these wars were won in spite of this system. I believe that this system has caused the unnecessary deaths of thousands and possibly millions of British servicemen. This system blindly ordered men to go "Over the top" and to their certain deaths in the trench-warfare of the First-world-war. The same system sent thousands of men to their deaths in Arnhem, during an unnecessarily risky invasion, which was necessary only to enhance Montgomery's ego, during the Second-world-war (despite this operation being pronounced a resolute success by Montgomery, it was widely regarded as a senseless waste of life by all involved parties). This system of simply winning battles by weight of numbers has been used as a poor substitute for tactical expertise by the British Army for centuries and it hasn't got any better, even though human rights laws have evolved dramatically in that time. To this day and into the future, the British Army will maintain that the only way to fight a war is to send as many men in as possible.

The problem is that the system cannot last forever because the manpower just isn't available. To call up the reserves and the TA as an invasion force shows just how desperately short of men the Army are, particularly when you consider that the next step beyond calling up the reserve is to source people from the general populace and that surely wouldn't go down too well. The British Army simply isn't capable of winning wars by weight of numbers anymore because the numbers aren't there to be called upon. It wasn't the first time that my mind had come to the conclusion that the British Army's system of operation is outdated. Unfortunately, due to the Army's strict policy of not listening to the thinkers in the ranks, they won't find this out for quite while yet.

My poor, bitter, defeated mind began to turn even further sour. My thoughts scoured the depths of the unfairness of it all before I came to a bizarre comparison. There were Iraqi soldiers deserting the Iraqi army by the dozen, every single day. They were deserting in protest to the regime in which they were employed. If these men managed to get on a flight to England, then they would have a right to claim political asylum, as they were fleeing from certain peril and would be entitled to live at the British Taxpayer's (Including me, despite my lack of pay) expense for life, as Britain apparently has a duty to offer salvation to such people, even though it cannot afford decent health or education services for it's existing population.

Conversely, if I managed to get on the same flight, upon landing, I would be instantly locked up and punished in the strictest way possible, by way of making an example of me and would have to live at the taxpayer's expense rather than return to my job, where I can earn a decent living and contribute to the economy, because I apparently had a duty to stay in Iraq. I didn't think it was possible to have less in the way of human rights than a deserting Iraqi soldier but somehow, I had managed it.

Although I had no job and the unit had said I could go home, confirming that I was never required in any official capacity, plus the fact that they hadn't paid me a single penny, I was officially bound by duty to stay in Iraq until the Army told me to go home, or sent me to Kosovo. That is how sensible the Army's decision-making system is, when the decision is made so remotely. It was costing the British taxpayer a thousand pounds per week (albeit mostly in accrued debt) to keep me there and a flight home would be four hundred pounds. None of this carried any weight because officially, the Queen had decreed that I should stay in Iraq. I felt sure that if anyone had had the guts to put forward my case to anyone in any sort of authority then I would have gone home well before that day. Sadly, that just wasn't the case. Sadly, the system wasn't even being challenged, nevermind beaten.

## CHAPTER 32; ADDING INSULT TO INJURY.

A WEEK HAD passed since the Army dropped the bombshell that I was to remain in their employment for a little, or maybe a lot longer than initially anticipated. I had tried, several times, in vain, to sort out the mess that was my wages. I had spoken to my mother, a senior financial executive at Royal Mail, no less, about my wages and she sounded distinctly unimpressed. According to her, if the Army's pay department were a civilian organisation, they would all have been sacked.

Still, it was nice to hear that she was as gentle as ever. I had attempted to persuade anyone who might listen that I should be sent home but I had achieved absolutely nothing. I was still sorting the mail and managing the odd repair job but basically, I was wasting my life away at her majesty's pleasure. Over that wasted week, my raging anger had subsided into a mild, resigned depression. Maybe I was close to being broken by the Army, despite the Psychiatrist confirming that I wasn't theirs to break. I didn't have much left in the tank.

I had been to see the Padre, he being the regimental vicar, in the hope that he might just have something up his sleeve. He didn't. The official statement was that if I wanted to go home early, then I would have to be declared mentally ill and I'd already explored that scenario. I did, however, manage to clarify the exact meaning of that over-used and clichéd term, a conscientious objector. When I explained my case and put across my views, which had been in place long before the conflict began, he agreed that in my case, the suggestion was true. I had been a conscientious objector all the time. I just hadn't known it exactly. I knew that in the future, should the government make further unreasonable demands on my personage, I would simply have to declare myself as such and face the consequences but it seemed that this time, it was too late. Still, it didn't hurt to talk, I suppose.

My father had appealed to the Reserves centre at Chilwell for my return on the grounds that the workload had picked up and that if I wasn't required in theatre, I was certainly required at work. It seemed like a perfectly reasonable request and whether it was entirely genuine, or probably linked to the fact that he wanted his son back, it fell on unreasonable ears and was turned down. It was fair to say that my father was similarly unimpressed with the "Bunch of fucking useless twats", as he put it. It was also fair to say that, for the first time in my life, advice given to me by my father had proved to be wrong. I think the guilt over that hit him hard. His view, that "a contract is a contract" had changed slightly, since he realised the Army's view that "Your contract terms are enforceable by law, ours aren't enforceable at all". Doubtless, he was suffering too.

The missus had managed to sell my car, for a little less than it was worth but in desperation, she admitted that she took the first offer. She had also taken a weekend job to earn a little extra cash, so it appeared that we might hang onto the house until my wages were eventually sorted out, whenever that might be. Needless to say, she hadn't exactly been bowled over by the considerate nature and professionalism of the Army either but it would be most unlike her to speak ill of the incompetent. Besides which, having had no contact with them whatsoever, she didn't even know who to speak ill of.

The newspapers bore the story of a small Iraqi boy, who had had both arms blown off, when the building he was in had been hit by an American missile. Apparently, as he was now in top-class care and was going for treatment by a top surgeon, he was a symbol of hope for the entire world to see. It signifies the true nature of the conflict when a child, horribly maimed by an invading nation, is seen as a symbol of hope. To me, it just looked like a symbol of the lack of control, which the Americans exercised over the obvious power they had. It was a shame for the boy. I wonder if, when all the sympathy and public gratification died down, he remembered why everyone was being so nice to him. Perhaps they told him to be grateful.

In another newspaper, there was a published list, mostly with photographs, of the British soldiers who died in the conflict. It seemed to be an attempt to give honour to the cause, which they had all fought for. I couldn't see any honour in the cause. It was most certainly right to honour their deaths. They deserved it and I would never question that, nor would I wish to dishonour the memory of anyone who died in the conflict but to me at least, it didn't seem like they died for world peace, or anything like it. It seemed to me like they died in service of a country that simply didn't deserve such commitment. It seemed to me that their lives were wasted in pursuit of something entirely different.

Basra had been all but completely liberated, by the time I'd arrived at the Airport, for the first time and within a few days, with the fall of Baghdad, the Americans had declared that Iraq had been liberated entirely. Perhaps this was an optimistic view. The conflict had gone very well, better than they had hoped, it seemed and things were beginning to settle down nicely into peacekeeping operations. It seemed that this was the time for decisions to be made on a governmental level and this was where the coalition went in slightly different directions.

The war-mongering Americans, having vented a little anger in Iraq, were beginning to seek their next victim. It appeared that, suddenly, Syria had a long history of terrorist intent and were known sympathisers of Osama Bin Laden. Apparently they had chemical weapons too. The plot was beginning to sound increasingly familiar and it sounded like motivation was building to attack them as well. I supposed that, as the Americans had travelled a long way and spent a lot of money, they thought that they might as well do a bit more for world peace before going home. Doubtless they saw it as a bit like a day-trip to France, when you're on holiday in the south of England.

I got the distinct impression, from George Bush's incredibly simplistic terminology, that he believed that this whole conflict was something similar to a film. It sounded to me like he thought that the good guys should win, no matter what and somehow, he gave the impression that they were the good guys. Perhaps someone ought to have told him that the huge, powerful empires, with the biggest, scariest weapons, who wantonly invade defenceless countries in search of resources, are usually portrayed as the bad guys. I wondered exactly how the coalition had been portrayed in the Iraqi press.

Conversely, the evil empire's sleazy cohorts (Namely the right honourable UK Plc) decided that it was time for a few cost cutting measures. With the conflict seeming to have been concluded in such a concise manner, it was decided that certain portions of the funding already allocated to the conflict, would be withdrawn, with immediate effect. The announcement was greeted with dismay by the Army's senior figures but from my point of view, it could only be seen as a bonus. It meant that the funding was no longer available for the extra manpower. The units would have to find the extra costs form their own budgets. Suddenly, regardless of whether the TA and reservists were actually needed, they weren't officially needed anymore. The prospect of being laid off has never been so appealing.

The absolute joy at my impending redundancy was tempered by the knowledge that, although we were to be sent home as soon as possible, due to funding difficulties, this would take time. As ever with the Army, the beaurocratic wheels turned very slowly. Nonetheless, it meant that I wouldn't be staying in Iraq, twiddling my thumbs for months on end, nor sent to Kosovo. It meant that I would, sooner, rather than later, be able to get back home and get on with my life. It also meant that I would be able to sort out my incredibly messy financial situation too. It was nice to see that the high-handed authority of the Army only extended as far as the government stipulated. Unsurprisingly, in this issue, they did precisely as they were told.

The downside of this, for some of my colleagues at least, was that it confirmed my point of view from the beginning. Some of the TA had been called up and were enthusiastic at being able to represent their country in such a way. They genuinely believed that their country needed them and that they simply couldn't have done it without them. To be sent home, just as indiscriminately as we were sent out, confirmed the fact that the decisions were made irrespective of manning needs, or the individuals concerned. To some, this seemed to de-value their efforts considerably. I had already de-valued mine. I knew I was an unneeded part, in a badly operated machine, which was being used for a dishonest purpose.

From there, there was little I could do but wait and carry on with my mail-sorting duties. There was nothing to argue anymore. There was no point to make. It was simply a case of sitting and waiting for the painfully slow, painfully disorganised "organisation" to get its arse in gear. This was a different kind of frustration. This was like being a young child, desperately waiting for Christmas, not really knowing what to do with the available time.

It was a long, sweaty and uneventful week later before any kind of decision was made. This was a welcome rarity and the news that the Army had a plan, albeit a vague one, to send home all TA and reservists represented all my birthdays and Christmases at once. It was going to take three to four weeks and we were well down the pecking order in flight preferences but we were, at least, on the agenda. We were going to be allowed home. Until then, all that remained to do was to sit around, drink tea and read four-day-old newspapers. Perhaps we may find ourselves the odd moment to complain, you never know.

The newspapers were surprised to find that the man whose helmet had apparently saved his life was having a bit of a joke. No one in theatre was surprised; everyone knew that it wouldn't stand up to anything bigger than an air-rifle pellet. They were equally surprised to find that the Americans were already planning to make a film about Jessica Lynch, the blonde-haired, all American girl, who was taken prisoner of war. I doubt it will be too graphic about the time she was held captive, as the American public probably wouldn't find such things acceptable, at least, not where one of their own is concerned. I'd say it would probably centre on the heroism bit, the bit which is clearly and so obviously false.

The British public, at least according to the newspaper, wanted a victory parade for our troops, to celebrate the liberation of Iraq. I personally could not think of anything that any member of the armed forces would want less. Ninety-nine percent of military personnel absolutely despise parades and they are even less popular amongst the ex-military people. I wouldn't have appreciated being forced to turn up to that one, after being allowed to return to civilian life. I think I would have found a way out of it, if asked.

In those few days, the general boredom of peace-keeping operations had set in quite firmly. Some delightful people, after the rush of the conflict, had become so bored with it all they had taken to shooting the wild dogs, simply because they were a nuisance. One in particular was wounded by a poor shot and took hours to die, howling all the time. No one seemed to care that the poor animal was obviously in agony. No one tried to end its' suffering. It was plain to see that people who have been fired up with such aggression cannot easily relax back into normal life afterwards, although the Army prides itself in its' counselling and support in such matters. These people had been made abnormal by their experiences and surroundings.

A brief abortive attempt at feeding everyone centrally, via the cook's tent, had brought with it an exceptionally widespread dose of diarrhoea and sickness. One by one, everyone had been taken ill with it but I hadn't developed any of the symptoms until after everyone else. After mocking people for days over their dodgy guts, it was my turn for a dose and it hit me for six. I've had bad guts and stomach upsets from being in foreign places before but nothing to rival this. This was like something from another world.

I couldn't keep anything down at all and my already heavily depleted underwear collection was beginning to suffer. At least I hadn't soiled the sleeping bag though, which, at the time, seemed like my only small mercy. What I referred to simply as a dose of the shits, turned out to be severe enough for me to be placed in isolation at the field hospital, with a drip in the back of my hand for a day or two, due to my body shutting down because of dehydration. I wasn't well, to say the least.

Unsurprisingly, the Army didn't offer to reimburse me for my ruined underwear.

My memories of these few days are hazy; suffice to say, I can remember complaining that the air-conditioning in the field hospital was broken and that the heat was making me feel worse, only to be told that it was officially working perfectly. I remember disputing this, pointing out that the temperature on the thermometer read forty eight degrees Celsius. I can even remember, despite shit trailing out of me like snail's trail, offering to repair it, for the good of all who were suffering due to the stifling heat, only to be told that, "No, the commanding officer says it's working perfectly". For the record, I never laid eyes on him. He never came into that part of the hospital. Quite how he knew it was working perfectly, I'll never know. I just remember saying; "Look at the flaming thermometer. I couldn't get it that hot, even if I crammed it up my arse". It seemed that the stupidity was even encroaching into my illness.

# CHAPTER 33; THE DAWN OF A FALSE HORIZON.

NEWS OF MY flight came as a complete surprise to me. The missus had managed to send me information about my interview for the Police. It had taken it's time coming around and my application was proving a slow process but it seemed that, having waited months, this interview, the next stage of my application, was a couple of weeks too early. If I missed the interview, it would have put my application back approximately six months, which I felt I didn't deserve.

I had spoken to the officer in charge of allocating flights a week or two earlier and put forward my concerns and although the Army unsurprisingly refused to budge an inch in the matter, he did tell me that if there were any last minute cancellations, for whatever reason, I would be the first to know. I had thanked him for his consideration but never genuinely expected a positive result from it.

Suddenly, I had four hours to pack all of my kit and equipment, bundle up my weapon for the flight and get myself up the Quartermaster's department, where I would be taken by bus back into Kuwait and flown home. I didn't care who had cancelled, or why and I certainly wasn't concerned that I didn't have much time to get ready. I would have willingly left everything I owned in theatre just to get home and have my life back at last. In fact I did have a ceremonial burning of a few items, just to commemorate the end of my "Glittering" military career.

My arrival at the Quartermaster's department was greeted with jeers from old friends from the workshops, who were just passing but as I was in good time, there were no problems with missing the flight. For a brief minute or two, I had to explain why I wasn't the person on the list and that I was his replacement but, to my surprise, this went smoothly enough and I was soon on my way. I was actually on my way to find a way of wasting a bit more time because the bus wasn't picking us up from there for another five hours. Army timing is certainly a funny thing.

I had plenty of time to say my heartfelt goodbyes all of the people from the workshop who had helped me through a difficult situation, so I set off for the Optronics section to offer my thanks and to see if there was anything I might be able to send out to them out after I got home. Sure enough, they requested alcohol and more alcohol and made sure I didn't leave theatre with anything that might have proved valuable to them and I was only too willing to oblige.

After a while, I left and set off back towards the Quartermaster's area, to see if there had been any changes in the flight situation. On my way there, I bumped into One Pip, who had recently become Two Pip and seemed to have grown up a little, at least in Army terms. He had become very frustrated with the Army system and expressed his deepest regret that he wasn't able to get a flight home for my mate Dave, whose wife was expecting their baby at any time. Needless to say, he was surprised to find out that I had managed to get one.

To me, it didn't seem right that the Army could be so inflexible as to not allow someone home for the birth of their child but as ever with the system, it was already set in stone and was seemingly unchallengeable. I instantly offered to give up my seat. I did it with great reluctance and no shortage of disappointment and he took me up on my offer instantly and ran away back to the control point, to make enquiries.

I followed, maybe a little dazed and unsure of exactly whether I really had said it. In truth, I was absolutely gutted at the prospect of not going home but I knew it was right. I would get a flight, within a week or two, which meant that I would miss my interview. Nonetheless, it was only right that a man should be allowed home for the birth of his child. So, doubtless, I was doing the right thing, even if it was at great personal cost.

The unfortunate problem was that the inflexible military machine simply didn't see it that way. As far as they were concerned, it was too late and I had only just made it at the last minute as it was. As was the norm, they refused to budge an inch, which meant that I would get back for something which was very important to me but as a consequence, Dave wouldn't get back for something considerably more important to him. Two-Pip was understandably angry. It seemed that the system had recently become a cause of annoyance for him too and he reluctantly conceded that there wasn't a way around it. It had taken him a while but he had eventually seen the Army system for all it was worth and suddenly, he seemed to have far greater potential in life. Suddenly, he believed in something other than the military handbook. "Told you it was wank, didn't I?"

With mixed emotions, I accepted that I was to be flown home. True enough, I was absolutely delighted at the prospect of going home but it was tempered by the knowledge of what might have been, or really, what should have been. It felt strange that after weeks of telling the Army that they were wrong to keep me there, I suddenly felt that they were wrong to insist on flying me home. This time though, it wasn't too difficult to accept and in all honesty, my mind soon wandered from Dave's predicament.

I found my way over to the Quartermaster's area and upon finding that nothing had changed; I sat down, behind a stack of pallets, near the Quartermaster's tent and began to think about my return home. My previous uncomfortable phone-calls to the missus had given way to relaxed conversation and I had started to get to know her again. Other than my messy financial situation (I still hadn't been paid a single penny), my life was beginning to look rosy again and I was about to have my own personal moment to celebrate.

In one of my bags, I had kept a can of John Smith's Bitter. It had been there since Germany and I was saving it just for such a special moment. Alcohol wasn't allowed in theatre officially and although most would have tolerated it, I wouldn't have had to look far to find someone who wouldn't. Hidden from prying eyes, I cracked open the can and, assuring myself that no one was looking I began to drink. It seemed to take only seconds for the entire content of the can to find its' way into my stomach, such was my ravenous desire to consume what seemed like the most delicious beverage I had ever come across in my entire life. I was going home and I even had a drink to celebrate.

After the allotted time had elapsed, a time which had been taken up entirely by thoughts of home, the transport came to take us to where the buses would pick us up. Oddly, instead of the buses coming to fetch us, a couple of lorries took us down to where the buses would pick us up. Irritatingly enough, it was fifty yards from the clerk's area, where I had set off from nearly six hours earlier (after a four hour wait). This did little to dampen my spirits, however.

It was also near something else I had promised to do only on my last day in theatre, namely the Burger King and Pizza Hut lorries. Bizarrely, these had turned up a week earlier and promptly begun to serve their varieties of fast food. It seemed strange to me that the Army was unable to provide us with fresh, hygienic rations and the fast food chains were there, serving it up in vast quantities. Nonetheless, these were a popular addition to the facilities, or rather, the facility already in place.

I had been to the Burger king only once previously and vowed not to return until my departure. It had been a source of disappointment when I got the window and ordered my food. I had requested a Double Whopper with cheese meal and for a second, I felt like a free man, in charge of my own destiny. I hadn't been able to choose anything for weeks and had been eating whatever was supplied. For one second, I experienced a freedom of choice I'd forgotten the feel of. The reply came back that all they were serving was Single Whoppers and that was all I could have. Suddenly, my freedom of choice was gone. For all I knew I could have been back in the clothing store in the first few days of basic training, receiving whatever sizes were available. It was a very deflating moment.

With my departure now imminent, it was time to spend my last few dollars on a pizza, by way of a farewell meal. I queued, like everyone else on the flight did and handed over my last money, like everyone else on the flight did. Then, like everyone else on the flight did, I went and sat down on the floor and ate it, whilst waiting for the bus to turn up. It wouldn't be long; we were assured.

After devouring my pizza, my drink and a couple of the million or so flies, which were swarming around my food, I sat and waited for the bus, which would be along in a few minutes (This time, we were assured that it really would be along in a few minutes). As I didn't know anyone else on the flight, it was a nice time to reflect on my situation and the time I'd spent in Iraq. I relaxed and began to look upon Iraq as part of the past. Just as my mind was drifting, I saw him, out of the corner of my eye. It was Two-Pip and he was walking in my direction. I wasn't going to need three guesses to find out what the useless twat wanted.

He came to ask me if I would consider giving up my seat for Dave. He explained the situation to me but I already knew it. I wasn't listening to a word he said. He made some promises about getting me the first available flight home but it didn't matter and I didn't really listen anyway. There wasn't anything he could offer me and I'd stopped believing the Army's promises years ago. The one thing I did hear was that he couldn't force me to give up my seat and that I would have to do it voluntarily. It would have been so much easier earlier, before I had said goodbye to the place and started thinking about home, before I had called the missus to tell her the good news which she had been craving for a long time, before I got the taste for it.

Looking at the other people waiting for the bus, it was plain to see that these people weren't so desperate to get home. The people I had spoken to were people borrowed from other units, who were returning at their CO's request. It wasn't as important as my reason and went nowhere near Dave's. It was grossly unfair that not one of these people would be asked to give up their seat. A few of them had even mentioned that they would have rather stayed. That didn't matter though because they simply weren't in the frame. Whether it was fair or not, the Army system would only be able to cope with one person giving up their seat for Dave and that turned out to be me.

I had spent five weeks trying to get a flight home. I had shed blood, sweat, piss, tears and who knows what else in my efforts to get home and finally, I had been rewarded with the one thing I wanted above everything else, my most treasured possession in the world, a tick in the box marked "home". I had achieved my goal and I was going. I had even begun to celebrate in my mind about it. Two-Pip was trying to offer me incentives to stay but there was nothing I could have wanted.

He made it apparent that this move hadn't quite been properly approved and that Dave's passage home could only be achieved by slightly underhanded means, not condoned by the hierarchy but he felt it would work. For once, he seemed to be right. He said I had the choice and it was a simple one. I could get on my incredibly hard-earned flight, to the disapproval of a few people I would probably never see again and be free of Iraq and the British Army forever, or I could allow a friend and a thoroughly decent man to see the birth of his child. It was as simple as right or wrong and no incentives could ever influence my decision.

It was fair to say that after weeks of being forced to do things against my will, the opportunity to make a decision without the overriding control of the Army was a major concern to me but the plain and simple truth of it was, whatever the Army had done to me and however badly the government had let me down, I just couldn't do it to someone else. After all the effort I had put towards getting a flight home and the grief I felt at being forced to stay, I finally, willingly, volunteered to stay in Iraq. I had been numb with shock at some of the Army's decisions and now I was about to be numb with shock at one of my own. I was in a state of disbelief that my mind was capable of such decisions.

I shook Dave's hand, when he arrived, ten minutes later. I wished him well and hoped that the baby was healthy. I genuinely meant it and although I was agonisingly disappointed at my own decision, I knew that, in the fullness of time, I would come to live with it and probably be pleased that I had managed to do something worthwhile with my time in Iraq. The one consolation, I would suppose, is that if it hadn't been for all my effort to get home, then Dave wouldn't have made it home for the birth of his child. The system said I should have flown home and I finally managed to overturn their decision. Who says you can't beat the system?

Poker-faced bastard that I am, I didn't show any emotion. I didn't cry, or even say much at all. I didn't even mutter any disappointment. After all this time and effort, I'd somehow justified my presence in Iraq. I'd finally done something worthwhile with my time there. I'd finally volunteered. This, for me, came at a price though and inside, I was devastated. As a child, I'd always dreamt of winning the world cup final, which, for me, would have represented all my dreams come true. This unfortunate little boy had just lost, to the Germans, who won it with a dubious penalty.

# CHAPTER 34; CHANGING FORTUNES.

SO IT WAS that I was driven back to the workshops, in silence, by Two-Pip. I didn't have much to say, to him or anyone. I couldn't decide whether I was numb with shock, or boiling over with anger, at my constant unchanging misfortune with the Army. My head was spinning. My arrival back at the workshops caused a few raised eyebrows and more than a few jeers at the irony of the arrival of the "new volunteer".

The OC workshops, still a man with whom I had not had a crossed word, praised my attitude and acknowledged the difficulty in the decision I'd just made. I called the missus, for a minute or so, to explain the bad news and although disappointed, she acknowledged that mine was indeed a noble act. I didn't think so, personally. I thought I'd done what should be expected of decent people but then, I wasn't actually sent there by decent people. I think perhaps I'd simply risen above something, rather than sinking to their level. It's difficult to feel any sort of pride though, when all you can feel is disappointment.

The jeers and the abuse, which came my way, did benefit my state of mind though and the Scandinavian soon suggested we play a little golf, with the camel spiders that come out at dusk. Mine was a seven iron and the pitch and distance I achieved with the first of these horrible creatures was quite magnificent. It flew a full forty yards, which, I'm told, was a record. A cup of tea was thrust into my hand by way of celebration and suddenly, things didn't really seem ever so bad. "Fucking Hell, he doesn't wanna gan home now". Offered a Geordie voice. Not quite true, but the people around you are certainly important in these situations.

Another "person" arrived, being the Sergeant in charge of Guard duties for the day. He strolled straight up to me and told me, cheerfully enough, that it "Looked like I was on guard duty all night", as, unsurprisingly, they were a man short. Wearily, I felt a resignation within me and was about to simply accept this when a few voices spoke up on my behalf.

"Fuck off, you miserable cunt, you can't treat him like that after he's just given his fucking seat up on a flight home. It's not fucking right. Get someone else."

There were several sentiments of agreement and even a couple of volunteers to take my place; such was the strength of feeling over this issue. I was quite surprised at this and stood in silence. For once, I didn't have anything to offer. I wasn't even sure what I thought about it. I couldn't think about it but everyone had an opinion and it seemed that in their opinion, this man was a "cunt". It seemed that, although my luck had picked up exactly where it left off, this time, there was more than a little opposition.

"I couldn't really give a fuck. It's his tough shit, isn't it?" He said to the group.

He didn't say anything else about it after that, as the matter was officially closed. He got up off the floor and wiped the blood from the little cut above his eyebrow. He looked a little dazed. He stood up, looking a little confused at receiving what was apparently the last thing he expected.

"Sarge, you cannot just try to fucking hit people like that. It's fucking bullying, like" Said the Wise man from the North East.

It suddenly became clear to him exactly what the group of half-a-dozen ore more had officially seen and what that was, was one man trying to bully another due to his position of seniority, nothing more, nothing less. Everyone muttered their agreement.

"I think you'd best fuck off and find someone else for that duty like, unless you wanna get off your fucking arse and do something yourself for a change" Seemed to signify the end of the debate. The matter was now closed. The official and the actual were, as ever, poles apart but this time, the official verdict was to my benefit. For me, everyone's opinion (above) of this individual was pretty much spot on. Later that evening, I was asked discuss the incident with the OC workshops and, somewhat surprisingly, he fell in with everyone else.

I slept surprisingly well that night, my first as a volunteer within the unit. It seemed that with the end of my resistance, had gone the anger and the stress that I'd endured throughout my time in Iraq. For once, I declared myself at peace with the Army. True, they had inflicted and continued to inflict a great many wrongs upon me but I didn't feel like fighting over it anymore. I started to simply get on with it again, until I got my flight. The time started to pass more easily. Surely the next available flight wouldn't be long.

On that subject comes the last (and it definitely will be) of the Army's broken promises to me. Two-Pip, in his desperation to persuade me to let Dave go home, had promised to get me on the first available flight home. Conversely, four days then passed, with me going quietly about my business, almost cheerfully, even managing a guard duty, definitely not flying home though. I decided that maybe it was time to remind him of this promise, which I, of course, never asked him to make. I decided, after all my efforts, that it was time for one last throw of the dice.

"Sir" (rare that I felt the need to address him so) "A few days ago, when you were appealing to me to let Dave go home instead of me, you made me a promise, which I never asked you to make. It wasn't even a factor in my decision but nonetheless, you made it."

"What was that then?"

"You promised to put me on the first flight home. I never asked you to but you did. I've had hundreds of promises from this organisation and they've all been broken, without fail. Is this just another one?" I asked this question, genuinely offering him a way out. I knew he'd promised something he couldn't deliver anyway.

"Corporal Jones, sometimes, the first available flight doesn't always mean the very first available, you know."

"No, I don't know. First available, is first available. It's quite clear, just as it's quite clear that I've missed four flights already, since then. I wouldn't ask, only I've got a job interview in less than a week. I've got a life away from all this shit that I want to get back on with please."

"You'll just have to be patient"

"Why? You made a promise to me. You seemingly made it in good faith. You tell me to be patient but why should I believe that, when I obviously can't trust a word you say?"

"Well, I know I promised…"

"I know you did as well." I cut in

"Well, I'll try to get something sorted."

"I don't believe that either. One thing you'll need to learn in life, if you ever want to get anywhere, is to deliver what you promise. Otherwise, everyone will just think you're completely useless."

"I think everyone already does." He offered, a sentiment which suddenly disarmed me a little.

"Maybe not everyone, I don't know. Mine is a simple situation. I've got a life that I really need to get back to and the Army is depriving me of it. I don't want to sit on my arse here. I want to start moving forwards again. I'm not asking for much, am I?"

He concluded that I wasn't. In truth, I was surprised he listened. Maybe he learnt something. Maybe he was a better person for a bit of experience. Then again, given that I had to wait another two days, missing another two flights and that I only actually flew home when all the rest of the TA and reserves flew home, maybe he was just better at paying me lip-service than I thought. And there was me, wanting to go out on a high note. Oh fuck it.

# EPILOGUE.

I BEAR NO malice towards any person involved within this text. I accept the failings of individuals as simply being part of the whole predicament. Conversely, the skill, courage and good humour demonstrated by the many should never be forgotten and I, for one, never will. The good men got me through it. Three years on and I find that I look upon this experience as a lesson well learned, rather than an embittering experience. I know life can be very unfair. People and Organisations can be dishonest. The world can be a very dark and scary place, if you allow it to be.

I find myself wondering if my chosen course of conduct was correct. It felt correct at the time and it is that which will be measured. I would ask the reader to consider this notion, in hindsight of the conflict. What if every soldier had done the same? What if everyone had refused to take part in the conflict? Obviously there would be legal complications against the people involved but that aside, would the world not be a better place, had the armed forces refused to co-operate? I doubt if it would be any worse. It is not that I think that mine was a stand of great principle either. I think the title bears this out. Certainly, I'm not the man I always wanted to be.

No one will ever have me believe that the invasion was for the greater good of mankind. True there is an inquest over the reasoning behind it but then, will it ever reveal the truth? I doubt it. There are a great many truths I will never know. For the countless uninvolved people, there are even more. The truth, that which we all seek in our readings and viewings of news items, seldom comes to the fore. I only know this; a great number of lies have been told by all involved parties. If these organisations see fit to lie about their own conduct, then where does it end and for that matter, where did it start? Could our whole civilisation be founded upon lies? Maybe it's a question of perception.

To illustrate the point, I propose this; Over the years, the Americans have made a huge number of western films, in which the Native American (Pause and consider the term) is portrayed as the villain of the peace. Ironic then, that these were really the indigenous population, to the White settler's illegal immigrant. Still, a few doses of Colt 45 and the west was "won", apparently. These immigrants are perceived as the "good guys", simply because the only available media strongly suggests that is the case. Perhaps the Native Americans had a different take on the subject. Perhaps, if their views were given equal platform, the perception could change.

Likewise, the British are apparently renowned throughout the world for their honesty and sense of fair-play, or at least we believe we are. We do find it odd that most of Europe can't stand us though. Perhaps they see a different side to us, one that the British government cannot influence. Perhaps they regard us as the nation that invaded everywhere and stole all their resources in the past. Perhaps they just see us as the people who insist everyone else speaks our language. Perhaps they perceive us as the louts we often are, I'm ashamed to suggest. I wonder how our conduct in this particular matter was really perceived.

We won't know. Nor can we, but we can suppose this; if we, as a nation, have any doubts over the grounds for the invasion of Iraq, then all the other nations who flatly refused to take part will have much firmer views, perhaps backed by the information provided by their own governments. Maybe they won't know the truth either. Indeed, I doubt they ever could but they will have been presented with information to support their government's views (I think that this is sometimes referred to as "Spin") and their perception will certainly be different to ours. I would warrant that the rest of Europe has less to trouble their conscience than we do, in any case.

I do not find my own conscience troubled. In fact after shitting blood for four months, my toe-nails falling off due to malnutrition, a few sleepless nights due to a mild does of post-traumatic stress and the sun-damage to my skin caused by the refusal to issue sun-cream, I found that I am at peace with myself and with the world over this. I do not feel burdened by my experience, or my own actions. I am free of this and have put it well and truly behind me. Maybe I'm even a stronger person for it.

There is one who should feel so burdened by his actions, however and it is this time that I choose to name the only person I will ever name. Surname of L*****bury. He didn't even go to the Gulf, yet still I find myself loathing this man. Having named him, I will not describe his conduct though, suffice to say, that he was and most probably still is, a complete and utter wanker. I dare say that their will be a knowing few who will confirm this. I shall not comment further on him.

Incidentally, three weeks after my arrival at home, I did actually receive my wages paid in full, in a settlement, which was substantially larger than Long John Silver's benefit claim. Oddly enough though, my wife also received the one communication from the Army, telling her that I was alive and well and somewhere in the Middle-East. It would have been a useful gesture, had it not arrived three days after I had returned home, safe and well but then, this just about sums up the Army's approach to looking after the families of their mobilised personnel, doesn't it?

I can even forgive the over-zealous store-man, who upon my return to Chilwell, demanded the clothes I was standing up in be returned (I didn't) and then refused to accept one of my mess-tins back because it was dirty. Given the length and nature of our engagement and that handing over the kit was the last part of it, I found it surprising that he sent me outside with a piece of scouring pad to clean it but then I probably wasn't as surprised as he was, when I returned ten seconds later, stating I'd lost the thing. For the record, it's most probably in the hedge, behind the cook-house but I didn't really see where it landed. Nor do I care. This, like the problems which continue in the Middle-East, is not my problem anymore.

The curiosity is that, amongst all the lies, the killing and the stupidity, there is a solution to this mess. I can remember when I was at school, on numerous occasions, being drawn into fighting with numerous people, largely for no significant reason. Most of the time, it was a squabble over something which was genuinely insignificant and every time it happened, the dinner-ladies would came and say "Pack it in or I'll bash your heads together." Or similar sentiments. Oddly, that usually brought an end to the violence, perhaps quickly followed by the realisation that it wasn't really worth fighting over anyway.

Perhaps the main protagonists of international politics (Are these not simply the biggest kids in the playground?) should have their heads bashed together by some international political dinner-lady type entity because none of this is really worth fighting over. It wouldn't really take much for everyone involved on either side of this "war on terror" just to wake up and smell the fucking coffee and wonder just why did the dinner ladies spent years telling us "There's no sense in fighting". It really is that simple, underneath everything and that, as we all know, is the truth of it. It doesn't really set a good example for the children either, does it? For me, all of this violence is for nothing. Really, if we were mature enough, we could all just sit down and have glass of wine and let everyone else get on with their own business. There wouldn't be any wars then. We'd all be too pissed.

www.ingramcontent.com/pod-product-compliance
Ingram Content Group UK Ltd.
Pitfield, Milton Keynes, MK11 3LW, UK
UKHW041847190726
13854UKWH00002B/761